"the story of all of us in different moments of our lives . . . I was deeply stirred"
> ann kiemel anderson
> *Author*
> *Idaho Falls, Idaho*

"honest and moving book . . . shows us God's biblical and powerful redemptive way to new wholeness"
> Leighton Ford
> *Evangelist*
> *Charlotte, North Carolina*

"Gordon MacDonald has discovered the ways required to restore health to a fallen Christian warrior"
> Stephen Strang
> *Editor, Charisma Magazine*
> *Altamonte Springs, Florida*

"written with gut-wrenching honesty by one who knows what he is talking about . . . for sinners only—but whom does that exclude?"
> James Packer
> *Regent College*
> *Vancouver, British Columbia*

"must reading for all Christian sinners . . . I read it twice!"
> The Rev. Bill Hybeis
> *Senior Pastor, Willow Creek Community Church*
> *Barrington, Illinois*

"for those of us who have walked through that dark tunnel of moral failure; and for those of us deeply concerned as we see our brothers and sisters entering—and wondering if they will emerge; Gordon's book is life to a dying man"
> Jamie Buckingham
> *Pastor and Author*
> *Palm Day, Florida*

"if you are looking for a 'confessional,' this is not it; but it is a light for the dark and divine guidance in the midst of personal confusion"
> Ted W. Engstrom
> *President Emeritus, World Vision*
> *Monrovia, California*

"nothing cheap or sensational in these pages, no short cuts, no easy formulas, only solid practical principles that all of us can apply by faith"
> Warren Wiersbe
> *Back to the Bible*
> *Lincoln, Nebraska*

Gordon MacDonald

REBUILDING

YOUR

BROKEN

WORLD

OLIVER
NELSON

A DIVISION OF THOMAS NELSON PUBLISHERS
NASHVILLE

Published in Nashville, Tennessee, by Oliver-Nelson Books, a division of Thomas Nelson, Inc., Publishers, and distributed in Canada by Lawson Falle, Ltd., Cambridge, Ontario.

Unless otherwise noted, the Bible version used in this publication is the HOLY BIBLE: NEW INTERNATIONAL VERSION. Copyright © 1973, 1978, 1984 by the International Bible Society. Used by permission of Zondervan Bible Publishers.

Scripture quotations marked NKJV are taken from THE NEW KING JAMES VERSION. Copyright © 1979, 1980, 1982, Thomas Nelson, Inc., Publishers.

Verses marked TLB are taken from *The Living Bible*, copyright 1971 by Tyndale House Publishers, Wheaton, IL. Used by permission.

"The Road Not Taken" is copyright 1916, © 1969 by Holt, Rinehart and Winston, Inc. Copyright 1944 by Robert Frost. Reprinted from THE POETRY OF ROBERT FROST edited by Edward Connery Lathem, by permission of Henry Holt and Company, Inc., the estate of Robert Frost, and Jonathan Cape Ltd.

Excerpts of Daniel Golden's June 3, 1984, article on the drowning death of Chris Dilullo reprinted courtesy of The Boston Globe.

Excerpts from SONG OF ASCENTS by E. Stanley Jones. Copyright © 1968 by Abingdon Press. Used by permission.

Printed in the United States of America.

LIBRARY OF CONGRESS
Library of Congress Cataloging-in-Publication Data

Macdonald, Gordon.
    Rebuilding your broken world / Gordon Macdonald.
        p.   cm.
    ISBN 0-8407-9086-4 : $12.95
    1. Christian life—1960-   2. Macdonald, Gordon.   I. Title.
BV4501.2.M2273   1988   88-22569
248.4—dc19   CIP
        3   4   5   6 — 92   91   90   89   88

To Gail
AND
THE "Angels"

*the inner core
of many who have
helped me rebuild
my broken world*

Contents

PART II

WHY WORLDS BREAK

PART V

PREVENTING A PERSONAL WORLD FROM BREAKING

> *Bottom Line #17:* We must assume the inevitability of attacks by an enemy hostile to our spiritual interests and build our defenses in the places he is most likely to attack.

PART VI

REBUILDING YOUR BROKEN WORLD

> *Bottom Line #18:* The grace that helps to rebuild a broken world is something given: never deserved, never demanded, never self-induced.

PART VII

SOME PERSONAL COMMENTS

> *Bottom Line:* When you have been pushed or have fallen to the ground, there can be only one useful resolve: GET UP AND FINISH THE RACE!

Foreword

As a young pastor, I read a very moving and reassuring sermon by that eloquent Scottish preacher-scholar, Arthur Gossip. After the agonizing death of his wife, he asked himself and his congregation, "When Life Tumbles In, What Then?" When for whatever reasons your personal world goes to pieces, is it possible to do more than simply manage to survive? If the whole structure of your existence is shattered, like a precious vase dropped on a hardwood floor, can those sherds be gathered up and by some recreative miracle be put together again into an object of beauty and usefulness? Once Humpty Dumpty has had his "great fall" are "all the king's horses and all the king's men" incapable of doing anything except lamenting as they consign his fragments into rubble?

That is precisely the problem God deals with in the book of Jeremiah. He issued a directive to his servant: "'Go down to the potter's house, and there I will give you my message.' So I went down to the potter's house, and I saw him working at the wheel. But the pot he was shaping from the clay was marred in his hands . . ." Let me break off the narrative at that point. When the recalcitrant clay resists the moulding hands of the potter, is the marred vessel thrown aside? By no means! Jeremiah's narrative continues: "So the potter formed it into another pot, shaping it as it seemed best to him" (Jer. 18:2–4). God's message to Jeremiah is centuries later God's message to ourselves through Gordon MacDonald, a message of recreative grace that inspires praise, humility and hope.

A few years ago if I had been asked to name ten outstanding leaders in America evangelicalism, I would have unhesitatingly included my friend Gordon MacDonald. I had known him intimately since his childhood. I had followed his development with as much pride as if he had been my own family member, a legitimate pride springing from gratitude to God for the fruitful giftedness of a choice and, I felt and still feel, a chosen servant. As the director of an outstanding campus ministry, a visionary churchman, a best-selling author, a lecturer in constant demand, and a devoted husband and father, he was a spiritual model, a dynamic spokesperson for the Gospel. Then overnight his world tumbled in. His career ground to a screeching halt. He became one more conspicuous casualty in the never-ending battle all of us carry on against evil within and without. But that, I rejoice to add, is not the end to the story. And that is why this book is such an inspiring message of hope.

Exercising what Dietrich Bonhoeffer calls "a certain manly reserve," my friend and brother wisely refuses to satisfy carnal curiosity. Yet with soul-searching candor he uses his own experience in order to help all of us who are his fellow sinners, fellow sufferers, and fellow strugglers.

Though he makes no pretense at being a psychologist, he probes the labyrinth of his own soul and ours too with a penetration reminiscent of Alexander Whyte or Oswald Chambers. He gives us a profoundly insightful analysis of the causes of our sinful wrongdoing, why it is we hypocritically contradict in behavior the norms and ideals to which we sincerely subscribe on a cognitive level. He analyzes as well the external factors that conspire with our own propensities to warp and wreck our lives. But he refuses to minimize in the least our own responsibility for sinful failure.

He does far more, however, than engage in such skillful analysis. He shares the story of a Spirit-guided restorative process, the emotional anguish of confession and repentance by which a broken world can be rebuilt.

Thus this book, born out of indescribable travail, is a message needed by every Christian (and there are really no exceptions) who, only imperfectly sanctified, battles with that unholy trinity of the world, the flesh, and the devil. A powerful testimony to our Lord Jesus as not only Redeemer of sinners but likewise Rebuilder of broken worlds, it is a remarkable twentieth-century testimony to the central New Testament truth that where sin abounds, God's grace superabounds.

Vernon Grounds
Denver Seminary

Introduction

> BOTTOM LINE:
> *"Think of me as a fellow-patient in the same hospital who, having been admitted a little earlier, could give some advice."*
> *C. S. Lewis*

When a much younger man, I had the opportunity to compete as a runner on the track and the cross-country course. Now, it has been decades since I last heard the starter's pistol and sprang away from the line and (with hope) toward the victory tape.

But a love for the sport of running has never left me, even though I am now merely a power-walker. That's a major reason why I was caught up with the drama of two races I saw in recent years.

The first was a cinematic re-enactment of a competition held more than sixty years ago. Eric Liddell, the subject of the film *Chariots of Fire*, was in a pack of runners and breaking for the lead. Suddenly he was thrown off balance, and he crashed heavily to the infield grass. The camera lens zoomed in on him as he lifted his head to see the other athletes pulling away, never looking behind.

The moment on the infield grass only lasted for a second or two, but from my perspective as I watched the film, it seemed as if it lasted for many minutes. Would he get up again? And if he did, could he even finish the race?

He got up! And the man began to run. The movie audience of which I was a part spontaneously cheered as Liddell assumed his famous awkward profile and tore after the now distant pack of competitors. The result? He won, going away.

The other race I often think about happened only a few years ago. Two world-class female athletes were competing in the Los Angeles Olympics. Millions of people around the world were fascinated by their rivalry and were tuned in when they and a host of other runners left their marks. Shoulder to shoulder the two ran together through the first one thousand meters. It was clear they were measuring one another and preparing for the strategic moment when each would try to break for the lead. And then suddenly, so quickly that the slow-motion replay cameras never fully showed what happened, one of them was on the infield grass just as Liddell had been sixty years before.

But this time was different: the runner on the infield grass did not get up. Just like in the movie, the camera zoomed in on a face etched with pain, rage, and instant defeat as the pack of runners pulled away Could she have gotten up, fought off the pain and the disheartening blow to her psychological edge and reentered the competition? I don't know. Perhaps she does not really know either. To her credit, there came another season when she went back to the track and proved that she was best in her class.

The figures of those two runners lying on the infield grass are drilled deep in my mind. They are visual symbols to me of what happens in the "race of life" when men and women crash either because they have made a terrible choice or set of choices or because they are jostled or upset by what someone else has done.

Those who have fallen to the infield grass in life also have a decision to make that is similar to the one those two runners had to make. Will they get up again? Or will they stay on the grass and pity themselves?

I have a name for men and women in that decision-making situation. I call them the broken-world people, for that is exactly what has happened to them. After years of dreaming, preparing, conditioning, and fighting their way to a particular point, they have (usually by their own initiative) fallen. This "world" they have constructed is suddenly shattered. And the only questions left are versions of the runners' question: Will they get up again? Will they rebuild their broken worlds?

I've come to a high point of sensitivity about broken-world people, for I am a part of those who look back into their personal history and recall with strong regret an act or a series of acts that have resulted in great distress for themselves and many others. And what is worse is the fact that such performances are a terrible offense to God.

What I have called a connection of broken-world people is not a formal or necessarily visible body of men and women. I'm simply highlighting a mass of people who live with a certain kind of suffering. Not the suffering that comes through bereavement, an injustice, a persecution, a painful illness, or poverty. These people suffer from self-inflicted wounds: mistakes, errors, bad choices. Another word might be *misbehavior*. The hardest but most descriptive word for such suffering-inducing actions is *sin*.

When God formed a nation later to be called Israel, one of the first things He dealt with through Moses, their leader, was the matter of behavior. There were ten laws, inviolable, nonnegotiable principles, which were designed to identify human performance that honored God and human performance that dishonored or offended Him and the community. What I call misbehavior, or what the Bible calls sin, flows from those laws and their derivatives.

In the majority of cases, then and now, when sin occurs, there are painful results. They can come directly from the hand of God. That was the case in numerous instances in the Bible: people suddenly struck down in a way that made it clear that the judgment was of divine origin. In other situations, the consequences for misbehavior are facilitated through other people: an enemy's invasion against a misbehaving nation, the justice meted out to a person or family by community leadership, or the pronouncement of consequence upon an errant king or a carnal church by a prophet or an apostle.

Many times, the consequences simply come through the resulting events that flow from misbehavior. God's laws must be obeyed because they come from Him and because, in the scheme of life, they make sense. When they are violated, they usually result in nonsense: people hurting one another, taking from one another, slandering one another, even killing one another. And out of all that flow pain, grief, anger, bitterness, and vengeance.

Misbehavior usually results in bad consequences rather quickly, but some people seem to get away with everything. It's as if they go through life unaware that they are, as we sometimes put it, "getting away with murder." They are unaccountable to anyone or anything as far as we can see.

In Psalm 73, the writer seems confused over this notion that some do get away with murder.

> I envied the arrogant
>> when I saw the prosperity of the wicked.
> They have no struggles;
>> their bodies are healthy and strong.

> They are free from the burdens common to man;
>   they are not plagued by human ills. . . .
> From their callous hearts comes iniquity;
>   the evil conceits of their minds know no limits.
> They scoff, and speak with malice;
>   in their arrogance they threaten oppression. . . .
> They say, "How can God know?
> Does the Most High have knowledge?" (vv. 3–11).

The psalmist is confused because he doesn't seem to get away with anything. Every misbehavior in his life seems to come under the scrutiny of God, and when he is found out, he pays for it. To him, God's dealings with humankind appear for a moment to be inconsistent, capricious, and maybe (in his finite mind) a bit unfair.

It is true. A study in the Bible of why and how God orchestrates the discipline and punishment of people who misbehave brings inconclusive results. One man murders and goes on to live a full life with God's continuing blessing; another gathers sticks on the Sabbath day and is executed. One king, by his wickedness, brings the judgment of total destruction on his city, but he personally repents and lives to an old age. A soldier hides a cache of war booty under the floor of his tent and is stoned for it.

It all suggests that no one can judge one kind of misbehavior as more serious than another on the basis of the consequences generated. The message? All misbehavior is serious and is sin in God's eyes. And no one knows what consequences are liable to be unleashed when a person steps beyond the bounds of right performance.

None of us would contest the fact that in a large majority of cases there are visible and destructive consequences when people choose sin. On some occasions the consequences result in the total devastation of everything someone has accumulated in the way of reputation, responsibility, or even material security. Integrity, respect, and credibility enter the loss column. Relationships can be dissolved: divorce, severed friendships or working relationships. The right to pursue one's vocation can be denied by professional governing bodies. These are all parts of a personal world that can be shattered into tiny pieces when misbehavior generates its consequences.

When the Chernobyl nuclear power plant in the Soviet Union blew up, not only the managers of the station suffered. Thousands of people who lived in the vicinity lost their homes, and the food supply of millions was affected by the spreading radiation. Just so, the broken-world experience damages not only the misbehaving person; the consequences can threaten scores of innocent people who live with what might be called the fallout. There can be a lot of losses when an ungodly act occurs, and the losses may spread across the network of one's relationships and even endure through several generations.

Of course everyone is a broken-world person in the strictest sense if we believe the Bible's claim that all have sinned or misbehaved. But in this book, I have had to draw an artificial line to identify acts or human performances that have brought about unusual consequences of scandal, major loss, or serious long-term pain. Beyond this, I must leave the definition up to the reader.

I am a broken-world person because a few years ago I betrayed the covenants of my marriage. For the rest of my life I will have to live with the knowledge that I brought deep sorrow to my wife, to my children, and to friends and others who have trusted me for many years.

It is a testimony to the ruggedness of the marriage Gail and I share that our relationship not only survived this damaging body blow but may have taken on extra sinews of strength and vitality in the aftermath as we rebuilt our broken personal worlds. Our rebuilding process began long before the news of my sin and failure was public. It centered on the acts of repentance, forgiveness, grace, and chosen new directions of performance. And it has provided us a costly love that has bonds of steel.

Rebuilding Your Broken World is not an autobiography of misbehavior. It is not a study in self-pity or excuses. *It begins with the premise that individuals who have misbehaved must present themselves before God in openness and acknowledge responsibility and accountability.* NOTHING IN THIS BOOK IS DESIGNED TO MAKE SENSE IF THAT PRINCIPLE IS NOT UNDERSTOOD FIRST.

I don't want to be misunderstood as I write about the sad dynamics of misbehavior. When I talk about some of the circumstances in which a person is more likely to misbehave, I don't want the reader to think I'm blaming the circumstances. But if, as C. S. Lewis says, I can offer a little bit of advice about what goes on in the hospital, then it will be necessary to muse upon the larger context that so often seems to surround the sinful choices people make.

This has been the hardest book I've ever written. It seemed at times as if there were an evil power that resisted any effort to write about restorative grace. And if that indeed was the case, then I must assume that some words here, words of comfort and words of grace, may be useful and gracious for others.

I've written it because I've become conscious of that connection of broken-world people out there. Many of them have written to me; some have called on the telephone if they could find my number; and a few others have visited. My perception is that broken-world people exist in large numbers, and they ask similar questions over and over again. Can my world ever be rebuilt? Do I have any value? Can I be useful again? Is there life after misbehavior?

My answer is yes. That is what grace is all about. A marvelous, forgiving, healing grace says that all things can be new. *And I would like to talk about the grace I have been given by God and by many others.*

As a child, I once knocked over a lamp that was precious to my parents. Its ceramic shaft cracked on one side when it hit the floor. Because I was alone in the room at the time, I was able to place it back on the table and turn the lamp so that the crack was not visible. It remained that way for days, and every morning I would wake up in fear that this was the day the crack would be discovered and I would face a parent's ire.

I froze every time my mother or father went near the lamp. I pictured the reactions in that upcoming moment when the inevitable discovery would occur. The longer the confrontation was delayed, the worse the consequences promised to be in my mind.

Then it came: the day my mother dusted the lamp and found the crack. "Did you do this?" she asked. I could only answer yes and brace myself, telling her what had happened.

But Mother never said a word. She took it to the kitchen, glued the pieces so that they once more fit tightly together, and within a few hours returned the lamp to the table. The crack was always there, but the lamp was rebuilt. And it served its purpose for years.

Broken worlds may always have cracks to remind us of the past; that's reality. But sometimes the grace of God is like the glue my mother used on her lamp. The bonded edges can become stronger than the original surface.

This book includes some of the bottom lines that have become important to me during this rebuilding process. I share them for the broken-world connection out there: the men and women whose cracked lamps have yet to be discovered or who are living in the aftermath of the discovery. I want them to know what I've experienced through the love and affection of lots of godly people: BROKEN WORLDS CAN BE RE-BUILT.

Perhaps I should have begun this introduction with words that may be fairly familiar to anyone who has been a part of Alcoholics Anonymous. I am Gordon, and I am a broken-world person. The great AA tradition says that anyone who speaks at a meeting of alcoholics will usually begin by saying, "I am G———, and I am an alcoholic. I took my last drink on. . . ." It makes a lot of sense to me that we ought to introduce ourselves in a similar way in the Christian community: "I am Gordon, and I am a sinner." That is our primary affinity when we gather before Jesus. Such a declaration doesn't make us sound very attractive, but then we aren't . . . until we get to the Cross. That's when wonderful things happen, and broken worlds start to be rebuilt.

There are probably few runners who haven't fallen to the infield grass at one time or another. And most of them have their stories of those agonizing moments, stories of the inside battle: to quit the race and head for the locker room or to get up again. This is a book written by one fallen runner in the race who is determined to get off the grass and get back into the race of life.

No one has helped me more in the writing of this book than my faithful partner in twenty-seven years of marriage, Gail. We have discussed every paragraph, prayed over every chapter, and combed the manuscript for any evidence of self-pity or excuse making. What fellowship we have had in its writing! I dearly love and admire her. She is more than a friend.

Beyond Gail is the encouragement of our children, my brother, our parents, the elders and senior pastor of Grace Chapel in Lexington, Massachusetts, and the men to whom, along with Gail, this book is dedicated: THE ANGELS, the incredible team of godly men who long ago surrounded Gail and me and determined that here was one broken world that was going to be rebuilt. Finally, for many years Victor Oliver has been my friend and my publisher. He helped make me an author, and I will never forget that. I owe all of these my life.

Gordon MacDonald
Canterbury, New Hampshire
May 1988

PART I

THE TRAGIC REALITY OF BROKEN WORLDS

CHAPTER 1

Broken Worlds

> BOTTOM LINE #1:
> *Broken worlds are not*
> *uncommon; they can*
> *happen to any of us. And*
> *if they do, we may not be*
> *able to control the*
> *damage. Don't let anyone*
> *tell you differently.*

Some people love disaster movies. I do not! But I am aware of such things because I've seen brief portions of a few on late night television when I couldn't sleep. I suspect that they tend to play upon a common fear: the threat of massive destruction of something we normally think to be indestructible. So there are movies about large ocean liners sinking, huge cities disintegrating in earthquakes, and entire nations suddenly being overrun by gigantic insects or prehistoric reptiles.

A science fiction version of this disaster theme features an object from outer space, a gigantic meteor or star, which is discovered as it travels along a collision path toward our planet. If the course of the threatening celestial visitor is not altered, the earth and all of its life-forms will be vaporized. Thus, the mission of the people in the grade-B movie is to find a way to prevent that from happening.

Another version of the disaster theme focuses on a fiendish, gangsterlike character who is bent on holding the world's population hostage to his threat to blow up the earth with a hidden explosive device. Only the villain knows where this megabomb is concealed and how it works. Usually, the movie's hero (or heroes) locates and disarms the weapon just before it can be triggered. A few of these films go a long way, and one is more amused than frightened as the plot unfolds and winds down to its predictable conclusion: everything turns out all right.

But, remember, these are old movies, the kinds that come to pleasant conclusions. I never remember any of them going so far as to permit the meteor or the villain to finish the job and smash the earth to pieces. But then I'm not a movie buff, as they say, and I can't be sure. I suspect that a modern disaster movie might end in a high-tech catastrophe designed to please an audience hungry for bizarre thrills.

As I said, disaster films do nothing for me. But I do see some of them as metaphors of life. They are visual symbols of what happens when our personal worlds are suddenly threatened and subsequently smashed into pieces, broken by the meteoric force of events that crash in upon us from beyond ourselves or broken by bomblike forces that come from deep within ourselves.

Out of these cinematic metaphors I first conceived the phrase *broken world* as an apt way to describe what happens when someone sustains a major blow in life that is either self-inflicted or the result of someone else's unfortunate or treacherous performance. I'm thinking of disasters in the inner spirit, to the mind, to the body, to relationships, to reputation, or to personal usefulness.

We usually use the word *world* to describe the earth and all of its ecosystems. But I have found it a helpful word when referring to the context of a person's being. *World* can convey the notion of a complex personal system of life and relationship, of ownership, of energy, of capability, of feeling, of pain and pleasure, of commitments and choices.

A rough guess would be that over five billion of these individual worlds (or micro-worlds) are alive and scrambling for space on the earth. Over five billion! And like the proportions of a typical iceberg, one-seventh of each personal world (the public world) is visible to others, and six-sevenths of each one (the private world) is invisible to most everyone but God.

The public sector of our worlds extends as far as our senses can take us, perhaps even to the edges of the universe if we can see that far. In this public part we intersect with other human beings and with the stuff of creation. And if we are interested and attentive, we may pick up the voice of God the Creator as He reveals something of Himself in all that He has made.

Then there is the private sector of our worlds. Beneath the surface of our skin, an inner space may be just as expansive in a spiritual dimension as the universe is in a physical dimension. In our private worlds, God, our Creator, is most likely to whisper in the gentle stirrings of conviction, guidance, and the experiences of grace. But also in our private worlds is the grim reality of darker, shadowy forces that we identify with the word *evil* or *sinfulness*. Not many people like to talk about this dimension of our inner selves, and our very ignorance or neglect of it may portend our vulnerability to brokenness. If God whispers, evil often shouts, and personal worlds break when that shouting gets our attention.

If you're a people-person as I am, you like to know something about the public and private worlds of the people around you. And that's pursued primarily by asking questions. "How is your world today?" I sometimes ask to get someone to share with me how he is feeling. And if I want to go beyond the superficial level of most conversations and find out what motivates or captivates a person, I might begin by inquiring, "What are the top two or three most important themes in your world?"

More than a few people have responded by saying, "No one has ever asked me that before." But questions of that nature usually give individuals an opportunity to range far and wide with answers and observations that fit their current mood and sort out their serious priorities. They may describe how they presently perceive events and circumstances, and in answer to the second question, they may share something that is significant to them but hardly ever gets the attention of others.

If you get into the habit of asking such personal-world-oriented questions, you will soon discover, as I have, that the worlds of people cannot be described only as part public and part private. More than a few of them will be broken, badly broken. Personal worlds are in many cases remarkably fragile, and they can shatter under stress much like an elegant goblet explodes under a barrage of powerful sound waves. I call people who are hurt like that the *broken-world people*.

The television camera zooms in on broken-world people on virtually every news broadcast. Personal worlds are broken in terrorist activities, in famines, in massive airline or train crashes, or in the horror of physical illnesses such as AIDS. Worlds can be ripped apart by the cruelties of rape, street muggings, wanton murders by drug-crazed or war-stressed gunmen, alcohol-related accidents, or missiles loaded with explosives or nerve gas. The list of ways to break up worlds is endless; the suffering is beyond description. And when such broken-world people survive, they are usually marked by lifelong trauma.

Homes on every city block, in every suburban neighborhood, and in every rural community are overshadowed by broken-world scenes. Family breakups are devastating to those making the decision to terminate the marriage as well as to the children and others in the extended family who must live with the long-term side effects. Firings and layoffs from careers and jobs are as much the fault of politics, economic downturns, and poor management as of incompetency or negligence. Personal worlds are broken without warning when health fails, poor decisions are made, or an accident happens. And one by one we discover that broken worlds do not just happen to someone else; they can happen to us.

Another, more specific kind of broken-world person is the one who makes a terrible choice and deviates from standards set by God, by himself, or by the system in which he lives. More often than not, he reaps the consequence of the choice. His world breaks apart, and maybe the worlds of a few of those around him break up too as they share in the consequence. Such an individual who brings his world to brokenness through personal error, weakness, or failure is my primary concern in this book.

If you are a student of American baseball, you'll remember the name of Ralph Branka, once an exceptional pitcher for the former Brooklyn Dodgers. Some will be aware that he pitched many winning seasons for the Dodgers; but most will only remember, if they're old enough, the autumn afternoon in 1951 when Branka pitched to Bobby Thompson of the New York Giants in the last inning of a National League championship game. The Dodgers were ahead at the time by a score of 5–3, and Branka's assignment was to make sure that Bobby Thompson did nothing to change it. But Thompson did.

Unfortunately for Branka, Thompson hit his pitch far enough into the outfield grandstands to score three runs and win the championship for the Giants. You could say that Ralph Branka's world (or at least part of it) blew up that day with one pitch. He had to stand there on the pitcher's mound and watch the ball fly out of the park while Bobby Thompson jogged around the bases to a triumphant reception at home plate.

Branka was never permitted to forget that moment. From that time forward, people never asked him about his long career as a successful athlete; they wished to hear only about the day he threw one bad pitch. He was nailed to that event.

That's just baseball, an American game, someone says. Hard for those of us who are not professional athletes to take Ralph Branka's personal disaster seriously. But not hard if you're a professional athlete. Then you understand. Pitching was the man's job, the source of his income, the basis of his public reputation. And it all seemed to disintegrate with the crack of a baseball bat.

Ralph Branka's broken-world moment was very public. Most broken-world experiences are less conspicuous, and they may occur over a longer period of time. But anyone's broken-world moment is just as real and just as painful as Branka's must have been. Sudden or gradual, when one's world has been broken, the question of hope usually arises. Is there a tomorrow? Will there be another chance? Is the damage permanent? Do new starts exist? *Can this broken world ever be rebuilt?*

There are some myths about broken worlds. Dangerous myths, I think, because they can disarm us, making us less vigilant on the one hand and less prepared on the other when worlds do break.

Broken-World Myth #1

One myth suggests that *broken worlds are the exception, not the rule*. They are merely anomalies in life, and the less we think about them the better. Broken worlds never happen to good people; only phonies, rebels, and those less than smart really go through broken-world moments. Furthermore, to spend too much time brooding on the possibility of broken-world experiences is to invite the event. It's better to think only happy, positive thoughts.

Broken-World Myth #2

A second myth presumes that *a broken-world experience can never happen to me*. This is a version of the typically human notion that we can live above all the odds, take all the risks, and avoid all the consequences. One senses this myth working when people mourn the death or the misfortune of a good person. "Why her?" they say. "She had everything going for her. Why not some loser, some evil person? Why do these things happen to the best people?"

Broken-World Myth #3

A third myth plays off the second. It is built on the assumption that *if and when my world does break, I can more than handle the results*. This myth is expressed in such "reasoning" as: I'm above the consequences; I have enough energy, resources, influence, and good performance stored up to reduce, if not neutralize, any bad effects; in fact, God owes me something.

We need to refute these myths by espousing some simple principles. If we do not, we are liable to find ourselves caught in some world-breaking ambushes from which we may not escape.

To the first myth (broken worlds are anomalies in life), one must say, *Know history.* To the second myth (it can't or won't happen to me), one must say, *Know thyself.* And to the third (I can handle anything that comes in my direction), one must say, *Know God's laws.*

KNOWING HISTORY

Far more of us live under the presumption of the first myth than we realize. Eschewing the gloom-and-doom prophets and reminding ourselves that the world and great success in general are inherited by those who think positively and act optimistically, we plan our futures and marshal our resources along the lines of what the planner calls "best-case scenarios." We are tempted to leave no room for the possibility of less than "best case."

One of the first jokes of the age of automation describes a planeload of people soon after takeoff. A voice comes on the plane's intercom, "Good afternoon, ladies and gentlemen. Welcome aboard. We are climbing to our planned cruising altitude of 39,000 feet. All of the plane's systems are working perfectly, and we expect to land at our destination on time. This is a fully automated plane. There is no pilot or copilot. Everything is guided and monitored by a computer. We want you to sit back, relax, and enjoy the flight. Nothing can go wrong . . . can go wrong . . . can go wrong. . . ."

For many years I served as a pastor, and one of my responsibilities was to officiate at weddings. There were always two moments as I worked with young bridal couples when I felt a brief bit of despair. One came during the process of premarital counseling. I almost never met a couple who wished to talk about the potential bumps and bruises of merging two lives into a permanent relationship. They were far too anxious to discuss plans for the wedding and the honeymoon.

Rarely was I asked in such conversations, what are the storm warnings for a destructive conflict? Or where are we likely to face temptations and seductions that might cause a drift from our commitments to God or to each other? I can hear someone grimacing, amused that I would seek such grim reality in the midst of youthful joy. Nevertheless, I stick to my original observation that it is not the nature of most of us to ponder the possibility of world-breaking events in our relationships.

A second moment of concern often arose during the ceremony itself as I laid my hands on the kneeling couple and prayed over them. Usually, the pastoral prayer was followed by a solo while the couple remained kneeling. Sometimes I would look down during this solo and note the bride and groom holding hands and snatching glances at each other. And my mind would turn to the morbid statistics that suggested hard times ahead, and I would wonder, "old man" that I was, whether they were ready, whether they had even thought of the potential of broken-world experiences.

The young person doesn't ponder the increased odds of physical or psychic danger when fooling around with alcohol or drugs. The middle-ager is most likely not thinking of the long-range implications of over-eating. Nor is the fast-track executive prone to plan for the day of a company downturn and the resultant firing. Each is liable to assume the best-case-scenario for all of life's events, rarely, if ever, contemplating the likelihood of struggle.

The Bible covers a period of measured history of several thousand years. From the first pages to the last, we are given insight into the noble behavior and the ignoble misbehavior of people from scores of generations, cultures, and classes. We are given family lines to study, intimate (no-holds-barred) biographies to poke into, and analyses of leaders, business people, and military personnel to evaluate. After reading through it all, we will probably be on fairly safe ground when we reach some conclusions about what life brings to human beings then and now in terms of possibility, success, and pain.

One of my conclusions based on the reading I've done is simple: *almost everyone in the Bible had a broken-world experience.* Virtually no one was exempt. In fact, it's tempting to reverse the myth that broken-world experiences are anomalous and suggest that everyone then and now will have a broken-world experience sooner or later. It may not always be the result of one's own performance; it can be just as likely that one has to live with the consequences of someone else's choices.

Furthermore, the Bible seems to suggest through the stories of various men and women that broken-world experiences are usually the turnaround moments ushering people into greater and more powerful performances of character, courage, and achievement. One by one they seem to illustrate exactly what a football coach was trying to express when he said of his team, "We learn almost nothing in victory; but we learn much in defeat."

Moses is connected, educated, and talented, but he amounts to little that means anything to God until his world has been broken and re-built, the work commenced in the desert and continued at the site of a burning bush.

Zechariah and Elizabeth, parents of John the Baptizer, seem to play no significant role in God's involvement with His people until they pass through a broken-world experience that drives them to a breaking point through the stress of apparent sterility and/or barrenness. Zechariah's world is further broken when he is struck speechless and forced to live in silence for the extent of Elizabeth's pregnancy. The young man they produced, however, went on to be, in the words of Jesus, the greatest of the prophets.

Saul of Tarsus (later to be St. Paul) is only one more fiery Jew in his generation until his pompous, religiously structured world is shattered on the road to Damascus, and he becomes silent and submissive before Christ.

Tell Moses, Zechariah and Elizabeth, and St. Paul that the broken-world experience is an addendum, an add-on, to life. Tell them that pressure, failure, and embarrassment are not part of the course of human development and maturation. They simply won't agree. They will say that sorrow, pain, and stress are the "graduate school" of godly character and capacity if people are willing to enroll. The problem, they may suggest, is that this school has too many no-shows and dropouts.

"Are you telling me," a woman asks in a group conversation, "that the things I desire most in terms of being a mature person can be acquired only through some form of suffering? I don't want to believe that."

I'm not about to offer a quick and easy yes to her question, but I know in my heart that the vast majority of people down through history who acquired or achieved the traits of character and endurance that she seeks passed through a broken-world experience to obtain them. I'm not sure I like it any more than she does, but when one knows their history, a startling reality appears. In pain, failure, and brokenness, God does His finest work in the lives of people.

George Matheson reflected this reality when he wrote:

There are songs which can only be learned in the valley. No art can teach them; no rules of voice can make them perfectly sung. Their music is in the heart. They are songs of memory, of personal experience. They bring out their burden from the shadow of the past; they mount on the wings of yesterday. . . .

The father is training thee for the part the angels cannot sing;

and the school is sorrow. I have heard many say that He sends sorrow to prove thee; may He send sorrow to educate thee, to train thee for the choir invisible. *(Streams in the Desert)*

In the 1680s John Bunyan wrote one of the world's great classics, *Pilgrim's Progress*, while he was in jail (talk about a broken-world experience), and one safely assumes that this book would not have been written in any other place. Earlier in his Christian life, Bunyan passed through a broken world of another kind—several years of deep, painful searching for a solid relationship with God. It was not that God couldn't be found; rather, it was that Bunyan had a lot of things to work through in his private world.

In his spiritual autobiography, *Grace Abounding,* Bunyan made no attempt to hide the fact that his younger years were characterized by attitudes and performances that can be labeled only as rank evil. And the consequences in his spirit broke his world apart. But Bunyan knew that those broken-world experiences were the foreground for his ultimate commitment to Christ. And he observed this when he wrote:

I never saw those heights and depths in grace, and love, and mercy, as I saw after this temptation: great sins draw out great grace; and where guilt is most terrible and fierce, there the mercy of God in Christ, when showed to the soul, appears most high and mighty.

Know history! Its startling lesson is that the great qualities of life usually come only when the pain has begun, pain we may bring upon ourselves or pain brought by events and circumstances over which we have no control. When we fight the brokenness, or when we curse it as having no part of our existence, we forfeit the opportunity for quality growth.

KNOWING YOURSELF

The second myth says, *It can't happen to me.* And the challenge ought to be, *Know yourself.* When we utter this myth silently or aloud, we become guilty of a subtle lie.

Simon Peter, to whom I will frequently refer in this book, is a perfect model of this myth holder. On the night of the betrayal of Christ, Simon said, "Lord, I am ready to go with You to prison and to death."

Jesus replied, "I tell you, Peter, before the rooster crows today, you will deny three times that you know Me" (see John 13:31–38).

I have often meditated on this interchange of opinions between Simon Peter and Jesus. Simon simply didn't know himself. Jesus knew Simon better than Simon did. That simple little matter about self-knowledge (or the lack of it) ought to be a cause for major thinking.

How should Jesus have handled Simon that night? Should He have practiced some sort of blind, tell-him-what-he-wants-to-hear affirmation on Simon that night? Should He have said, "Simon, I love your courage, your intention. Keep thinking that way, friend, and you'll make it through just fine"?

Apparently, Jesus didn't think so. He did two things that many of us wouldn't have considered doing. First, He countered Simon's naivete with candor: Simon, you're going to make some major errors tonight; not just once, but several times. How could Simon have missed the pointedness of Jesus' warning? How could he have been so blind to his own weaknesses? His performance record on other stressful occasions was unquestionably poor. Hadn't he learned his lesson yet? No! And it would take a world-breaking experience of major proportions—humiliating, devastating, complete—to develop the kind of character Christ wanted from him.

Second, Jesus let the man fail. He let him pull a sword in the garden after he'd been taught for two years that you don't pull swords when you follow the Lord. He let him run away into the darkness without reminding him of his promise to stand firm. And He let him make a fool of himself as he denied three times an association with Christ, each time more profuse and profane in his denials. Then He let him cry bitterly in the night and sweat out the situation for a while before He restored him. You have to conclude that Jesus thought the broken-world experience was absolutely necessary to the formation of Simon Peter the apostle.

A soccer coach senses that his goalie isn't handling himself well during pregame warm-ups. And since he's not paid to lose games, he sets the goalie on the bench and substitutes another player. But Jesus didn't put Simon Peter on the bench that night. He permitted the broken-world experience because, unlike the coach, Jesus' objective is to build men and women, not simply to win games. And so when the key moments came, Jesus said to Peter and the others, "Rise, let's go forward," and they did: right into a broken world. I doubt if Peter was ever fully caught off guard again due to a lack of self-knowledge.

Almost every personal defeat begins with our failure to know ourselves, to have a clear view of our capabilities (negative and positive), our propensities, our weak sides. Furthermore, in the larger sense, some of our broken-world experiences result from our failure to estimate the performance capabilities of others. Although Jesus loved every person with whom He came in contact, it is also clearly stated that He "would not entrust himself to them" because "he knew all men" (John 2:24).

This reasoning could lead, of course, to the notion that we should invite pain or defeat, even rejoice in it, if we wish to achieve the character level we seek. And that is a false objective. Rather, we should realize that broken-world experiences are most likely to happen to all of us sooner or later, probably sooner to those who pretend they are infallible or untouchable.

This reasoning could lead to a patent mistrust of others, and that is not the point, either. Jesus wasn't a suspicious person. But He was realistic, and He understood that every man or woman regularly faces moments when failure is a strong possibility. However, He seemed to be less concerned about the failure and more concerned about the ability to learn from the failure and receive the grace that is offered when one is properly humbled.

Oswald Chambers frequently pressed his readers on the matter of self-knowledge. Not always a pleasing or simple exercise, he admitted. But a necessary one. Not to take into account and be prepared for the exposure of our weak sides was to invite a broken-world experience sooner or later.

> Always beware of a friendship, or of a religion, *or of a personal estimate of things* that does not reconcile itself to the fact of sin; that is the way all the disasters in human friendships and in human loves begin, and where the compromises start. Jesus Christ never trusted human nature, but He was never cynical, He trusted absolutely what He could do for human nature. (*The Place of Help*, emphasis mine)

Broken-world experiences happen to almost all of us. We need to major in knowing ourselves to have fairly accurate estimates of where they are likely to happen and to know how we will respond both preventatively and remedially.

KNOWING GOD'S LAWS

The final myth is, *I can handle anything that comes in my direction.* And its challenge is, *Know God's laws.*

This myth spotlights a foolish optimism. It builds upon the assumption that when the time comes, we can bargain with God, manipulate circumstances and, if necessary, tough it out.

Ask Lot, the nephew of Abraham, about such optimism. If you could, he might relate his calculation of the risks when he moved his family toward the fertile plain of Sodom, toward the attractive city of Sodom itself, toward the society in that city, toward the values and perspectives pervading its marketplace.

Lot had spent a considerable amount of time with his uncle and had thrived spiritually and materially. When he stepped out from Abraham's family umbrella, he obviously took with him a high degree of bravado: the world was his oyster; there were pearls to be found.

But the man lost everything when his world broke. The brotherhood of the community, the respect of his sons-in-law, his material assets, his wife, his good life. Smashed! And there was no damage control throughout the process.

Lot reminds me of a certain Wall Street personality who one day is participating in the purchase and sale of junk bonds, who manages leveraged buyouts of reputable companies, who amasses millions of seemingly easily gained dollars. And then one day we see this same man grimly surrendering to U.S. marshals to begin a five- to ten-year prison term and agreeing with the courts and the government never to work in the financial world again.

Stanley Jones was fond of telling audiences, you can make your own choices; you cannot control the consequences of those choices. Lot learned that principle the hard way.

I know I have also. Too many of us have experienced our own broken-world moments, and even more of us have witnessed the broken worlds of those we love. One major experience teaches us something we usually never forget: the consequences are rarely capable of being controlled. They have an energy of their own, and no one—except God—knows where the effects of a broken world are likely to stop.

Our Lord was never seduced by these three myths. His life patterns strongly declare that He understood that broken-world experiences are a part of life. It's what we do about them that counts. He knew history. And His personal awareness of pain and suffering assure us that He came to our world knowing that He was not exempt from the realities facing every person. He knew Himself and others. And He accepted the consequences of a broken world: the consequences of other people's anger and hatred, the consequences that were poured out upon Him when He took upon Himself the sins of the world. He knew that God the Father had to pour out upon Him the consequences of the evil of humankind. To live genuinely as a Christian means to live on the truthful side of these myths and not be deceived by them.

When Ralph Branka went to the pitcher's mound on that autumn afternoon almost forty years ago, he may have dared to assume that he was only a few pitches away from athletic stardom. Throw hard; bear down; keep your emotion under control. And then that one pitch. And his world broke.

Our planet is rife with the sad stories of men and women who have been hit by something like a meteor or an imbedded explosive device. Yesterday's world so bright and vigorous lies today in pieces. What happened?

Perhaps the myths were too blinding and deceptive. Perhaps one didn't know where the meteor was coming from or where the bomb was planted. Perhaps one didn't know how to mount the proper defenses.

Can a world under threat of breaking be defended? Yes, emphatically yes. Has it been done before? Many times. The precedents abound.

But if my personal world breaks, is there still hope? Can that broken world be rebuilt? Again, the answer is yes. God has put all the pieces in place, and the process for rebuilding has been time-tested and proven authentic.

CHAPTER 2

A Broken-World Sampler

> BOTTOM LINE #2:
> *The pain of a broken-world experience is universal; the ancients knew it as well as any of us.*

I have had many enjoyable occasions visiting the personal worlds of people who were at the peak of their success. I've been in the locker room of an acclaimed professional athlete; I've ridden along in a corporate jet with a company CEO; and I've sat at the table with a notable person as everyone stared with admiration at him and then with consternation at me wondering who in the world I was. All in all, those occasions are associated with pleasant memories.

But I've had many more opportunities to enter the personal worlds of people who were in the pit of despair. People hurt and grieved because they were left or cheated or badly defeated in a contest of wills. People grieving over the death of a loved one. People whose life savings were obliterated because of a downturn in a business or market.

I've seen worlds broken because of seemingly random events that offered no satisfactory explanation or answer to the question *why*. I remember standing with a farmer as he watched a vicious hailstorm wipe out an entire season's wheat crop, and as a result his annual income, while his neighbor's field just a few yards across the section road remained untouched. Why? He didn't know, and I certainly didn't. If there was an answer, it lay in the physical interactions of the elements above. And that didn't help much.

But the most common broken world—the primary one I've chosen to write about—is the world that shatters because some-

34

one has made a series of bad choices, misbehaved, and now has to live with what he or she has done. No one else to blame; no handy excuses; no injustices to identify.

Sometimes the choices of the broken-world person are premeditated in the darkness of the heart; sometimes the choices seem impulsive and utterly absurd. But the results can be (and usually are) loss of integrity and credibility, humiliation, grief, regret, remorse, fear, and more than a little self-dislike.

And what of those who live with the side effects of broken-world choices? The betrayed spouse? The cheated business partner? The exploited friend? The deceived employer? They often live with a pain they can hardly describe, and they ask hard questions about their rights and their responsibilities. In the final analysis, few broken worlds touch only one life. Like a hand grenade, the effects of one person's terrible choices explode outward to wound many others. For a genuinely sorrowful broken-world person, this unintended wounding of others often brings untold grief.

What happens when personal worlds explode, when circumstances get out of control and all hopes and expectations lie in pieces? How do broken-world people feel? What do they think about? And what are their temptations in terms of defending or excusing themselves?

These are hard questions to pin down with adequate answers. We can take only a few sample runs at them and get a general idea of how people in the past acted when their worlds broke because of misbehavior. The Bible abounds with examples of men and women whose worlds crashed from self-inflicted causes, and their responses range within great extremes.

On the dark side of those extremes is the case study of Cain. Jealous of his brother, Cain killed him, denying continually that he was answerable for his attitudes and actions. As far as we know, he never brooded on the warnings that could have helped him avoid the tragedies that occurred. He appears to have ended up living a thoroughly wasted life. Cain represents the rigidity, the hardness of inner being, that can appear when the heat is on and the consequences set in. Cain is not alone when it comes to those who will not accept accountability for their actions.

On the brighter side of the extremes, a woman, Mary Magdalene, came through her broken-world experience permitting the moment to become the beginning of an entirely new life. She was one of numerous New Testament characters who pursued lives of gross immorality and who virtually personified the energy of evil itself. She was obviously living in a kind of human bondage with no hope. No one had to tell her that her way of living was taking her downhill fast, that changes had to be made, or there would be no way back. When Jesus offered the opportunity of liberation to her, she accepted what was given and rebuilt her broken world into something beautiful.

So there is Cain: stiff-necked and unrelenting. And there is Mary: open, unfisted, and ready to submit. All of us have seen samples, perhaps in ourselves as well as in others.

There is nothing to envy in the experience of someone whose world is in the process of breaking up. It is similar to what happens when an airplane is purposely flown into the center of a hurricane for research purposes: tossed and flung about as circumstances and consequences have their way. We are talking of a person who loses much of the control over his life that he has formerly enjoyed.

Initially, the broken-world experience is usually private and very personal. It may include a period of resistance to the truth, shocked disbelief that anything like what has happened could have occurred, and anger at the possible consequences and anyone who might make sure they happen. We call this living in denial. He may attempt to blame others and interpret events so that he is able to see himself in the most charitable light. He may do this to avoid the awful feelings of guilt and self-recrimination. But if this thinking continues, it will lead to nothing good, certainly no hope of a broken world that is capable of being rebuilt.

The more healthy but nevertheless very painful part of this secretive phase occurs when the broken-world person faces facts: a self-realization of what has actually happened and his responsibility for it. There can be times of churning fear and feelings of cheapness, self-dislike, and quiet turmoil when topics too close to his experience are raised in conversation. It can be a time of depression; a period in which there is an overwhelming desire to escape, even hope that somehow life would come to a sudden end in an accident or a physical illness. He may work harder than ever in an attempt to outrun the anguished thoughts or to try to atone—as if he could—for what has happened.

These are the terrible, lonely moments for a broken-world person, and many of us know what they are like. Relief comes only when the individual looks heavenward and treats the matter for what it is: a serious offense against God and His standards. Then, in such an acknowledgment, the initial stages of healing and rebuilding are likely to begin.

This may be the time, a second stage of the broken-world experience, when a man or woman then turns to others who might be willing to forgive and provide the comfort necessary for the rebuilding process to begin. A spouse; close, intimate friends; a pastor or counselor. Ultimately, rebuilding broken worlds can never happen alone. It is a team effort, and it has to be accomplished in concert with those who can give grace and affirm progress.

When we purchase something of value that is fragile or delicate, it comes in a carefully designed box and is packed in various forms of Styrofoam to protect it against all but the most crushing blows. A whole industry is dedicated to such packing and protecting. A broken-world person needs the same kind of protection. That is why Paul called for the Corinthians to forgive and also to comfort a broken-world person in their congregation (2 Cor. 2:7).

Naturally, there are some downside risks when misbehavior and its consequences become known. Perhaps someone who cannot forgive wishes to punish or hurt the broken-world person in return. There is the risk that some relationships will never be restored, that silence and antipathy will be the way of the future. Divorce, lawsuits, periodic acts of vengeance, are some grim possibilities. The broken-world person may not be able to do anything about these unfortunate reactions. Apart from confession, expressions of sorrow, and the pledge to change, it is difficult to see what the individual can offer an offended party that will elicit restoration if the other does not wish to give it.

A possible third stage of the broken-world experience is the one anyone would dread because of the magnitude of its humiliation. And that occurs when news of one's misbehavior reaches a larger public. No matter how one might wish these things would never happen, with public knowledge may come serious damage to one's reputation, the loss of credibility, the requirement to relinquish public responsibilities of leadership, and the loss of some friends who find it expedient to withdraw because they are hurt or feel betrayed. Add to all of that the pain of gossip, of people feeling that they can be perfectly free to discuss and analyze the misbehavior in any forum of their choice.

When my sinful act resulted in a personal broken world, Gail and I chose to wrestle with a significant question that one of our pastoral advisors placed before us. The wording went something like this: *will you concentrate on the pain of this broken-world experience and resist it, OR will you permit the pain to become an environment in which God can clearly speak to you about matters He deems of ultimate importance? The choice is yours.*

How often Gail and I have walked the woods around Peace Ledge, our New Hampshire home. Here and there are the junctions of trails and what the township calls "Class-six" roads. Each fork reminds me of Robert Frost's famous poem about choices, "The Road Not Taken," part of which reads:

> Two roads diverged in a yellowed wood,
> And sorry I could not travel both
> And be one traveler, long I stood
> And looked down one as far as I could
> To where it bent in the undergrowth;
>
> Then took the other. . . .

That choice, Frost concluded, "has made all the difference."

We were going to have to make a choice. I was the broken-world person living with self-inflicted wounds. Gail was the victim of a broken-world set of choices. Would we fight the pain of the aftermath of my sin, or would we permit the pain to be part of the rebuilding process?

It wasn't a one-time choice. We made it again and again as time passed. A score of ways could be found to bring back the pain. And each time the choice had to be made again. Would we fight the pain or permit it to be the environment in which God speaks? Usually, we chose the latter. And when for a moment we strayed toward the former, something seemed to happen to soon remind us that there was a better way.

During those dark hours I spent large quantities of time scanning the Scriptures. I looked at familiar, biblical biographies in a whole new light. What startled me more than anything else, however, was one insight regarding the great personalities of the Bible. Almost every one of them had experienced a broken-world moment. As I said in the preceding chapter, I could hardly find an exception. Failures, sufferings, oppositions and oppressions, outright sins of great magnitude, sicknesses, rejections, marital and family catastrophes, and grave moments of spiritual crises.

As I studied the record of these broken worlds, I found comfort. Others had gone through my pain; others had experienced the same feelings I knew; others were at one time or another as undependable as I saw myself to be; others had received great grace and healing as I hoped to receive. And, finally, others had gone on to the greatest moments of their service to God. Permit me for a moment to use my imagination and create some conversations cast in contemporary language that might reflect the broken-world thinking of ancient biblical personalities.

THE BROKEN WORLD OF MOSES

Take, for example, the world of Moses. His world broke into pieces for the first time when he was forty years old.

And what a world it was! As an infant, he'd been marvelously delivered from a pogrom of sorts when the Pharaoh of Egypt decided to slaughter all male Hebrew babies. His mother, determined to protect him, had hidden Moses along the banks of the Nile River, placing him under the care of his older sister. The two of them, baby boy and sister, just happened to be at the right place when an Egyptian princess wandered by and became enchanted with the child she saw in the floating basket. Moses was taken to the palace of the very Pharaoh who was trying to kill him and other Hebrews his age. There he grew up apparently enjoying all the privileges and opportunities of a member of the royal family.

Then in his fortieth year he began to be sensitive to the oppression under which his people, the Hebrews, were living. One day when he saw an Egyptian guard mercilessly beating a Hebrew, he took upon himself the role of liberator and sprang to the defense of the victim, killing the guard.

Give Moses an *A* for caring, for courage, and for the willingness to risk everything that meant security for him as a human being. Give him a much lower grade for acting without thinking. A swell idea soon exploded in his face.

Within days the Hebrews had made it clear that they weren't interested in his sort of leadership and deliverance. Why, I'm not sure. Fear and cowardice, I suppose. They just weren't interested. Suddenly, Moses was a criminal among his own people and among the royal family with whom he'd grown up. He had no recourse but to run. Talk about a broken world.

That's where my imagination takes over as I ponder the kind of conversation that he and Jethro, his future father-in-law, were likely to have had when they met deep in the desert for the first time.

JETHRO. We don't see many men like you out in these parts. Sure you fit here?

MOSES. Probably not, but then again I guess I don't belong anyplace these days. What causes you to say I don't fit here?

JETHRO. It's obvious. All anyone has to do is listen to you talk, and they'll know you didn't grow up in these parts. You're a city man. You've lived the good life.

MOSES. I *was* a city man, you mean.

JETHRO. What made you leave?

MOSES. I tried being a hero.

JETHRO. A hero?

MOSES. I'd had it up to here with the way the Hebrews were being treated by the system. You must know the situation. And one day I reached my limit. I was headed for an appointment, and I came across an Egyptian foreman beating a Hebrew senseless. The Hebrew was defenseless; I thought he was going to get killed.

JETHRO. So you decided to intervene.

MOSES.Yeah. I didn't even stop to think about what I was doing. I tried to stop this guy, and he pushed me away and started in on the Hebrew again.

JETHRO. And you got mad.

MOSES. I was furious! I jumped the Egyptian from behind and got him down and just started swinging. Before I realized what had happened, I'd hit him too hard and he was dead. There was nothing to do except to bury the guy and hope that no one found out.

JETHRO. Didn't you have enough self-control to . . .

MOSES. No, I didn't. But that wasn't the worst of it.

JETHRO. What do you mean?

MOSES. Well, I thought that maybe the Hebrews who knew what I'd done would realize I was on their side and they'd support me. We could have pulled off an exodus out of Egypt or something. I guess I really thought they'd listen to me.

JETHRO. You mean because you'd defended one of them?

MOSES. Yeah. But you can't believe what happened.

JETHRO. Try me.

MOSES. A day or two later I'm out in the same area, and now I see two Hebrews fighting. So I try to step in and put an end to it. You know, I'm sure they'll recognize me and do exactly what I say.

JETHRO. That's reasonable.

MOSES. Do you know what they did? They turned on me! One of them says, "Who in the world made you lord over us? We know what you did with the Egyptian; you going to kill one of us too? Is that the way you solve everyone's problems?" I couldn't believe it. I was speechless.

JETHRO. What did you do?

MOSES. I panicked and ran. I just ran. Until I got to here. I thought those slaves would pick me up and put me on their shoulders and give me a victory parade. And instead they tell me to bug off.

JETHRO. Are you sure?

MOSES. I'm sure. Before long the Egyptians would have been looking for me, and the Hebrews weren't about to take me on as one of theirs. I knew I wouldn't have a friend in the entire country as soon as the word got out. And it was obvious it would get out.

JETHRO. Are you sure that the Hebrews wouldn't protect you?

MOSES. It couldn't have been clearer. They weren't taking any chances. Their game plan was to save their own hides. No risks. And I was a risk; you can be sure of that.

JETHRO. You must have felt about as low as anyone can feel when you headed out of town.

MOSES. Well, I can tell you one thing: there's no way I'm ever going back in that direction again. No one could ever get me near that palace or those Hebrews again. No way!

For forty years Moses lived with the consequences of a broken personal world. He had had good intentions at the age of forty, but everything had gone wrong. Knowing the rest of the story as we do, we are tempted to exonerate him. After all, he may have made a bad mistake then, but he finished his life strongly with many quality contributions. But if we had lived in Moses' time, our judgment would quite likely have been that Moses was a hot-tempered zealot with an uncontrollable character defect.

When the Bible picks him up again at the age of eighty, we get the feeling that Moses wasn't interested in rebuilding his once broken world. He no longer had a dream for liberating his people. The desert may not have been the most hospitable place in the world, but the man had made it his home. And when God suggested that the world of Moses was to be rebuilt starting back in Egypt, Moses was hardly interested in getting burned again.

What's it like to have your world break up? For Moses, it meant being hunted and chased, losing everything that had meant security for the first forty years, forfeiting his access to power, changing vocations dramatically, and living among people who had little respect, if any, for his former reputation and social position. But that broken world was rebuilt, and the new Moses was a man who presently owns a large piece of history. The people who initially rejected him made him a great hero.

THE BROKEN WORLD OF JONAH

Centuries later another man, now quite famous, saw his world fall apart in a rather unique fashion. If Moses ended up deep in a desert when his world broke, Jonah the prophet ended up deep in the sea, and it's likely that he thought he would never see land again. Again, my imagination attempts to penetrate some of Jonah's more difficult moments, wondering how and what he thinks about.

REPORTER. Mr. Jonah? Sir, I'm from the *Jerusalem Post.*

JONAH. How in the world did you guys find me here?

REPORTER. Little bit of luck, really. We got word that you'd gone overboard in the storm last week, and when the search was called off, we printed your obituary. Then someone up here who saw your picture with the obit called and said that he saw you staying at this inn.

JONAH. So everyone down there thinks I'm dead? Well, I suppose I might as well be dead for all that happened.

REPORTER. That's it. We'd really like to get your story on what happened and how you got here. I mean, this is some distance from Joppa. Someone must have brought you up here.

JONAH. Actually, I came by whale.

REPORTER. Right. Say, could you go into that one a bit?

JONAH. Look, years ago I made a commitment to the God of Israel that I'd live in total obedience to His purposes. That I'd never shrink from saying what He put in my heart. That I'd go anyplace, say anything, and do it at any cost.

REPORTER. OK. So what about the whale?

JONAH. That commitment meant a lot of tough days for me. Being a prophet is not a glamorous life.

REPORTER. How does this connect with the whale?

JONAH. I'm coming to that. You've just got to understand that when God said, "Go to Nineveh," I . . .

REPORTER. You said, "Nineveh"?

JONAH. That was my reaction too. Nineveh? I mean, I haven't made it a habit of questioning God before, but I did then. I protested with energy in me that I didn't know I had.

REPORTER. What were you supposed to do in Nineveh?

JONAH. Preach. What does any prophet of the Lord do?

REPORTER. Preach what?

JONAH. Repentance; offer a promise from God that if the city would repent, God would spare it from judgment.

REPORTER. How does that link up with going overboard in a storm? Could you get to the whale?

JONAH. Frankly, I decided that I wasn't going to Nineveh, that God was going to have to find Himself some other prophet dumb enough to go there. And so you could say I resigned from prophethood.

REPORTER. And the storm?

JONAH. Well, you don't really resign from prophethood exactly. You run, and I ran for Joppa and found the ship that was sailing the farthest the soonest.

REPORTER. And it sailed into a storm.

JONAH. In more ways than one. Those guys thought they had a storm going. I had one far larger inside me.

REPORTER. Inside you?

JONAH. You make a choice, a bad choice, like the one I did, and you suffer for it. I walked around in a daze. I was angry with myself. I was full of self-doubt. I was scared. Here I was leaving everything that was important to me, running to a city I'd never seen before. All I knew was that I was angry with God for the trip He was trying to send me on. And I'd dug in my heels and said no.

REPORTER. Did it work?

JONAH. It worked until the storm hit outside too. I was in such denial that I'd gone to sleep down in the ship after it left port. I found that I could sleep almost around the clock. Apparently even through the early part of that dumb storm. Then the captain woke me up and seemed to think that I somehow knew something about that storm. And if I would help the others on top pray, he'd be very appreciative. Of course he was right; I did know something about the storm.

REPORTER. So what did you know?

JONAH. That the storm outside was merely an extension of the storm inside. So I had them throw me overboard.

REPORTER. They threw you overboard?

JONAH. I made them do it. I felt so cheap and worthless. My sin of rebellion and disobedience was hurting other people. They were about to die in a storm that I had created. If I was devastated, what do you think they were as they watched their world breaking up? I had

no recourse but to force them to throw me over. The outside storm
cleared up for them immediately.

REPORTER. And for you?

JONAH. You could say that the storm lasted for three more days as God
let me live inside a whale and think over whether or not I still wanted
to live in rebellion. He just crushed my world; that's what He did.
And I had to make a big decision. Would I keep on fighting Him or
finally realize that His way was the best?

REPORTER. What did you decide?

JONAH. I'm here, aren't I?

REPORTER. What happens next, Mr. Jonah?

JONAH. You see that road over there? It leads toward Nineveh.

THE BROKEN WORLD OF SIMON PETER

As I've already mentioned one of the saddest descriptions of a broken
world is that of Simon Peter. I'm thinking of the moment when Peter
heard the rooster crow for the third time and realized that it powerfully
underscored his denial of association with Jesus. Of that moment of
supreme personal failure, Matthew wrote, "He went outside and wept
bitterly" (26:75).

Most scholars agree that Matthew got his description of that moment
from Peter himself. One can almost hear the dialogue between them as
Matthew sought to recapture the hour when Peter so completely caved
in.

MATTHEW. How did you feel when you realized that you had blown it so
badly?

SIMON PETER. When I heard that rooster, bells went off inside me.
Loud bells! I remembered that Jesus had warned me the night before
that this was exactly what was going to happen. But who was listening? I'd been so excited and determined that I was going to be a
better soldier than anyone else that I simply didn't listen to a word of
what He said.

MATTHEW. So you suddenly saw what He'd been trying to tell you?
That you were capable of failure?

SIMON PETER. Saw it? Saw it? I couldn't believe it; I was so shocked at
my spinelessness, I was speechless. You think you can handle anything, and then the moment comes and you can't do anything right.

MATTHEW. So what did you do? Did it occur to you to go back and try
and set the record straight?

SIMON PETER. No. I wish I would have, but I didn't. I was so devastated, I just made for the door as fast as I could and found the darkest spot I could find where I could be alone.

MATTHEW. So then what happened?

SIMON PETER. I guess I can only tell you that I cried more tears than I'd cried in an entire lifetime.

MATTHEW. Cried? I've known you for almost three years. You're not the crying type.

SIMON PETER. Matthew, I was so torn up inside; so embarrassed; so angry; so confused; so mystified at my own cowardice and stupidity. There was absolutely nothing I could do except cry. Look, I'd made a total jerk out of myself. I mean, in a matter of minutes I had self-destructed. Everything important to me was in shambles. Nothing was left. I could imagine how Jesus felt; I mean, you should have seen how He looked at me. Can you imagine how badly I had let Him down? I was so heartbroken that all I could do was cry.

And that's why Matthew wrote of the moment: "He went outside and wept bitterly." Peter could only blame himself for his dismal performance. In a strange way, his failure should be a comfort to many friends or spouses who have been betrayed by a broken-world person. All too often an insensitive world looks on in the wake of bad consequences and says, "if he or she had been a better spouse," or "if he or she had been a better friend." But who could have been a better friend to Peter than Jesus? And still the fisherman stumbled.

When Moses failed, he disappeared into the desert. When Jonah failed, he put to sea in more ways than one. And when Peter's world fell apart, he ran off into a back alley and subsequently to Galilee where he thought he could get lost back in the fishing business. Who would ever want to hear from him again? It was a reasonable question. The answer is that at least one person wanted to hear from him: Christ. And that was no small thing.

Broken-world moments (or hours) were known by virtually all of those whom we now look upon as saints. It wouldn't be safe to say that such disasters are a part of faith. But it would certainly be accurate to say that they ultimately developed faith. And the men and women who went through them and handled them correctly were the better when the matters were ended.

In the darkest moments of Gail's and my broken world, no modern author offered more consolation and hope than Amy Carmichael, a woman who served as a missionary in India for more than fifty years. Carmichael's last seventeen years of life were broken-world years, for she suffered intensely from a combination of illnesses and the effects of a serious fall. During that time, she hardly ever saw life beyond her bedroom.

Nevertheless, Amy Carmichael's broken world became a pulpit from which, through her writing, she poured faith and hope into tens of thousands of people. And her ministry continues until this day.

Speaking of broken-world moments, she wrote:

> The plant called heartsease often grows where we should not expect to find it. And it says, after these sad days have passed you will look back and wonder how you were carried through. It will not always be so hard as it has been of late; for after the darkness cometh light and after tempest cometh calm. And this is no fantasy. It shall be so. (*Gold by Moonlight*)

And so it was for Moses, for Jonah, for Simon Peter, and for countless others.

CHAPTER 3

Impenetrable Airspace

> **BOTTOM LINE #3:**
> *An unguarded strength and an unprepared heart are double weaknesses.*

Military experts say that the Russians have developed and positioned the most effective anti-aircraft system in all the world. Powerful radars probe the air above major Soviet cities, and missiles are poised to bring down enemy aircraft at any altitude. None of the cities is more heavily defended in that system, it is said, than Moscow and its famous Red Square just outside the Kremlin, the seat of the Communist government.

That explains why the world was shocked (and more than a little amused) when a young German piloted a small rented single-engine airplane from Denmark into Soviet territory and buzzed the Kremlin before landing in Red Square. Before he was taken away by the police, he managed to greet some surprised Muscovites who just happened to be in the area at the time. He even signed a few autographs. And when the incident was over, the youthful German was elated; the Russian government was embarrassed; a couple of top generals were abruptly sacked; and the world laughed.

When I read the first accounts of this daring escapade, I smiled with everyone else and mused upon the kind of courage (or foolhardiness) that would make it possible to do something so bold. But almost instantly it occurred to me that a parable of sorts arose out of this bizarre venture.

I thought about a city dumb-founded that its most powerful de-fenses were thwarted; a city suddenly forced to brood upon its own vulnerability. After all, if an adolescent could land a plane in Red Square without being fired on, what could a dedicated enemy, bent on destruction, accomplish?

As my imagination tuned in on the picture of the plane in Red Square, I also began to see the figures of men like Moses, Jonah, and Simon Peter. Something penetrated their airspace too; something that made it possible for them to make poor choices in a moment when better performance could have been expected. And then I realized that this is what happens to every broken-world person. Personal airspace is violated by temptations from without or by strange stirrings from deep within. And the result is the seedbed of misbehaviors sometimes of the worst possible sort. If that is our own case, we are likely to respond much like the Russians: we can't believe that this can be happening to us. That any of us should be so self-assured as to think that broken-world choices cannot happen to us is a point of maximum danger or double weakness.

I wasn't in Moscow the day the young German made his flight to Red Square so I don't know precisely what happened. But my strong suspicion is that no one in the Russian air defense command was ready for this sort of "invasion." All of their equipment and training was prepared for big, fast-moving, bomb-laden planes. And perhaps it was a nice day, and the people at the radar sets were somewhat relaxed. So when the blip of a tiny airplane was picked up on radar screens here and there along the air route, people reasoned that it was nothing. Nothing worth getting excited about; nothing worth doing anything about.

And then the harmless little aircraft landed just outside the door of the office of the general secretary. Suddenly the matter escalated from a harmless incident to an event of world-shaking significance.

As I already indicated, the Soviets' responses to the failure of their defenses were swift and retributive. General officers were fired; command structures were reorganized; many vituperative speeches were made. Somebody was mad!

When the personal airspace of someone we admire and love is penetrated and there is gross failure, we are usually numbed to the core of our beings. We're liable to pass through a series of reactions as we respond to the bad news, whatever it is: *dismay* and *sorrow,* first; perhaps then *anger* at feeling that our trust has been betrayed; next, a sense of *despair* if we think a good person or effort has been neutralized; and then maybe *fear,* fear that we may be vulnerable to the same failure.

The most important reaction will be the last one, and that, hopefully, is *the perspective and performance of grace.* A great and unique reaction of the Christian toward an individual's broken-world experience is the gracious one: treating someone not as he deserves to be treated but as he needs to be treated in order for his broken world to be rebuilt. Knowing what it is like to receive much grace, I'm deeply aware of its power to heal or redeem when given to a repentant person.

Those first reactions in the chain are human, predictable, and understandable. The act of grace, however, is a supernatural reaction to sinfulness and obviously the superior one in the long run. It is the biblically prescribed reaction, for it sets the scene for the healing and restoration of the one whose world is in pieces. Without grace, broken worlds do not get rebuilt.

Unfortunately, frequent alternatives to grace are gossip and slander. Some people surmise that scandalous news, if it is reasonably true, is fair game for conversation. But the Bible never discriminated between facts and fiction about people when it pointed out that all kinds of gossip and slanderous conversation are, by heavenly standards, wrong.

In her book *A Closer Walk*, Catherine Marshall deals with this matter in a transparent manner:

> These further insights have come as I pondered Satan's inroads into my own heart and will:
>
> 1. When we rejoice over, or look for, or repeat with relish negative news, then we have placed ourselves on the side of evil.
>
> 2. It is possible to take this negative stance so often with regard to situations and persons that this becomes a way of life. Negative thinking is really a weapon of Satan. WE call it "realism"; Christ calls it "not believing the truth."
>
> 3. We do not realize how definitely our mind-set—that is, what the mind picks out from all the news to highlight—reveals *whose* side we're really on.

These responses are similar when we are the ones whose worlds have broken up. Until someone has had a broken-world experience, it may be difficult to realize that the chain of responses—dismay, anger, despair, and fear—may be nearly the same for the one who has failed as he or she comes to an awareness of what has been done.

Talk to broken-world persons who have honestly faced up to the realities of the situation, and they will admit that they were unprepared when it happened, disarmed as it did happen, and terribly disillusioned about themselves after it happened. Quite likely they will say, "When I talk about what happened, I almost feel as if I'm speaking about another person. I want to believe that it couldn't be me."

The word *scandal* is often employed for such occasions of optimum failure. It suggests the revelation of an act or actions entirely opposite our convictions and expectations. Because of the nature of human beings, we will always have scandals with us, and—sorry to say—it is always possible that we will be the scandal.

The point then is this: *although we may not like it, we must assume that disasters that break up personal worlds—small/large, publicized/privatized, self-inflicted/inflicted-upon-us, mega-consequences/minor-consequences—will always be with us, and we must accept them as a tragic part of life.* That means we must comprehend the reasons for and the results of world-breaking moments; we must be prepared so that we can prevent them from happening to us and others; and we must know something about how to restore to fellowship and bring to wholeness those who pass through the experience.

Oswald Chambers urged his readers toward this full-orbed alertness about the power of evil or sin and its capacity to invade personal airspace either from the external world or from deep in the internal or private world. He was more than blunt when he wrote:

> It is *not being reconciled to the fact of sin* that produces all the disasters in life. We talk about noble human nature, self-sacrifice and platonic friendship—all unmitigated nonsense. Unless we recognize the act of sin, there is something that will laugh and spit in the face of every ideal we have. Unless we reconcile ourselves to the fact that there will come a time when the power of darkness will have its own way, and that by God's permission, we will compromise with that power when its hour comes. If we refuse to take the fact of sin into our calculation, refuse to agree that a base impulse runs through men, that there is such a thing as vice and self-seeking, when our hour of darkness strikes, instead of being acquainted with sin and the grief of it, we will compromise straight away and say there is no use battling against it. (*The Place of Help*, emphasis mine)

The failure to understand this distressing reality often paves the way for those who have been offended or disillusioned by the performance of a broken-world individual to become unredemptive or vindictive persons. It can even include those who secretly revel in the misfortunes of others because they feel superior and look good for the moment. Sometimes it can mean a kind of unfortunate amusement as some scoff at those who momentarily look like fools.

François Fénelon, the great French mystic, wrote:

> When the world triumphs over a scandal it shows how little it knows about mankind and virtue. Those who know the depths of human frailty and how even the little good we do is a borrowed thing, though grieved, will be surprised at nothing. Let all men prove themselves mere men—God's truth will not be weakened and the world will show itself as more hateful than ever in having corrupted those who were seeking after virtue. *(Spiritual Letters to Women)*

As I've already observed, in most biblical cases we know more about people's errors and tragedies than about their successes. This is another way of saying that they were, for the most part, rather salty characters. Bold, daring, venturesome to be sure; but well acquainted with what it means to be humiliated and stripped of everything thought to be worthwhile in life.

Like runners who have sustained terrible falls in a race, they sprint toward the finish line with grass stains, dirt smudges, and bruises all over them. For most of them, the fact that they appear in the Bible at all is based on the fact that they ran, fell—usually more than once—got up again, and finished.

I find that rather comforting. It suggests that God communes with and uses people not because they are perfect and antiseptically clean in life but because they have painfully discovered the way of grace. They live as men and women who know they can keep going only because of divine affection and empowerment. Nothing else sustains or strengthens.

The fact that the God of the Bible loves and offers second chances for rebuilding to people who have failed doesn't justify their sin. And we should never fall into the trap of suggesting that the more we fail, the more God will like us and favor our lot in life. Not at all! It is to say, however, that sin and failure is a common event in human history and also that God makes great room in His agenda for those hapless failures who are committed to keep on going. This is a God of the second chance! Consequences? Of course. Restoration and hope? Most definitely. No one need run or hide. His grace calls us out into the open, to a fresh start.

Perhaps we need to reaffirm that Christ called men and women to be godly, not Godlike. Godlikeness is an impossibility; godliness is a description of a particular maturing process that causes people to reflect some of the Creator's personality qualities. There is a significant difference between the two. Each day I can ask the heavenly Father to help me be a godly man. But I will never be Godlike.

When I first read the story of the little plane on Red Square, I applied the parable to my own broken-world experience. I began to see in a clearer light how often our inner space can be invaded from without or from sources deep within us. And when our defenses are inadequate and we are not alert, the results can be as humiliating as the Red Square incident was for the Russian defense ministry.

It was a stunning new reminder that I am actually what the Bible says I have been all along: a sinner. If not in act, then in thought, I have managed to break every one of the Ten Commandments, sometimes in the most subtle ways.

The study of those standards God gave Moses for Israel on Mt. Sinai makes for a frightening but nevertheless illuminating self-measurement. The study suggests that I do not stack up well. No one else seems to, either.

James points out in his New Testament writings what compounds the matter of my culpability as a sinner. If I have broken any of the commandments, I have actually broken them all: "For whoever keeps the whole law and yet stumbles at just one point is guilty of breaking all of it" (James 2:10). Before God, we are all lawbreakers, whether or not our misbehaviors have received special public attention. And Christians must recognize that as the primary affinity bringing us together before Christ.

But the Scriptures do not focus on the individual actions or attitudes of sin; rather, the focus is on the underlying condition of evil or sinfulness that leaves us all morally and spiritually vulnerable to misbehavior. It is a human tendency, however, to want to spotlight certain misbehaviors that seem worse than others. We do this because they are particularly repugnant to us in our generation or because we perceive that they have greater consequences than others. And when people are exposed or confess guilt in these categories, we refer to them as fallen. But the truth is that we are all fallen people, whether or not we have been guilty of a major misbehavior.

For all the talk in the church about sin and misbehavior, we probably do not take the matter of our vulnerability seriously enough. By unconsciously "grading" certain misbehaviors as more significant than others, we bypass central biblical doctrines: ALL are sinners and stand on equal ground at the Cross; ALL are in need of equal amounts of forgiving and restorative grace; ALL of us are always in danger of the little invaders that enter our airspace and render us to a fallen state; and ALL of us need to learn more about how to defend when the attacks come.

Chambers wrote:

> You hear of one man who has gone safely through battles, and friends tell him it is in answer to prayer; does that mean that the prayers for the men who have gone under have not been answered? We have to remember that the hour of darkness will come in every life. It is not that we are saved from the hour of sorrow, but that we are delivered in it. (*The Place of Help*)

A few years ago I gave a speech at a college commencement. Before the festivities began, a member of that school's board sat with me in the president's office. We'd never met before, and we were asking questions of each other that might help us get better acquainted.

Suddenly, my new friend asked a strange question. I've thought about it many times since then. "If Satan were to blow you out of the water," he asked, "how do you think he would do it?"

"I'm not sure I know," I answered. "All sorts of ways, I suppose; but I know there's one way he wouldn't get me."

"What's that?"

"He'd never get me in the area of my personal relationships. That's one place where I have no doubt that I'm as strong as you can get."

A few years after that conversation my world broke wide open. A chain of seemingly innocent choices became destructive, and it was my fault. Choice by choice by choice, each easier to make, each becoming gradually darker. And then my world broke—in the very area I had predicted I was safe—and my world had to be rebuilt.

In another deeply insightful piece of writing, Oswald Chambers commented on an Older Testament military figure, Joab, whose record of loyalty to David, his commander-in-chief, had been exemplary. One test of his character had come when Absalom, David's son, mounted a rebellion that could have catapulted Joab into greater power. But he resisted the seductiveness of it all and remained faithful. Later the same man, now known for the strength of his loyalty, faced the same moral test but failed. He made a bad choice and joined Adonijah's rebellion against David. Joab's greatest strength became his weakness (see 1 Kings 1:7).

Chambers commented on the tendency of men and women to lose major personal battles not at the points of their weaknesses but, strangely enough, at the points of their perceived strengths. He wrote, "The Bible characters never fell on their weak points but on their strong ones; unguarded strength is double weakness" *(The Place of Help)*.

Funny! During my earlier years I'd thought we were most vulnerable at our weakest points, but Chambers said the opposite. I wondered why until I realized from personal experience that where we perceive ourselves to be the strongest is where we're least likely to be prepared for a battle that isn't psychological or emotional. It's spiritual! And when we are unprepared, even our most fortified defenses are in serious jeopardy. Let no person ever say, "I can't be taken." Or as St. Paul wrote, "So, if you think you are standing firm, be careful that you don't fall!" (1 Cor. 10:12).

A tiny airplane buzzes Red Square in the center of Moscow. You don't see tiny planes over the Kremlin very often, I'm told. The airspace is restricted, and the air defense system all the way to Denmark makes a violation of territory impossible. The military is strong and determined; no intruder could ever make it to Red Square. But still that plane circles the area. And then it lands . . . right there next to the Kremlin Wall and Lenin's Tomb. A kid gets out and signs autographs. And the Soviets are humiliated.

And so are the rest of us who have allowed our worlds to be penetrated when we never thought it could be possible.

CHAPTER 4

Why Do Worlds Break Up?

> BOTTOM LINE #4:
> *Personal INSIGHT is not only momentary; it is a healthy way of living. Insight is the first step in rebuilding.*

Among the many stories Jesus told is that of the young man who chose to break with his family and move away. For reasons we do not understand in our culture, he felt within his rights to demand his share of his father's estate. This he apparently turned into cash suitable for traveling and immediately left for another part of the world.

Jesus said nothing about the plans the young man had as he left his father. We only know he wanted to be free from family responsibility, to be independent. And with his father's money, he set out to achieve his goal. We also know nothing about why he picked the city to which he traveled. Perhaps he was drawn by a first-century brand of glitter. Or perhaps he heard of desirable investment or employment opportunities. But when he got there, fun quickly became the primary issue.

It is reasonable to believe that the young man we know as the prodigal son did not plan on, nor did he anticipate, losing his entire nest egg to games and girls. But he did. My imagination suggests that he was the guest of honor at all the parties until his cash flow dried up. Only then did his propped-up personal world collapse. In actuality, it had been breaking up for a long time. It just took certain circumstances to verify the fact.

Once rich (at least in money if not in maturity) and now penniless, the young man had to face a broken-world scenario that included a stint on a pig farm, which would have been just about the worst predicament the Jewish hearers of this story could have imagined. It was Jesus' way of saying: we are talking about a man who has hit bottom.

As the Master unfolded the story, listeners could grasp the consequences of loss, hunger, and humiliation suddenly piling in on the young man and bringing him to a moment of deep personal insight. Jesus described that moment this way: "When [the man] came to himself" (Luke 15:17 NKJV). Only then did he begin to think clearly about what home meant, what personal relationships meant, and—most important—*the implication of the values by which he had lived and the choices he had made.*

Call it the occasion of PERSONAL INSIGHT, the instant of ruthless truth! It's a startling moment. When it's experienced, one will never forget it, especially if one has been avoiding the truth for a while and has gotten out of the habit of facing personal facts. It's an event that almost everyone who has had a broken-world experience would wish had come much earlier so as to avoid the choices that led to terrible consequences. Usually, there are such chances; but the reality is that in those moments, when a different outcome could have been arranged, the person in question, like the prodigal, wasn't watching or listening.

This INSIGHTFUL MOMENT—biblically speaking—is the occasion when individuals see *the truth* for what it is; when they see *themselves* for what they are; and when they see what I would like to call the *environments of choice* for what they make possible.

The first of these, *the truth*, is really God's law, His specification by which life can be lived to produce the maximum amount of personal health and stability. This truth is noncompetitive; it is nonnegotiable; and it is, in the long run, unavoidable. When it is respected and obeyed, everyone wins, and God is honored.

Seeing ourselves for what we really are is another story. Humbling, in fact. In this aspect of insight we human beings quickly discover and affirm that we do not have life all put together; left to ourselves, we are quite liable to drift from what are healthy values and choices and end up dismantling ourselves and the resources God has entrusted to us. History testifies to that. And so does the prodigal.

Being sensitive to the *environments of choice* for what they make possible means realizing that there are times, places, and moods of spirit when we are more likely to make certain choices—good choices *or* bad choices—we might not make on other occasions. For example, it is reasonable to assume that the prodigal would almost certainly have never made the foolish choice of squandering his financial resources if he had elected to remain in his home environment. At home he would have been restrained by the natural accountability he had to loved ones and wiser people who cared for his welfare. Presumably he would have enjoyed the benefit of their counsel and rebuke. But in the environment of a strange place, uncaring people, and unrestrained revelry he formed the choices that lost him everything, including his integrity.

Unfortunately, he came to himself *after* the loss. Naturally one would have wished that the moment of insight had come *before* the accumulated choices. And therein lies the simple answer as to why many personal worlds break up.

I wouldn't be writing this book in quite this way if I hadn't gone through a broken-world experience. Burned into my mind is the occasion when I came to myself, that of personal insight.

You could say that I was in a pigpen mentally and spiritually. I must emphasize that no one around me realized my mental and spiritual location, and I wasn't prepared to reveal it. Rather, I expended great amounts of energy for a brief period of time to mask a torturous inner struggle.

INSIGHT: "he came to himself." I would like to suggest that the moment of insight follows a rather standard order, and men and women who have made poor choices down through the centuries and then come to insight have followed that order almost to the letter.

When I think of this process, I'm reminded of what a person generally goes through in a visit to the dentist because of an aching tooth that has a cavity. A standard process involves locating and probing the extent of the decay, drilling to clean the tooth out, and filling it with a substance that will return it to strength and health.

In coming to oneself, as in the experience of the prodigal, there is first an awareness of mounting circumstances that are more than unpleasant and never anticipated. Call it a massive "ache of the spirit."

For a while, perhaps, the prodigal may have thought that the adversities he faced could be managed and that with a little bit of good fortune, the damages or losses could be repaired or at least concealed. But that wasn't possible for him, and it usually is not for any of us in the long run, though many of us try. Isn't this similar to those days when a tooth hurts, but we keep putting off a visit to the dentist because we hope the pain will go away? Occasionally it does; usually it doesn't.

Then comes the conclusion that one has made a massive error in

judgment and choice. Usually a trust has been violated, resources mis-
handled, or a wrong road of decision making taken. The prodigal in the
pigpen now knows this and begins to have remorse that it ever happened. The problem, the ache, must be examined and treated.

But the insightful moment continues. Who is responsible for this
choice? Me? Others? Bad timing? And this is often a crossroads in the
process of insight. If the prodigal had chosen to blame his performance
on others, he might have guaranteed another cycle of brokenness, the
second perhaps worse than the first. No, this is one of the moments of
supreme inner pain. The prodigal must point the finger at himself and
acknowledge that he alone is responsible for his choices.

The drilling is often an anguishing experience. Acknowledging guilt
and accountability before God; standing before Him, as it were, offering no excuses and sorrowfully admitting that one has done wrong. It's
a very difficult moment, perhaps the hardest of the human condition.
The Bible uses the word *repentance* to describe this action.

Repentance is a rather dramatic word. It refers to the act of traveling
in one direction and then suddenly changing to go the opposite way.
Both John the Baptizer and Jesus used repentance as the centerpoint of
their teaching because they were talking to a generation of people whose
personal worlds were terribly broken. Yet the people would not face up
to the changes necessary to make their worlds come back together
again. Stubborn people do not repent very easily, and those people were
stubborn.

Repentance is activated, first, in the act of confession: the candid
acknowledgment before God, and perhaps to others, that one has
sinned and is in need of forgiveness. Both by example and by teaching,
the Scriptures place a high priority on confessing, for in so doing, one
actually reveals the secrets of the heart. And until the heart is volun-
tarily opened up, the process of rebuilding a broken world cannot begin.

Our Christian traditions seem to have gone to unfortunate extremes
on the matter of confession. The Roman Catholic church has maintained the confessional booth for centuries. But in most places now, the
confessional booth appears to be diminished in significance, if not
phased out entirely. This is understandable if the encounter between
priest and penitent sinner had become incidental and devoid of mean-
ingful restoration, understandable if the act of confession had become
an empty obligation, a religious nuisance.

On the other hand, the Protestant penchant for privatizing faith and relegating confession to a singular transaction between that person and God has meant a loss of accountability and a loss of helpful new direction that confession ought to make possible. Anyone can breathe a silent prayer that amounts to little more than a "Sorry, God" and presume to get on with life. How, if things are to be so private and "under the table," is the sinner and the sinned against to know if there has been genuine sorrow and change of heart? All too often this undefined process drifts along as the pursuit of cheap grace.

There needs to be a moment in the life of the Lord's followers where they can clearly acknowledge those things they know to be an offense against God and His church and then hear the words: *"you are forgiven in the name of Jesus."* This need not be the mystical priestly absolution of which Protestants have been afraid for centuries. No, it can be the affirmation from one fellow believer to another that God is faithful to forgive when we are humble enough to confess. How that should actually happen in each of our lives is a question of great importance.

Finally, just as the cavity in a tooth must be filled, so the broken-world person must finally enter into something the Bible calls restoration. Restoration means rebuilding. Some of that one can do for oneself, but the final part must be done by others.

As we will see later on in greater detail, restoration looks to the damage done in a broken-world experience and asks how it can be repaired. Broken relationships must be examined and, if possible, glued back together again. Forgiveness must be requested *and* granted, and that requires people to come together and offer mercy and grace to one another. These are not simple or easy things to give, and sometimes they require time.

But restoration is one of the unique acts of the Christian community. In the final analysis, it cannot be demanded or even earned by the broken-world person; it must be freely given as God once freely gave grace to whoever wished to receive it.

If restoration is genuine, it may provide a rebuilt relationship that is beautiful to behold. I think of this when Gail takes a special glue out of the tool cabinet to join the broken pieces of a cup back together. "This glue is so strong," she says, "that the new joint will be the strongest part of the cup." She has described the possibilities of restoration.

It all began when the young man came to himself: INSIGHT. The logic of insight suggests that we get into trouble when we permit a blindness about the inner world to occur. For it is in the inner world that we handle *God's truth,* we remember *who we really are* with our propensities and weaknesses, and we monitor the *environments of choice*. So if we are not in touch with our private worlds, we are liable to have a broken-world experience.

That's what happened to Israel's King David. He seemed to fight the process of insight all the way, and that is understandable because David seems to have had a problem with insight. Reading David's poems, we note that he frequently talks about the problem of insight, almost as if he's fighting to remind himself that he's stubborn about facing his inner self and that he needs a lot of help in this area.

In one of his most favored psalms, the 139th, David talks about such insight: "You have searched me and known me" (v. 1, NKJV). It isn't clear at first if David likes the fact that there is a God who knows him as well as He says He does. But before the psalm is ended, David is inviting God to a further search. Search my heart (my inner being); search my ways (my outer performance). Let me know if there are errant ways in need of correction.

Like the prodigal son, David had made a series of terrible choices at one time in his life. The most significant bad choice we all know about was his illicit relationship with Bathsheba.

The story might have been different if David had had insight about what was happening in his private world the day he first experienced temptation. What might have changed if he had identified the boredom and laziness that apparently were taking over in his inner being? Would he have been more careful if he had chosen to recognize that he was vulnerable to poor choice making when his key companions and advisors were gone to the battlefield leaving him alone in his palace? If there had been insight, would David have been more on guard and sensitive when lusts and passions from his innermost being attempted to take over and affect his choices?

Since these things did happen, we wish that David had come to his moment of insight soon after he realized he had sinned with another man's wife. But he still didn't! And from all we can surmise, he apparently planned to deliberately cover up his law-breaking performance with Bathsheba and hope that nothing bad would occur.

But something did; she sent him a message informing him that she had become pregnant as a result of their meeting. Her husband, Uriah, was away at battle, and in a short time it would become obvious to everyone who cared to notice that he had been betrayed.

David had to face external consequences. Before that moment the consequences seemed internal and private, relatively simple to handle (albeit painful) if he so chose. The king would have had to deal only with God, Bathsheba and her husband, and perhaps a few others. Now the consequences were soaring out of his control. Others would soon get into the act.

That could have been the time for his moment of personal insight, but it wasn't. David took the wrong fork in the road and chose the cover-up policy again. David invited Uriah home from the battlefield in hopes that he and his wife would spend a few days and nights together. *Surely that would make the consequences go away,* David apparently thought.

But David's cover-up scheme fell apart when Uriah refused to visit his home while on temporary duty at David's palace. "Why should I go home when my comrades are in battle and do not receive the same privilege?" he asked (see 2 Sam. 11:11).

When Uriah intentionally or unintentionally foiled David's cover-up plan (some think that Uriah suspected the plot all along), David had another chance to enter into the further process of insight. But he took the wrong fork again, (deliberately mixing my metaphors) refused the dentist's drill, and arranged a simple plot to make sure that Uriah would be killed on the battlefield.

The perimeter of effects from David's original broken-world choice expanded when he wrote a note to Joab, the commander of the troops on the battlefield, directing that Uriah be assigned to a position of maximum danger. Joab had to know what was going on when he read the unusual request, but instead of confronting David, he complied and participated in the next phase of David's attempt to make the original offense and its consequences go away. Soon Uriah was dead.

With Bathsheba's husband gone and no one asking any questions, David thought that his problems had ended and that his personal world would not break up. He was free to marry Bathsheba, and he did. If you could have entered David's inner space and read his mind for the next few months, you would have probably monitored the thoughts of a man living with a temporary sort of double-mindedness. One part of him was in misery, knowing what he'd done; the other part felt somewhat defiant and clever because of how he'd manipulated people and events to cover his original *indiscretion.* (I use that lighter word for a gross sin because the mind of a person covering up usually likes to diminish the nature of sin at every possible chance.)

A year passed. A year of routine activity. Running the nation; making decisions; writing psalms, although we have to wonder about how many and what kind of quality. A year in which it appeared as if a bad choice was finally history. We can't be sure, but we get the impression that David finally thought he had managed the external consequences to their termination. After all, he had kept people (and God?) from finding out what he'd done. At least it seemed that way.

You enter again into David's mind to learn how a broken-world person thinks. Did the king get to the point that he rationalized the original adulterous meeting? Did he manage his mind so that he justified Uriah's death, perhaps forgetting that the real reason for assigning Uriah a place at the most dangerous part of the battle was not a military decision but a cover-up decision? Did he ever get to the point that he was "uninsightful" enough to thank God for making all the external consequences go away?

Broken-world people can indeed think that way. "Uninsightful" minds that have not "come to themselves" are capable of turning any event toward a favorable interpretation to make themselves look blameless. Human beings are adept at such cover-ups.

Anyone who has studied the mind-set of the Nazi leaders in wartime Germany will remember their effort to justify the killing of the Jews and other enemies under holocaust conditions. They told themselves that this was a difficult but nevertheless heroic act for which generations in the future would thank them. This is how the "uninsightful" mind is capable of thinking.

Back to David. Did his conscience ever bother him during this time? Did he ever replay the events of the previous year like a slow-motion tape in a VCR? How hard did he have to work to keep from "coming to himself"? How much energy did he waste keeping the lid on inner thoughts bursting to be heard?

These might have been the days when he wrote the words:

> When I kept silent,
>   my bones wasted away
>   through my groaning all day long.
> For day and night
>   your hand was heavy upon me;
> my strength was sapped
>   as in the heat of summer (Ps. 32:3–4).

People whose worlds are beginning to break apart understand that language. They know the discomfort of glancing within and not liking what they see. They know the loneliness of sleepless nights when a carousel projector whirls round and round in the mind playing pictures of the past when choices were made that cannot now be unmade. They visualize an accusing finger pointing at them every time someone raises the subject about which they feel the most guilt.

People like David suddenly realize that they no longer have integrity, that they are not whole or healthy persons. And people like David become increasingly weary of making sure that no one ever discovers the origin of their discomfort.

In David's case it appears that he could or would not make a connection between whatever bad feelings and convictions he had in his inner being and the truth of the past. I reach that conclusion after studying the approach of Nathan the prophet who came to see David about his evil acts of adultery and murder.

Would Nathan have gotten through the door if he had sent a letter to David suggesting a conversation about his sin? I suspect not! Would he have been invited to sit down if he had walked into David's office and said, "I've come to talk with you about a grave offense in your recent past"? Probably not!

Nathan was smart enough to know that David remained in cover-up, impervious to insight. So he entered the back door of David's life by telling him an innocent, though tragic, story. And David was hooked.

There were two men in a certain town, one rich and the other poor. The rich man had a very large number of sheep and cattle, but the poor man had nothing except one little ewe lamb he had bought. He raised it, and it grew up with him and his children. It shared his food, drank from his cup and even slept in his arms. It was like a daughter to him.

Now a traveler came to the rich man, but the rich man refrained from taking one of his own sheep or cattle to prepare a meal for the traveler who had come to him. Instead, he took the ewe lamb that belonged to the poor man and prepared it for the one who had come to him (2 Sam. 12:1–4).

That was all David needed to hear. Soon he was expressing outrage. I wonder why. Was this the emotion of a man feeling deeply about acts of injustice? Were they the righteous sentiments of a man who was truly indignant about the crime of stealing? Or were these the signals of anger that he really had against himself for what he had done to another "poor man" named Uriah?

We have seen this sort of thing happen many times. Haven't most of us realized that we often become most irritated about characteristics in other people that we really haven't faced in ourselves? On a more public scale, haven't we all seen the occasional public figure who goes to extraordinary lengths to accuse or criticize another and later is exposed as being guilty of a similar offense? What is happening?

Perhaps it's a pattern we are more used to seeing in the life of an alcoholic who has just come off a binge. He swears in his heart that he will never do it again, that the most recent event was really the last time. And for a few days or even weeks, he reinforces his desire to cease and desist from drinking by expressing strong hostility toward all alcohol and drinkers. In so doing he thinks to distance himself from something that has previously victimized him.

But all of the anger he expresses toward someone else is really anger expressed toward himself; it is a subconscious effort at seeking a false kind of cleansing; it is an insufficient attempt to rid himself of his guilt. If he gets mad at the error he has committed, maybe it and its consequences will go away. But they won't.

Nathan picked the moment of David's supreme anger toward a stranger whose sin was infinitesimally smaller than his original sin. He said, "You are the man." And David, like the prodigal, came to himself.

Insight! Its moment has arrived long after it should have.

"I have sinned," David said. And the search for truth, an objective assessment of self, and the matter of restoration begin. Or to put it in its metaphorical setting: the "tooth" was examined, the drilling began, and at the right moment, the filling was accomplished.

No broken world ever begins to be rebuilt until this moment of insight is initiated. And the longer it takes to reach that moment, the more difficult it will be to rebuild a broken world and minimize the consequences.

Perhaps the metaphor of a tooth with a cavity in need of filling is not a pleasant one to most of us. That is why it may be the most apt one for this difficult subject. But I cannot leave the metaphor without remembering the moment when a dentist used the drill on one of my teeth. A rather unpleasant odor arose as the drill probed the cavity of the tooth seeking every bit of decayed material. It was an undesirable event in every way. But necessary!

The moment of insight is not necessarily a pleasant moment. But this book has no value if we do not go deeper into subjects that many people in our day have found distasteful. And so I wish to take the drill and examine what happens in the moment of insight. If insight in the biblical sense means knowing myself for what I am and then knowing the environments of choice making for what they are, I have an outline for the next couple of chapters.

In my mind I watch the prodigal wend his way from pigsty to home. I think that the story Jesus told that day was a true one, and those in the crowd who heard Him tell it realized that He was rehearsing the experiences of a neighbor. Perhaps the father or the son was there listening. The story is entirely believable. And I ponder what the young man thought about as he headed for the homestead.

Did he think back on the events that led up to his decision to leave home? Did he think through the various moments in his stay in the "far-off" land when he made a chain of seemingly innocent but increasingly dangerous decisions? Did he count the losses he sustained of monies not really his own? And did he consider in his new insight how much he must have hurt his father and anyone else he really loved very much? Of course he did. All of us broken-world people know he thought those thoughts.

CHAPTER 5

Life on the Underside

> **BOTTOM LINE #5:**
> *Almost no one bears a heavier load than the carrier of personal secrets of the past or the present.*

Years ago I had a prolonged experience of lower back pain. After all attempts to live with it failed, I went to see a physician who treats bad backs. I paid him forty-five dollars to tell me to go to bed for fourteen days of rest and not to get up except to take long hot showers. But it wasn't a bad deal because his prescription for my problem worked, and I was soon on my feet again.

The doctor warned me that I would meet a thousand fellow lower-back-pain sufferers who would want to commiserate with my plight. He was concerned, he said, that I not take their home-grown diagnoses and remedies too seriously. "There are some pretty dumb ideas out there," he said. I wasn't sure I knew what he was talking about until I left my bed and the hot showers two weeks later.

The doctor was right; I think I met all one thousand sufferers. It was as if I had been inducted into a society of people whose sole affinity was sore backs. As the man had predicted, every one of them seemed to have an explanation for my discomfort, and each one had a proposal for what I should do about it. Some explanations seemed to make sense; others did indeed seem dumb.

In his most recent book *Recovering the Christian Mind*, Harry Blamires admits to the same experience: "I found I had entered via a slipped disc into a world-wide fellowship in which the password 'back trouble' would key off reminiscences of extraordinary variety and length."

Many years later, I became aware of another more unfortunate society when I experienced a discomfort that was far more serious: my personal broken world. I call this group *the society of secret carriers.*

Like the back-pain sufferers, they had been there all the time; I just hadn't known how many there were. Some of them found ways to communicate with me through the mail, others in conversations when possible, and still others over the phone if they could get my number. The code words that almost always introduced a secret carrier began, "I know exactly what you've been going through . . ."

I had been a pastor for more than twenty-five years, and during that time I'd probably come into contact with literally tens of thousands of people. Although I was always aware that congregations were full of men and women who were living with self-inflicted or other-inflicted wounds, I never (never, never, never) had any idea of how many more secret carriers there really were and how deep were their shame and their pain. I began to learn as I identified this most sorrowful of all societies.

Recently, I turned over a two-by-six board that had been lying on the ground behind our home for a long time. I was startled to discover an enormous city of bugs hiding underneath. It seemed as if there were thousands and thousands of them dwelling in that dark and damp place. And it was clear that they did not appreciate my exposure of their life on the underside of that board.

As I watched them scurry for cover, I thought of what might be called the underside of the church: those numberless people who walk into sanctuaries all over the world carrying their secrets behind bright clothing and forced smiles. They sing the songs, pray the prayers, listen to the sermons. And all the while the secrets fester within the private world causing either a constantly broken heart or a hardened heart. They come in fear of their secrets being exposed, and they quite likely go in fear that they will have to live this way for the rest of their lives. Believe me, the underside of the church is there, listening and watching to find out whether there is anyone with whom their secret might be safe if revealed.

Several kinds of people are in this society of secret carriers.

THE CARRIERS OF SECRETS OF THE PAST

The first group of secret carriers living on the underside of the church maintain an active memory of an event or events in the past for which they have consuming regret. They live in the constant fear that their secret will come back to haunt them with consequences that will shatter not only their worlds but the worlds of loved ones and trusted friends.

Their agenda regarding the secret of the past could simply be called BURIAL. In other words, they try to live as if the event(s) never occurred. These secret carriers live in the hope that the past will never penetrate the present. It's a very unpleasant way to live because they can never be sure that someone will not find out what has happened and reveal the secret for them.

The BURIAL scheme is not at all prudent but it often seems to be the only way when one knows his personal world is in trouble. It is usually pursued when one does not feel that there is a place to go and find forgiveness or acceptance, or when one is terrified of hurting those who would be affected if his secret of the past was disclosed. Of course some of these carry their secrets defiantly and conclude that what's done is done.

When I think of these secret carriers, I'm reminded of Edgar Allan Poe's grisly short story, "The Tell-Tale Heart." Poe wrote of a man who had killed another and buried him beneath the floor of his home. Soon afterward he was interrogated by the police. At first he was absolutely confident that he could conceal his secret even from the authorities. So confident that during the questioning, he seated himself in a chair directly over the place of the dead man's burial.

> In the enthusiasm of my confidence, I brought chairs into the room, and desired them here to rest from their fatigues, while I myself, in the wild audacity of my perfect triumph, placed my own seat upon the very spot beneath which reposed the corpse of the victim.
> The officers were satisfied. My manner had convinced them. I was singularly at ease.

But his coolness evaporated as the conversation went on. Soon he sensed a strange pounding noise in his head. But then he realized that it was coming from beneath the floor where the corpse was located. He was sure that it was the beating of the dead man's heart. He wondered why no one else noticed what he was hearing.

> No doubt I now grew very pale;—but I talked more fluently, and with a heightened voice. Yet the sound increased—and what

could I do? . . . I talked more quickly—more vehemently; but the noise steadily increased. I arose and argued about trifles, in a high key and with violent gesticulations, but the noise steadily increased. Why would they not be gone? . . . Oh God! what could I do? I foamed—I raved—I swore! I swung the chair upon which I had been sitting, and grated it upon the boards, but the noise arose over all and continually increased. . . . Was it possible they heard not?

Finally with a shriek the secret carrier confessed:

"Villains!" I shrieked, "dissemble no more! I admit the deed!— tear up the planks!—here, here!—it is the beating of his hideous heart!"

It is an extreme picture, but it nevertheless faithfully portrays the awesome power of a conscience in revolt. Secret carriers expend tremendous psychic and emotional energy to keep the past from interfering with the present. There is the energy of fear that something from "beneath the plank" may come back to haunt the present. No wonder most secret carriers are not integrated or peaceful people.

SECRET CARRIERS IN THE PRESENT

A second kind of secret carrier lives with hidden matters in the present, covert activities and attitudes that one is consciously attempting to conceal from those in the closer circles of acquaintance. The agenda for this person is COVER-UP.

This present secretive dimension of life might include a destructive habit, a relationship that betrays other covenants, or entrapment in an addiction or an eating disorder. Harder types of present-tense secret carrying to identify are inner attitudes of anger, resentment, or jealousy (there are many others) that can lodge themselves in our private worlds where we think no one can see us as we really are.

Active secret carriers become experts in deception to survive. Large amounts of energy once funneled toward creativity and vital living get siphoned off in the constant planning and implementing of elaborate schemes to cover tracks. The drinker uses vodka to keep from having breath that will tell the story; liquor is squirreled away in obscure places where he or she can sneak an occasional drink. The unfaithful partner creates all sorts of fictional situations to explain blocks of times when he or she has dropped out of sight.

I've known a couple of men who fell into the habit of borrowing money from friends and not paying it back. When pressed for repayment, they would write a check backed by insufficient funds in the bank and then frantically rush about town borrowing more money from others to cover what they had just written. One of those men sometimes drove hundreds of miles between banks each week, moving money back and forth so that checks wouldn't bounce. What a torturous life-style of secret keeping he lived! I understand his is not an uncommon predicament.

When secret attitudes and feelings lie deep within the heart and mind, members of this society will often cover up by exhibiting behavior that appears on the surface to be just the opposite of the truth. Instead of anger that boils within, they may feign calmness and tranquillity; instead of resentment, they may engage in a form of flattery; instead of deep fears and insecurity, they may hold others off through a constant use of humor or talkativeness.

One turns back in the Bible to the story of Achan who disobeyed an explicit order from Joshua (who got it from God) that no one should seize and retain booty from the fallen city of Jericho. But Achan quietly defied the order when he saw things he wanted for himself. He buried the loot under the floor of his tent, where it remained for some time.

Did Achan frequently check the dirt to make sure no one would detect that a hole had been dug there? Did he unconsciously stand over the spot, like a goalie in a hockey game, when visitors came to his home? Did he lie in bed at night and ponder the possibility of digging up the stash and returning it to its original place in the ruins of Jericho? Did he come to a point where he said to himself that having the treasure was no fun anymore?

The startling lesson about Achan's secret was that God would not permit the Hebrew people to advance a step further into the Promised Land until the stolen goods were accounted for. And when he was unmasked, Achan and his family lost everything (see Josh. 7).

HE WHO CARRIES SECRETS FROM HIMSELF

A third kind of secret carrier may be the most frightening of all. This person's secrets are so deeply concealed that they have become mysteries to the carrier himself. This takes a bit of explaining.

I'm thinking of the man who lives in what some call denial. This person has permitted the facts of errant behavior or attitude to become so intertwined with life that the conscience has ceased to send out cease-and-desist signals. He hears no tell-tale heart; he no longer imagines that the dirt on the floor of his tent appears freshly dug. He has gone past the point of covering up to others; he has covered up to himself. His agenda is BAU: BUSINESS-AS-USUAL.

A cartoon shows a group of Danish knights sitting around a table in the castle's great room. At the head sits the king who says, "Then it is unanimously resolved that there is nothing rotten in Denmark; things are rotten everywhere else." So might go the thinking of this kind of secret carrier.

When I was a teenager living in Colorado, some of us used to hike to a Rocky Mountain ghost town where an aged woman lived a hermitlike existence. Should anyone go near her shack, she would shout and make threats to drive would-be visitors away. Naturally, we were driven by our curiosity concerning this unusual person and what made her the way she was. On the few occasions that I actually saw her from a distance she was always wearing a black hat.

Memories of that hat came back to me when I heard, years later, that she had been forcibly taken by the local authorities to a hospital. The nurses attempted to remove her clothes in order to bathe her, but her hat had been on her head so long that her hair had grown up through the fabric and colonies of bugs free from disturbance had made nests underneath. To remove the hat and get rid of the bugs, they had to cut away her hair.

The story of that sad, lonely woman reminds me of the secret carrier who lives BAU. His secrets have become secrets even to him. He lives with these destructive performances and attitudes day after day until they simply blend with every other part of his life just as hair grew through the fabric of a hat. He has no notion of how much he hurts others with his actions or his perspective; he cannot be confronted; he rejects the notion that he is the one needing most to be healed. More than likely, he is an angry person who resists any approach by friends or loved ones wanting to get to the core of things.

The ironic thing about this third kind of secret carrier is that his secrets are usually secrets only to him; unlike the situations of the other two kinds, the people around this man usually know more about him and his patterns than he does. He is frequently labeled a fool.

As I've become acquainted with the society of secret carriers, I've seen more than a few of them living BAU. Certain patterns of behavior are consistent over the years, and the results produce long-term pain for loved ones and friends. I know of several men who have established ten- and twenty-year patterns of marital unfaithfulness. Starting and stopping these intermittent relationships of infidelity, they are always one step ahead of those with evidence of their misdeeds. Confronted with the facts, they constantly defend themselves with bland denials. They may even go on the offensive, claiming that they are persecuted and the target of spiritual warfare. They lie to others and to themselves.

It's hard to know where to stop when we think of all the possibilities for living BAU. We are talking of people who possess abrasive and intimidating personality styles, but they will not face what is inside them that causes such hurt for everyone.

Studies suggest that more than half of American mid-life males live with at least one secret in the past of their personal lives, and these men believe its revelation would bring about catastrophic consequences for them and those close to them. If this is true, a lot of people are living unhealthy inner lives today. We need to look hard at the nature of our relationships *to see if we encourage secret carrying by making it difficult for people to come to the truth about themselves.*

The list of possible secrets carried by these three kinds of secretive people is almost infinite. It includes the secrets of people's fears and resentments, their anger, and their memories of devastating experiences in the past. It takes in covert and overt acts of vengeance, outright dishonesty, and sexual promiscuity.

We're thinking of people who permit their life-styles to become increasingly materialistic and try to justify their values and choices on the basis of spiritual terminology. The variations of secret carrying go on and on. We can make a case that one form of it or another touches all of us sooner or later.

Every group of secret carriers is likely to include women who have had secret abortions and who die a little inside every time someone talks about killing or murdering fetuses. There will be men and women who have grown up with the anguish of molestation and abuse in their childhoods. Some people will be struggling with the secrets of substance abuse and other disorders.

As I've already observed, every group includes single and married men and women who live with the bitter memories of indiscretions or infidelities. And every group includes people who are living in serious doubt about their faith, but they feel bound to keep up the outward motions for the sake of a spouse or the children. They and many others are secret carriers; their society is larger than I had ever imagined.

Secret carrying may be a spiritual epidemic. It just might be the common cold of Christian living. Why? Because it is so easy, so natural for all of us. Men and women have tried to carry and live with secrets ever since Adam and Eve tried to hide from God when He sought them in the garden.

"Why are you hiding, Adam?" God asked. He was hiding because he was keeping a secret, and he was ashamed to expose it.

Cover-ups are accomplished in a host of ways in the church. Some do it with the facade of an unusually passionate concern for theological and doctrinal correctness. They keep everyone on the defensive with their accusations and suspicions. Some cover up by being extremely emotionally expressive in their spiritual lives. We find it hard to doubt the sincerity of someone who seems able to weep or rejoice at key moments. Others cover up through a style of never-ending busyness and activism. Who can find fault with someone who is always serving, always giving, always leading? We've already noted the cover-up of leading by righteous indignation or pointing out the sins and irregularities of others. *All of these categories include individuals who are absolutely sincere and genuine in their pursuits of life and faith;* but people who have secrets to keep can abuse church- and spirit-related endeavors.

The Bible speaks often about secret carrying. It is most likely to come out in verbs like *deceive* or *lie,* or in nouns like *darkness* or *hardness* (as in hardness of heart). And when one studies the great biblical biographies, it's not unusual to see a secretive phase in almost every person's broken-world experience.

But why secrets? The answer has to do with *truth.* We acquire secrets when we do not wish to face or reveal the truth. We do a subtle thing when we play with the truth, but we do it all the time. So much so that few people think seriously about how much the systems in which we live constantly manipulate the truth.

We expect the politician to play with the truth, to tell us what we want to hear. In a recent presidential primary campaign, one candidate seeking his party's nomination was forced out of the process in its earliest stages because, the press said, he was too truthful about his assessment of our national situation and his convictions about what should be done to make corrections. The inference is that we, the public, are not prepared to hear the truth put so clearly.

We expect advertisers to bend the truth, and the Isuzu people have capitalized on this. They would never lie (the FCC sees to that), but we know that claims are usually exaggerated to the furthermost possible point that legality permits. And thus we become quite cynical about the promises and possibilities of any product. In effect we have made room for the half-lie when we listen to commercials on television, and we have developed highly sophisticated screening mechanisms in our minds to filter out the mindless and the truthless.

As men and women, we feel at liberty to play with the truth about ourselves. An entire industry panders to the desires of women to distort the truth about their aging bodies. Men have learned to cover the truth about their real feelings. We learn these capacities at an early age. We are brought up to be skilled liars about some things.

John Gardner noted this spiritual malady when he wrote in *Self-Renewal:*

> Self-knowledge, the beginning of wisdom, is ruled out for most people by the increasingly effective self-deception they practice as they grow older. By middle age, most of us are accomplished fugitives from ourselves. Yet there's a surprising usefulness in learning not to lie to yourself.

Of course all of this happens in the church also. A dangerous margin of mistruth is permitted over and over again in our hymnody if we sing with straight faces the words and phrases we never really intend to carry out. "Take my silver and my gold, not a mite would I withhold," we might sing with all the signs of serious conviction. One Sunday morning Gail and I were standing with the congregation singing the final verse of a five-verse hymn. I suddenly realized that I had sung the entire song, verse by verse, and hadn't contemplated the meaning of one word. And the words were actually frightening in terms of the response they were asking of me. I was glad that the song hadn't carried with it— humanly speaking—the force of a signed contract. But come to think of it. . . .

Have you ever wondered how many people in an audience are actually concentrating on a prayer being prayed? Or (am I losing friends) on a sermon being preached? How many of us have learned appropriate postures and angles of head and neck that indicate involvement but actually mask the secret that we are a hundred miles away solving a computer problem, worrying about a wayward son, or picking the color of a new car?

The day I sang the hymn without recalling any of the words, Gail and I spoke of what had happened all the way home from church. How is it, I asked her, that I can become so used to singing something that the words lose meaning? Perhaps, I reasoned, this is symptomatic of a faith that is cast in revolutionary terms but is usually practiced by people whose best interests are grounded in the status quo.

That helped me to understand a fundamental reason why some churches and groups of Christians struggle for spiritual vitality today. We have too often created an atmosphere for low-level lying in our prayers, in our sermons, in our singing. We actually may encourage the secretive way of life.

This issue of secret carrying and its opposition to the truth is at the very core of broken-world experiences. Personal worlds enter into the first phases of breakup when people consciously or unconsciously decide to compromise the importance of truth, most specifically the truth about themselves. Thus the proposition in the previous chapter: PERSONAL INSIGHT BEGINS WHEN WE SEE THE TRUTH FOR WHAT IT IS.

Alexander Whyte wrote:

> To know myself, and especially as the wise man says, to know the plague of my own heart, is the true and the only key to all other true knowledge: God and man; the Redeemer and the devil; heaven and hell; faith, hope, and charity; unbelief, despair, and malignity, and all things of that kind . . . ; all knowledge will come to the man who knows himself, and to that man alone. *(Bunyan's Characters)*

There are many fraternities and societies in this world. The informal network of lower-back-pain sufferers with their diagnoses and remedies. Others who fellowship around sports, vocations, and causes. And then there is the quiet, desperate society of secret carriers. How great their need for the liberation that begins the process of rebuilding.

CHAPTER 6

The Pain of Secret Carrying

In June 1984, the *Boston Globe* reported the tragic story of the drowning of eight-year-old Chris Dilullo. He had been lost in eight feet of water while on a hunt for golf balls at a local country club.

Chris had been accompanied by three friends who said that when he slipped into the pond, they thought he was playing a trick on them. But the boys were secret carriers.

They turned the truth into a secret: One of them had pushed Chris in. They didn't realize that by trying to protect each other, they kept a secret that would wreck their own lives, multiplying the tragedy of Chris' death.

> **BOTTOM LINE #6:**
> *The person who carries a secret has sentenced himself to a dungeon.*

It was almost two years before the secret was uncovered when the fifteen-year-old boy who had pushed Chris into the water confessed his guilt to a friend. Soon the police were investigating the incident and charging him with manslaughter.

Since the drowning, all three witnesses [to the drowning] have suffered emotional instability, according to their parents, police and their own stories. Their distraught parents say the boys are withdrawn and have nightmares. They are no longer friends.

One of the three "began crying frequently after Chris' death and had to sleep with his mother. . . .

Once he cut his head when he ran full-speed into a dumpster." A second, an eighteen-year-old, was fired from a job "because he would stay home from work on days when he felt 'angry and disgusted' about telling a lie to protect a friend." The third boy started "hearing voices and seeing visions and barely talked to his parents." He later entered a hospital for emotionally disturbed children.

Secret carrying is an ancient activity and a modern one. The story of the drowning of Chris Dilullo is simply a dramatic example of what members of the society of secret carriers live with every day. It is more vivid and heart-wrenching because it involves youngsters who were not as adept as many adults at handling their secrets.

King David was a secret carrier. For a year or more he tried to live business-as-usual hoping that the secrets of his recent past would remain in the past.

But when Nathan the prophet confronted David about his BAU agenda, he was able to get the king to dig things up. Psalm 51 was David's subsequent prayer of repentance. It is no accident that David mused on this subject of the truth when he said to God, "Surely you desire truth in the inner parts" (v. 6).

David was dealing most painfully with the fact that he had lost his integrity. Truth on the surface of his life and truth in the inner parts hadn't been connecting. The corrective that had to take place occurred when David stopped lying to God, to himself, and finally to the rest of the world. Whenever God becomes involved as a rebuilder in a person's world, the issue of truth will surge about in the innermost being.

To get the inner and the outer parts together, David had to deal with truth. A friend of mine calls and talks about some painful discoveries he has been making about himself in recent days. He has come to IN-SIGHT, and in that process he realizes that he has spent a large part of his adult life "changing the furniture," as he puts it, on the surface of his public world. "But while I've been so busy decorating the surface, I've seriously neglected the facts about the ugliness inside. Now I'm looking in, and I've come to realize that until you *name* what is in you and face it, you cannot change anything."

Lodged in the hard disk of my computer is an *integrated system* of programs. It combines computer programs for spread-sheet calculations, word processing, data base formation, communications, and time management. It is called an integrated system because all aspects of the program must fit and be capable of supporting one another with processes and information that will serve me, the user, well.

Each of us is created to be an integrated system of personal and corporate life. The truth by which we live in our public worlds must be the truth by which we live in our private worlds. The gap or the difference between the two will largely determine the state of our personal health.

I've been greatly impressed by the work of Alcoholics Anonymous. And as I've read of the twelve great principles followed by that organization, I cannot escape the fact that this entire process of introducing addictive men and women to the possibility of recovery is based on the notion of the truth and the dissolution of secrets. You cannot adequately aid a secret carrier.

I'm told that it is customary when a person stands to speak in an AA meeting, he introduces himself by first name only and the words, "and I'm an alcoholic." Then he states specifically when and where he had his last drink. There can be no cover-up at an AA meeting. The truth is faced over and over again, and the strengthening fellowship of AA'ers is based on that truth telling.

> After years of drinking, we alcoholics become cognitively impaired. In plain language, we can't think straight. The root of 'intoxicate' is the Latin word toxicum—'poison'. We have systematically poisoned ourselves, damaging the central nervous system.

So said a retired physician who is a recovered alcoholic. Another recovering alcoholic admitted, "I was committing chronic suicide. I was putting a liquid bullet into my brain every night." *(Getting Better)*

One of AA's two founders, Bill Wilson, wrote of the principles that became the original foundation for this remarkable program. Among them are these:

1. We admitted that we were powerless over alcohol—that our lives had become unmanageable.
2. We made a searching and fearless moral inventory of ourselves.
3. We admitted to God, to ourselves, and to another human being the exact nature of our wrongs. (From *Getting Better*)

As I've pondered this remarkable basis of fellowship in AA, it has occurred to me that we would be far more genuine and authentic as brothers and sisters who follow Christ if we introduced ourselves with a similar phrase, "I'm Gordon, and I'm a sinner." The church is made up of sinners; there is no other primary basis for fellowship in the church than that. And once having affirmed the truth about myself—I am a sinner—I move to the next affinity point with my fellow followers of Christ, the Cross.

When I was a secret carrier, I occasionally told people who were to introduce me as a speaker for a meeting to simply acknowledge me as Gordon, a sinner. Usually there was polite laughter; all thought it was a humorous way of expressing humility. Little did they know that it was the truth. I found it instructive for myself that some people who thought my suggestion was merely a joke really did not want to introduce me ever again when they learned I meant what I said: I was a sinner.

Insight then, as I wish to use the term, is the act of constantly aligning our two worlds, private and public, with the truth. *Secret carrying,* on the other hand, is the act of stretching the two worlds further and further apart.

Aaron, brother of Moses and high priest among the Hebrews, was a short-term secret carrier. His specific responsibilities were those of leading in the religious ceremony of the people. When Moses excused himself to go to the top of Mt. Sinai for a conference with Jehovah, Aaron picked up the added responsibility of overall leadership. You might have assumed that the people were in good hands, but they weren't.

A score of days passed. Moses was gone longer than anyone expected, and fear began to trickle through the camp at the foot of the holy mountain. People speculated on the possibility that Moses was dead, that they no longer had a leader, and that, in fact, they could not count on a relationship with a trustworthy deity. In that agitated condition they turned to Aaron and proposed the creation of other "gods who will go before us" (Exod. 32:1).

It could have been Aaron's grand moment for a display of moral and spiritual courage. But it wasn't. He could have managed the moment by pressing the people for patience and fidelity. But he didn't. Instead, the man caved in to their demands. "Take off the gold earrings that your wives, your sons and your daughters are wearing, and bring them to me," he said (Exod. 32:2).

The people did as Aaron instructed, and before long a calf of gold shaped with a tool (the Scripture is explicit about this; only later do we find out why) was erected in their midst. With that done, Aaron announced a religious festival for the next day. Everyone came, and the Bible describes the event as something akin to a pagan orgy.

At the top of the mountain God was aware of what was going on and angrily expressed Himself to Moses. In a strange but merciful conversation, Moses appears to have taken the role of intercessor and appealed to God's patience and promises, and the situation was momentarily cooled. That was until Moses came down from the mountain and saw for himself what was happening. Then it was his turn to fume.

Storming the camp, Moses destroyed the idol, ground its gold into powder, scattered it in water, and forced the Israelites to drink it. The immediate result was extreme humiliation and embarrassment, not to speak of the loss of lots of gold jewelry. The longer-term forfeit was a powerful judgment unto death for many of those who had acted so uproariously.

But the camera eye of the writer focuses on the conversation between Moses and Aaron. "What did these people do to you, that you led them into such great sin?" Moses asked his brother (Exod. 32:21).

Watch the deception, the distortion of truth, in Aaron's attempt to give an answer that might salvage his dignity.

> *Do not be angry, my lord. . . . You know how prone these people are to evil.* [Deflect accountability by blaming the offense on others.] *They said to me, "Make us gods who will go before us. As for this fellow Moses who brought us up out of Egypt, we don't know what has happened to him."* [Is Aaron hinting that part of the problem might even be Moses' fault for staying away so long?] *So I told them, "Whoever has any gold jewelry, take it off." Then they gave me the gold, and I threw it into the fire, and out came this calf!* [The deceptions grow. Aaron would like Moses to believe that the golden calf was the fault of whatever happened in the fire. Amazing!] (Exod. 32:22–24).

The final sentence makes the reader understand why the earlier part of the account emphasized that the calf was made with a tool. Aaron was lying! The man was simply refusing to deal with truth. He was secret carrying! Perhaps it was part cover-up and part BAU, business-as-usual.

His explanation would be hysterically funny if it wasn't so tragic. Aaron appeared to believe what he was saying to his brother.

What was happening? DECEPTION. Aaron's heart was so twisted that facts made no sense to him whatsoever. Many thousands of years later we look at his ridiculous explanation and laugh. But for Aaron, it was serious business. He was following the track of his darkened heart.

A replay of Aaron's performance prompts three questions. First, why would Aaron so easily betray his brother by yielding to the opinions of the people when they suggested Moses had turned out to be undependable? Second, why would he so quickly betray his brother by directing the creation of the golden calf and the ceremony that heralded its existence? And third, why would Aaron betray his brother by lying about what he'd done when Moses returned from the mountain?

Aaron's performance simply doesn't make sense unless we take into account the biblical theme of deception. The dark side of Aaron's inner being clouded his thinking and his values, and in a clutch moment he led the people into a serious fall.

Jeremiah probably describes the dark side of the human heart as well as any writer in the Scriptures:

> The heart is deceitful above all things
> and beyond cure.
> Who can understand it? (Jer. 17:9).

It isn't a pleasant or an upbeat analysis of the human condition. But a careful reading opens one to a profound reality. Jeremiah seems to suggest that there is no murkier place in all of the universe than the depths of the human heart. And darkness goes with deceit and lying.

The dark part of Aaron seems to have taken over in the incident. It's likely that he rather enjoyed the attention he received, and it wasn't difficult, therefore, for him to interpret Moses' extended absence as a sign that he wasn't coming back. Furthermore, it was probably easy to give in and supervise the development of the golden calf because it made the people like him all the more. Step by step, the power of deceit from the depths of his heart was taking control. By that time, Aaron was lying to himself. So when the moment of exposure came, it isn't hard to understand why Aaron would twist the truth and attempt to lie to Moses. Having lied to himself, he had no problem lying to Moses.

This is the consistent story of deception. All of us battle it every day. And it is the seedbed of virtually every evil act in the human repertoire. No wonder that one name for the arch enemy of God, Satan, is "slanderer" or "deceiver."

Deception is never more ugly than the moment we reenter the light and realize how we have been living under the influence of a series of inner lies. How could I have believed that? we ask ourselves. How could I have fallen for that line? How could I have ever assumed that what I did in that encounter was OK? How could I have forgotten the potential consequences of such a despicable act?

Why we permit the power of inner deception to gain control is discussed in another part of this book. For now, it is important to point out that this is where a fall of greater or lesser consequence begins. Twisted thinking that encounters questionable opportunities means disaster.

I know what it is like to live with a secret. And having dissolved that secret before God, my loved ones, and the church, I know what it is like to live once again in the light.

But I've never forgotten the loneliness of those secret-carrying days. And they have made me highly sensitive to the scores of people in the society of secret carriers who still walk in that darkness. What energy they expend; what fear they experience; what prisons they make for themselves. But what liberation when the secrets are jettisoned and they walk out of the darkness into the light.

As a policeman put it when the tragedy of Chris Dilullo's death came to light:

> All of them tried to suppress the information, but they couldn't do it. They're just children. They held their secret so long out of fear and guilt, guilt over what had been done and fear of being punished. I couldn't think of a juster outcome than to help those boys overcome those feelings.

CHAPTER 7

Implosion

BOTTOM LINE #7:
*"The one spiritual disease
is thinking that one [is]
quite well."* G. K.
Chesterton

Fifty thousand people in Boston were recently treated to a spectacular sight: the instant wrecking of a twenty-story skyscraper. It once took two years to construct the building, but it took less than fifteen seconds to topple it.

The job was done by implosion. Hundreds of dynamite charges were attached to the skeletal structure and then set off in a sequence that caused the skyscraper to literally fall in upon itself. It wasn't long before the building lay in a heap of rubble not more than fifty feet high.

Television crews filmed the event with high-speed cameras and then in slow motion played and replayed the event for viewers. Frame by frame we saw every part of the destructive process.

The flashes of light when the explosives were detonated, tiny but enlarging cracks in the outside wall, and then a slow-motion plummeting of debris, straight down, followed by a massive cloud of rising dust.

By now you've probably realized that I tend to see a parable or metaphor in almost everything. And this was no exception. For me, the specter of the building's collapse was one more picture of a personal broken world. As the stone blocks toppled downward, I saw a vivid picture of a human life imploding, breaking up, lying in a heap of consequences and sadness.

I saw a strong Samson, for example, making a series of strange, irrational decisions, the consequences of which stripped him of everything that he had formerly achieved and left him in humiliating weakness. A crafty and heroic Gideon whose earlier successes were greatly diminished when he permitted people to build shrines to his accomplishments. And a Solomon in whom God had invested awesome wisdom only to see it slowly dissipate in the king's growing preoccupation with the sensuous life.

In the drama of the imploding building I saw myself and a numberless host of broken-world people who have made terrible choices that may or may not have had anything in common with their previous life-styles. Why do human "implosions" happen regularly? What can we learn from such history?

The experience of INSIGHT in the pigpen where the prodigal son came to himself involved a stunning awareness of the terrible choices he had made, and it also meant that he had to face hard realities about his private world. As he himself admitted, he was no longer worthy to be called his father's son. He had made a deliberate decision to leave the home of his youth, to demand what he had not earned, and to waste it on things he could not really afford. He'd made those choices; no one else made them for him. As he lived among the pigs, there was really only one useful question left: *what had been inside him that had caused this series of choices, and what could he do about it?*

There is really only one adequate answer to such a question, and it is a discomforting one. One word does it all: *evil*. Some may be more accustomed to the word *sin*.

Evil is a distasteful subject to modern people. Not an agenda item on the cocktail circuit to be sure. And in my opinion, evil (or sin) is usually treated with considerable shallowness even among people whose theological convictions affirm its reality. Listening to the judgments and opinions of some who try to analyze and explain the bad choices of others leaves me cold, for I've learned that most of us understand very little about one another. We would do well to think very carefully before we claim to comprehend the reasons why someone has performed in the way he has when implosion happens.

When it comes to talking about the evil of the human heart, some in our world would probably reflect the opinion of the eighteenth-century Duchess of Buckingham. When she was asked to go to a George Whitefield evangelistic service, she wrote to her hostess, the Countess of Huntingdon:

> It is monstrous to be told, that you have a heart as sinful as common wretches that crawl on the earth. This is highly offensive and

insulting; and I cannot but wonder that your Ladyship should relish any sentiments so much at variance with high rank and good breeding. . . . I shall be most happy to accept your kind offer of accompanying me to hear your favorite preacher, and shall wait your arrival. The Duchess of Queensbury insists on my patronizing her on this occasion; consequently she will be an addition to our party. *(George Whitefield)*

Having made her protest concerning her aversion to the subject of sin and evil, the Duchess went to hear Whitefield anyway, if only to be seen in the company of the Countess. But she does represent a large segment of people who find that the best way to deal with evil is simply not to talk about it. Maybe, they seem to assume, it will go away. But it doesn't!

On the other hand, Velma Barfield, a twentieth-century convicted murderer, had an opposite opinion on the evil in the human heart, her own heart to be exact. Some will remember her as the woman who was executed by lethal injection in 1986. Shortly before her life was ended, she wrote:

I . . . want to make it clear that I am not blaming . . . drugs for my crimes. I am not blaming my troubled childhood or the marriage problems with [my husband] Thomas. Someone said to me, "Velma, you had a lot of pain and hurt and anger and you never found any release for it. You kept pushing it back and it was like a time bomb. It finally went off and exploded." Maybe that's right. I don't know. *I bear the responsibility for the wrongs I have done. I know those things influenced me, but they are my sins and my crimes.* *(Woman on Death Row,* emphasis mine)

The subject of evil has never been new to me. Growing up in a religious context, I heard about sin from my earliest days. But many years later, in my moments of broken-world INSIGHT, I came to a deeper awareness of the topic that seemed to eclipse all earlier knowledge. Previously, by contrast, the matter of evil had been almost academic; now in a broken-world state of my own it was an issue known through anguished experience. Apparently some of us concentrate most carefully on the subject of evil only when we have entered into one kind of pigpen or another.

Oswald Chambers understood this process:

When God wants to show you what human nature is like apart from Himself, He has to show it (to) you in yourself. If the Spirit of God has given you a vision of what you are apart from the grace of God (and He only does it when His Spirit is at work), you know that there is no criminal who is half so bad in actuality as you know yourself to be in possibility. *(My Utmost for His Highest)*

My insightful moments—does one dare to call them pigpen moments in remembrance of the prodigal?—forced me to look back and replay the history of a series of bad choices and ask the question *why*. Why am I indeed, to use Murray's words, twice (and more) as bad as any criminal?

In pursuit of that uncomfortable question I commenced a journey within myself. What I found was quite mysterious and more than a little distressing. I discovered in my meditations and my readings that the inner space of my life was far *greater* in scope and *evil* in quality than I had ever imagined.

But it made sense to me, nevertheless, that I must vigorously explore my inner space if I was to come to conclusions about why a personal world might implode. The exploration of such space is obviously a life-long project. I'm not sure a lot of people ever begin the journey.

This is the journey of which David, the born deceiver, spoke:

> Search me, O God, and know my heart [the inner space];
>   test me and know my anxious thoughts.
> See if there is any offensive way in me,
>   and lead me in the way everlasting (Ps. 139:23–24).

Teilhard de Chardin described the beginning of his personal quest into inner space in words like these:

> For the first time in my life perhaps (although I am supposed to meditate every day!), I took the lamps and leaving the zone of every day occupations and relationships where everything seems clear, I went down into my inmost self, to the deep abyss whence I feel dimly that my power of action emanates. But as I moved further and further away from the conventional certainties by which social life is superficially illuminated, I became aware that I was losing contact with myself. At each step of the descent a new person was disclosed within me of whose name I was no longer sure. And who no longer obeyed me. And when I had to stop my exploration because the path faded from beneath my steps, I found a bottomless abyss at my feet, and out of it came—arising I know

not from where—the current which I dare to call my life. *(The Divine Milieu)*

As I said, many of us would be uneasy to make the inner voyage of exploration that David requested of God and that Teilhard described. Most would dare to barely descend beneath the surface. Excuses might include "not enough time" and "it seems so morbid a project." But the thing that makes us most likely to resist David's "search-me" prayer is the dread we have of finding out too much about what's below. Too painful, too humiliating, too demanding for change. And to the extent that any of us avoid the journey, we invite shallowness of personhood and the ultimate possibility of a broken-world experience.

As Teilhard made the descent, he obviously grew wary of the uncharted territory. One is reminded of the oft-noted fact that medieval mapmakers would write on the edges of their maps where land and seas were unexplored, "Here be dragons and wild beasts."

Inner space was meant to be the territory, an inner temple or sanctuary if you please, in which God our Maker would make His interior residence. Here He would commune with us, give empowerment for us to reflect His image and His glory. Here would be the wellspring for thoughts and deeds showing forth what the Bible calls holiness, life after the character of God.

But in my INSIGHTFUL moments, as I began my journey to discover the mysteries of my broken world, I was quick to affirm that this terrible force called evil had violated the inner temple, seizing most if not all of the space for itself. It was as if the dragons, like modern-day terrorists, had hijacked my soul and were holding hostage all the good qualities and attitudes that God intended for each of us when He made us.

As you can see, I end up resorting to fantasy and metaphors to describe the almost indescribable; I end up going along with the modern hijackers and the ancient mapmakers saying, "Here be dragons and here be wild beasts; they seek to kidnap your world and shatter it." That seems to be what makes up the drama played out in a large part of this dark inner space.

A human tendency is to try to build a security gate near the surface of our lives, a gate to protect us from dealing with anything that might arise out of inner space. And it isn't unusual for us to be reasonably successful in keeping the dragons out of sight . . . for a time.

Individuals with material resources are often capable of building strong and high gates that last for some time. That's why life in an affluent neighborhood seems at first glance not to be as evil in appearance as life in the poorer sections of the city. Where money and opportunity are, the gates will often contain or at least hide the inner dragons of people for a time.

In the inner city, the resources to cover things up aren't available; thus, we often see the ugliness of man's heart for what it is first in those places. But get into the private lives of the uptown or suburban residents, and we see that the dragons are there; they are just being bought off for a time.

But dragons inevitably break through the strongest gates, and they have no respect for our timing or our convenience. When they come, most of us are shocked beyond words at the thoughts, the motives, the attitudes, and the distorted values that they bring with them.

Godly men and women have had the painful experience of discovering deep anger, violent and vulgar profanity, suspicion, and accusation flowing from their mouths when the filtering mechanisms of their conscious minds have been inoperative for a time during a serious illness. Where did the words and thoughts and attitudes come from, they wonder? Answer: from some form of inner space with its dragons.

Earlier I mentioned that I'd had an experience with lower-back pain some years ago. One of the interesting things the physician explained to me about the difficulty of diagnosing back problems was that the point of pain in a back was not always the point of the problem. In other words, a problem in the upper back might show up as pain in the lower back.

How similar, it occurs to me, such elusive pain is to the spiritual ailments of many misbehaving people. We are drawn to the point of the pain and try to address that situation when all the time the point of the problem is far deeper inside, where inner evil spawns its dragon-like influences.

St. Augustine was no stranger to sighting dragons or questioning the origin of pain in his inner space.

Who am I, and what manner of man? What evil have not either my deeds been, or if not my deeds, yet my words; or if not my words, yet my will? But thou, O Lord, art good and merciful, and thy right hand had respect unto the profoundness of my death, and drew forth from the bottom of my heart that bottomless gulf of corruption: what was to nil all that thou willedst, and to will all that thou nilledst. (Confessions)

These were the sorts of discoveries I too began to ponder in my insightful moments. There came a time when dragons, if you please, had come through my gates and had caught hold of my mind and my choice-making mechanisms. And I had translated the evil in my inner space into actions in my outer space.

Jesus was referring to this origin of personal performance when He said to His disciples regarding the heart:

> Don't you see that whatever enters the mouth goes into the stomach and then out of the body? But the things that come out of the mouth come from the heart, and these make a man "unclean." For out of the heart come evil thoughts, murder, adultery, sexual immorality, theft, false testimony, slander (Matt. 15:17–19).

In one of his excellent writings, Lewis Smedes brought the issue into even finer focus for me. He told of a woman in a German prison camp who stood watching a friend being beaten by a Nazi guard. She was filled with rage and hatred toward her friend's oppressor. But insight soon followed, and it neutralized her desire for vengeance, for a voice said, "Remember, there is also a Nazi in you."

As I read of that woman's insightful moment, I was seized with the fact *that there was a Nazi in my inner space too.* Perhaps it's more accurate to acknowledge that there was a "Hitler" in me, and given the right set of circumstances, I was actually capable of doing everything he did *and much more.* It was a frightening revelation, and the effect upon me cannot be exaggerated. So, I reasoned, the dragons really are that bad.

I had always subscribed to the essential teaching that all human beings are born sinners, that our misdeeds are the product of a nature prone to disobedience and rebellion against God. But somehow there seems to be a difference between understanding these things from a doctrinal orientation that you might learn in a Sunday school and coming to understand them through a terrible experience of failure where you discover that this *energy of unrighteousness*—what the Bible calls sin—is capable of destroying everything good within and without you. And that doesn't take into account the destructiveness to the personal worlds of "innocent bystanders."

The wrecking crew that expertly took out the skyscraper in Boston without damaging any other building was far more masterful than we sinners who usually manage to hurt lots of other people when we implode. Sin is indiscriminate as to who it hurts.

With a fresh awareness of myself as a sinner I took the Scriptures and began to read St. Paul's letter to the Roman church. As this experience of personal insight within me grew, I read the book straight through and discovered a simple agenda that I had never quite grasped before. I'd read and studied Romans many times in the past, but this time I read it not as a preacher, a small-time theologian, or even a veteran Christian. I read Romans as it was meant to be read, through the eyes of a prodigal who needed help in finding out what had happened and how to get home.

When I was through, I turned to Gail and said, "I see it now. This book was written by a man who had come to the simple realization that he was a broken-world person, that the people he was writing to were broken-world people, and so his subject had to be personal worlds broken by sin and what can be done about them."

Paul knew by personal experience and by the revelation given to him that evil was a force that had to be dealt with. To ignore it was to court disaster, a personal broken world. And so he began that letter with a careful exposé on the subject. Where did he begin? By suggesting that evil has its origin in the decision of humankind to suppress the truth about God and His mighty acts of creation and redemption. History, Paul observed, is one big cover-up, a failure to face the truth.

The result? The systematic breakdown of civilizations and cultures, the destruction of the orderly life-styles of individual men and women. Hatred, corrosive competition, misuse of bodies, hypocrisy. And so we see it today, just as Paul said it happens when evil goes unrestrained.

He concluded his thoughts on the universality of evil in the heart of every human being by writing:

> What shall we conclude then? Are we any better? Not at all! We have already made the charge that Jews and Gentiles alike are all under sin. . . . Now we know that whatever the law says, it says to those who are under the law, so that every mouth may be silenced and the whole world held accountable to God (Rom. 3:9, 19).

Silenced! No excuse! No plea concerning mitigating circumstances.

What was needed was insight, an awareness that humankind individually needs to come to the Cross wherein God has more than adequately and lovingly provided a remedy for the reality and effects of evil within us. God was choosing to deal with our evil through His grace.

What I've been trying to say here violates the suspicions of many Christians. Those with orthodox views are always ready to affirm the doctrine of original sin, but somehow some of us would like to gloss over the truth about how capable we really are of succumbing to that sin.

St. Paul wasn't lying or being falsely humble when he counted himself as the "chief of sinners." His point was not that he had been or was the worst sinner in the world, but rather that he had no illusions about the potential for evil within himself and that he marveled that God's grace was great enough to choose him for an apostle. In Romans 7 he vividly described the inner battle he had with evil. He admitted to being a desperate man who, apart from the empowerment of Christ within him, would not have amounted to anything.

I don't wish to be unfair to Paul, but I suspect that he had a particular ability to be abrasive, argumentative, and intimidating in certain social situations. His brittleness in turning away from young John Mark and the compassionate Barnabas makes one wonder if poor Paul wasn't often victimized by an unforgiving and judgmental spirit. And did the old Apostle suffer from this character defect? My opinion is that he did and that he often asked God for its removal. Could it have been his famous thorn in the flesh? A problem of character and personality rather than a problem of a physical nature?

THERE IS GOOD NEWS

The predicament of evil in the inner space of Paul and in the rest of us was not the way things were meant to be. Perhaps one of the reasons we do not take evil seriously enough is because we fail to realize that the human life was created by its Maker to be something entirely different. The Bible makes it clear that *a single human being is the most beautiful, the most valuable, and the most potentially powerful thing (or being) that God ever created.*

That may be a strange point to make when discussing a gloomy subject like evil. But the gloominess will not be properly handled until we realize what were the original creation intentions of God our Maker and what we have forfeited by diverging from that original design. So we must make this affirmation: human beings were created to be beautiful and integrated, individually and in community with one another, their mission to discover, enjoy, and reflect the glory of God.

This beauty was violently damaged by evil much as the magnificent *Pietà* was damaged in the Vatican a few years ago by a crazed man who charged through the barriers and slammed away at it with a hammer. With the pieces of the *Pietà* on the floor and the world of art in shock, the question became, can this magnificent work of art be restored? And the great question of the Bible after the worlds of the first man and woman were shattered was, can these worlds be rebuilt? And in both cases the answer was yes.

Art experts have since restored the *Pietà* so that the damage can hardly be detected by anyone but the most knowledgeable. And the genius of the Christian gospel is that the beauty of humankind is also restorable or "rebuildable" no matter how badly one's world has been damaged in one's past experience.

It might be useful to meditate on why the art world could be so devastated when something like a marble sculpture was desecrated, but most people hardly wince at the thought that humanity has been ravaged by this inner and outer spiritual energy called evil.

The restoration or rebuilding process in the human experience, St. Paul taught, is in two parts. A "present-life" part in which our original beauty is slowly reformed but some effects of the damage of evil still can be seen. And a "future-time," the day of Christ, when all effects of the original damage evil caused will be erased, and our humanity will be perfected as if nothing wrong had ever happened. The Bible refers to this two-part rebuilding process as the great hope, and it is available to all who seek it through faith in Christ.

A legend from the sheep counties of England exemplifies the process. Some centuries ago two men were arrested and convicted for stealing sheep. The magistrate sent them to prison for several years and decreed that the letter *S* should be burned into their foreheads with a hot iron. He determined that no one should ever forget their crimes.

When the jail terms were ended, one of the two left the area and was never heard from again. The second, being greatly sorry for his thievery and having dedicated his life to God, chose to remain in the community and offer himself in service to people. As the years passed, everyone fell into his debt because of the ways in which he freely gave himself to aid them in their sicknesses, their family crises, and their difficulties in their work. Soon no one remembered or spoke of his earlier crime of sheep stealing. They spoke only of all he had given them out of a heart of grace and love.

The legend concludes with the conversation of two small boys who because of their young age knew nothing of the past. Seeing the now aged man pass by, one asked the other, "Why do you think he has an *S* on his forehead?"

"I'm not sure," the second replied, "but from what my mum says about him, I think it must mean 'Saint.'"

THERE IS ALSO BAD NEWS

My inner-space exploration taught me that the evil within me is not going to go away in the present time. However, with the appropriate energy, a gift from God's Spirit, it can be MANAGED. But while the capability of inner evil to upset things will be checked, it will not be obliterated. I must learn to be aware of evil and vigilant for its attempts to betray me much like I might carefully monitor a chronic infection that can be kept under control if I am careful.

Perhaps it is here that many people calling themselves Christians are most apt to get into trouble. Pinning their hopes and expectations on a conversion experience and the seemingly fast changes that often happen in the first phases of a new Christian life, they too easily forget that evil lies miles deep in inner space. Just because the first "two feet" of our inner space have been sifted and momentarily cleaned up does not mean that the miles below are not going to make their contents known sooner or later.

Where are we most likely to see the signs of evil that roar up from deep within? There are probably many answers to that question. But let me suggest a few common times and places when and where we will probably see a side of ourselves that can be unpleasant.

1. When We're "Ambushed"

We are likely to discover what is deep within, first of all, when we react in moments for which we are not prepared. For example, that night in the Garden of Gethsemane Simon Peter was suddenly awakened from a nap he shouldn't have been taking, and he realized that men were coming to arrest Jesus. In the fogginess of the moment, Peter grabbed a sword and started swinging, the very thing he'd been taught for three years not to do. Under pressure he reverted to type; the dragons came up from beneath.

C. S. Lewis in *Mere Christianity* speaks of the sinfulness within inner space that is uncovered in the sudden experiences. When he notes sullenness in himself or he snaps at a person, he admits he is likely to reason at first that his reaction is not a demonstration of evil within; rather, he was just caught off guard. But more reflection tells him that he is wrong. What I've called the dragons within, he calls the rats in the cellar.

If there are rats in a cellar you are most likely to see them if you go in very suddenly. But the suddenness does not create the rats: it

only prevents them from hiding. In the same way the suddenness
of the provocation does not make me an ill-tempered man: it only
shows me what an ill-tempered man I am. The rats are always
there in the cellar, but if you go in shouting and noisily they will
have taken cover before you switch on the light. Apparently the
rats of resentment and vindictiveness are always there in the cellar
of my soul. Now that cellar is out of reach of my conscious will. I
can to some extent control my acts: I have no direct control over
my temperament.

2. When We Perceive That We've Been "Mistreated"

We will also find out what is deep within when we've been put at a
disadvantage by others: their fault or ours. Some of us will find a desire
for vengeance, to fight back, to defend ourselves with endless protests
and explanations. We will fantasize about ways in which we can gain
back our due and at the same time discredit the other. And if we have
been in the wrong, we will carefully think through the way others have
responded to see if there is anything we can expose about their lack of
grace and forgiveness that we insist we need.

3. When We Are Treated as We Deserve to Be Treated

A friend tells me that you know whether or not you're really a servant
by the way you react when you're treated like one. And I suppose that
there is a corollary: you know if you have accepted yourself as a sinner
when people help you find out just a little bit more concerning your
sinfulness.

Stanley Jones speaks of a Brahmin convert who began to live at the
ashram he and others had founded in India. Everyone was expected to
participate in the community chores, including the cleaning of latrines.
At that task the former Brahmin stopped short, claiming the job was
beneath him. When Jones insisted that in Christ there were no tasks
unsuitable for humble people and that those converted to His lordship
should have no trouble cleaning latrines, the Indian responded,
"Brother Stanley, I'm converted, but not that far."

I've discovered that I do not mind sharing the fact of my humanity
with people; however, I do have problems when people highlight *my*
humanity and the evidences of its faults and flaws for me. That's when
I'm reminded once again that evil dwells deep within.

4. *When We Are Drawn to the Evil That Other People Are Doing*

To the Roman Christians, Paul wrote much about evil, and he did not make the issue easier to accept when he suggested that people who "approve of those who practice [evil]" (Rom. 1:32) are telling on themselves.

Why are we drawn to the amusements and spectacles that portray people in real life or in fiction doing things we do not believe in doing ourselves? Our choices of amusement in sports, the theater and the cinema, and literature may in fact tell on us. The "deep" within us subtly calls out to things of evil about us, and the two entities feed on each other.

In my conversations with secret carriers, I've learned that many people, whose lives appear to be exemplary on the surface, are drawn to pornography (soft if not hard), violence and explicit sex in films, and places where all sorts of illicit activities take place. Cable TV has brought into many homes the information and stimulation that can only couple with the dragons within and hasten choices and values that create implosion and a broken world.

Thus, I came to newly affirm that the evil within is matched by the energy of evil in my outer space. The two forms could be said to attract each other. The inner comes in a spirit of rebelliousness; the outer in the form of attractive temptations, usually appealing to aspects of my emotions, drives, and intellect that will give a hearing. I don't know how to say it any better when I observe that there is a conspiracy between the two sources of evil.

Sometimes the evil from without comes to us through another person or through an appealing goal or objective or the temptation to a pleasurable experience. Samson met his Delilah; Gideon heard the crowd's applause; Solomon grew bored and had to keep pressing out the boundaries of sensation. These things and persons became attractive to these men, and the energy of inner evil provided an impetus to destructive choices. And because they were not on top of the situation, managing what was inside them, each imploded and fell in a heap like the building in Boston.

St. John wrote of Jesus that He trusted Himself to no man because "He knew what was in man" (2:24 NKJV). What did our Lord know? What Jeremiah said: that the heart was deceitful and that no one could figure it out. So I am impressed with the notion that if there is a sense in which Jesus can trust Himself to no one in terms of opinions and whims, then there is a sense in which I should not trust myself, either. I must assume that left to myself, energies within will quite likely betray me and urge me into a pattern of drift in life that will eventuate in implosion, a broken-world experience. G. K. Chesterton must have been thinking about this when he said through the words of his famous character, Father Brown, "The one spiritual disease is thinking that one [is] quite well."

This has been a most difficult chapter to write. And even as I finish it, I'm not satisfied with its contents. The subject of the evil within is far too illusive to handle adequately in a few pages. The unattractiveness of the subject is so clear that one is reluctant to write for fear that the reader will drop the book and not read on. The pessimism of the subject is so awesome that one fears a gloominess of soul. BUT EVIL MUST BE NAMED, not only in its generic presence within the inner space but in its specific dragonlike appearances. It must be acknowledged, confronted, managed, and hated.

I add the last word because I am impressed with the words of a young evangelist I deeply admire. When I asked him at breakfast one day what made him go to the streets and campuses day after day and represent the gospel of Christ, he said very simply, "Because I hate sin, and I have something in the gospel that can do something about it."

I was rebuked by his response to my question. The simple fact was that I didn't hate sin enough. I do now!

I watch that building in Boston collapse into rubble. It wasn't the most attractive building in the city over the years of its life. But because I tend toward the sentimental, I think of the architect who designed it, the builder who built it, and the owner who first cut the dedication ribbon and opened it up. I think of all the people who worked there, made friends there, achieved or lost great fortunes there. The building had a million memories imbedded in its walls. And now it's gone; it has imploded. Like a broken-world person who didn't know that the evil within has devastating power.

CHAPTER 8

Unhealthy Environments

> BOTTOM LINE #8:
> *Influences and moods,
> people and atmospheres,
> pressures and weariness:
> some or all of these, like
> a smoke screen, can
> distort what might
> otherwise be good
> thinking.*

In 1952, when I was barely an adolescent, my family and I moved from east to west and settled in Denver, then a modest-sized Rocky Mountain city. Since I had spent my earliest years in the urban sprawls of New York and Cleveland, Denver was a dream come true.

The mountains to the west of the city were almost always in full view; the dry, clear air was part of a very appealing climate; and the city possessed a western, rugged quaintness that fit the image of a Roy Rogers culture. The informality of those early 1950s days can best be illustrated by my recollection of walking unannounced into the Colorado governor's office (we called the governor Big Dan) and spending twenty minutes in conversation with him while he sat with cowboy-booted feet propped up on his desk. I was thirteen years old at the time. Denver was a great town for a boy.

All of that former desirability of climate, clear air, and western folksiness sprang out of my memory recently when my mother called to say that she and her husband were planning to move away from Denver. When I asked why, she told me that her physician said a move would be necessary.

"I have weak lungs," she said.

"But is there a place in the world better for someone with weak lungs than Denver?" I asked, remembering the way we all used to boast about the advantages of the environment.

"Well, the doctor says that Denver's air is now so polluted during much of the year that people with respiratory problems like mine can't live here anymore. It's unwise for us to stay."

Basically, my mother was saying that one's health can be adversely affected if one lives in an environment whose elements weaken the body and make it susceptible to other sicknesses and diseases.

This is ironic, I thought as my mother went on to tell me about moving plans. What had once been a city to which people would come in the *pursuit* of good health was now a place they had to leave to *preserve* good health. That's why many cities, like Denver, now have daily environmental reports. "Today we have an air pollution warning," the radio newsperson often says. "Health officials are suggesting that anyone with breathing problems should stay indoors."

If my mother has become sensitive to the quality of an environment because she has undependable lungs, I wonder if there is some value in giving attention to the kinds of environments that could be beneficial *or* detrimental to our spiritual lives. That thought takes me back to the young man who left home for the big city and the good life and ended up with the pigs and lots to think about.

The prodigal son broods in the pigsty. His world is broken into a thousand pieces, and in that shattered condition he slowly comes to INSIGHT. He has begun to measure his thinking against the truth. What his father had taught him and warned him about was in fact the real story of life. But he hadn't accepted his father's perspective.

Now in his INSIGHT he sorts out his willful blunders: his arrogant, know-it-all attitude; his demanding ways; his choices; his selfishness; his blindness to the occasional warning signs. He sees his inner deceit for what it was and is. Perhaps he occasionally gets up and stomps about in angry frustration as he ponders his own stupidity. Now he can see how much he hurt his father; what he lost by not remaining where the love was genuine and the life-style stable and nourishing; how he has accrued consequences to himself that he may have to live with for the rest of his life. The evil in his heart is apparent now; and the cost of permitting it to go unmanaged is quite clear.

The drilling on the cavity of his heart goes deeper and deeper, and as always, the process is terribly painful. But for the first time he is thinking with clarity. Eventually the cavity will be clean; eventually it will be time to rebuild his broken world.

Now having admitted to himself that he is not worthy to be a part of his father's family, he may be ready to go back and think through the realities of the spiritual and moral environment in which he made his decisions. Having dealt with his interior situation—the evil in his heart—he is ready to look at the exterior, the contributing elements that may have conspired to make his foolish choices possible.

He will begin to think about the city he chose to live in when he left home. Why that one? He'll look with fresh eyes on the people with whom he chose to spend his time. Why them? The places he chose to go; the things he chose to do when he got there. What was in my mind? he may wonder. Why is something that once seemed so satisfying now so distasteful? He has no good memories. The noise, the glitter, the sensations, have lost their appeal.

My imagination sees the prodigal coming to the realization that he had placed himself in an ocean current of influence and activity much like an undertow gradually sweeping him away until the consequences were out of control. Does he not ask himself more than once as he walks among the pigs and occasionally nibbles at a cornhusk, why couldn't I have seen it all as clearly as I see it now? I was warned about these things. I had seen others implode. Did I really assume that I was the great exception?

I strongly believe that our Christian view of human performance must always take into account the decision-making environments if we are to understand why people have broken-world experiences. Most broken-world people who are terribly remorseful will say that the choices they made are now mystifying even to them. As they look backward, they discern conditions that affected the way they thought and acted. And with such hindsight they see things *now* that they did not look far enough to see then. Influences and moods, people and atmospheres, pressures and weariness: some or all of them, like a smoke screen, distort thinking.

This is an extremely delicate subject, this business of environments. In even raising the topic, I run the risk of seeming to provide an excuse for errant behavior. And so, make no mistake, that is why I wrote of the evil in the heart first. I wanted to make sure that I was not misunderstood. Before God, *there is no excuse for evil choices.*

We do no one a favor when we offer excuses for evil performance. *But we also do no one a favor if we stop at the subject of evil or sin and say nothing about what assists a person in making an evil choice on one day that he or she would never have made on another day.* The evil in our hearts and the environments of our worlds are a combination that must be studied and mastered to appreciate how worlds break up. Unfortunately, there is too often a tendency to pay attention to one at the expense of the other.

Perhaps I can best illustrate this point about environments by taking a few samples and then showing their relevance in a conversation I recently had with a broken-world person.

People who frequently travel for business purposes are quick to agree that they often live with heavy moral temptation while they are away from home. Why? *The environment is different.* The away-from-home environment fairly invites various forms of broken-world choices by the unsuspecting.

In the environs of home life with family and friends, there is a schedule of routines, a set of support systems, and a way of doing things, all of which lends encouragement to responsible living and, conversely, restraint against irresponsible living. Virtually all of these external systems fall away when a person is hundreds of miles from home.

Thus, one may have only internal values and convictions upon which to rely for guidance in choices and commitments. If those have been carefully developed and nourished, they are more than adequate. But if they have been ignored? Then the greater susceptibility.

What are some of the specific external supports the traveler misses? INTIMACY, for one. A strange environment stimulates forceful feelings of loneliness and a desire to be in contact with someone who cares. Loneliness is largely a feeling of valuelessness, a "disconnectedness" in which a person feels cut off from spiritual and psychic forms of energy that make him feel whole and special.

RESTRAINT is often missing. In familiar surroundings, an individual has a sense of responsibility to people and systems that he would not want to violate, perhaps for fear that he would become unacceptable in a community where he has to get along. A child, for example, behaves when he knows that his misbehavior will bring a bad report to his parents. This assumes, of course, that he cares what his parents think and fears (in the right sense) their corrective actions.

A traveler, on the other hand, is very much aware of a high level of anonymity. No one will know or care what I do, a small inner voice, not of God, is liable to say. I won't be found out. This message is tempting to the rebellious part of human nature. In other words, one might wrongly conclude, there appear to be no consequences that I have to fear when I make certain unsavory choices.

A third environmental element the traveler sometimes misses is an ACTIVE MORAL CULTURE. He finds just the opposite culture vying for his attention for its own profit. He walks through the hotel lobby on his way to his room and sees the cocktail lounge. Drinks are available at the bar and in most hotel rooms, which may lower one's level of prudence in responsible choice making. Soft-core pornography is there for the asking on the room's television for only a few dollars. And if one is in the company of others, some of them may be only too ready to urge one another on to activities that none of them would be willing to do alone, much less in familiar surroundings.

All of these elements are apparent when I visit with a remorseful frequent flyer who shares with me the story of an illicit encounter with a woman. It occurred when he was one thousand miles from home. He is absolutely horrified when he recalls what happened. "It's hard to believe that that was me," he says. "I've never done things like that before in my life. There's nothing to justify what I did."

He was maintaining a booth for his company at a trade convention. Each evening he returned to his hotel after twelve hours of what felt like nonstop talking with conventioneers who only amplified his sense of loneliness by their seemingly obnoxious treatment of him.

On the third evening he found himself in conversation with a woman who sat a few feet away from his dinner table in the hotel restaurant. "She said things that got me talking about myself. And I have to admit that I enjoyed the conversation. It was great to talk with someone who was attractive and appeared to be attracted to me. I hadn't had a decent personal talk with anyone, it seemed, for three days."

He tells how they talked for a while and then he invited her to his room. He knew logically that such an invitation was poor judgment. But another part of him seemed to take increasing control and drown out the normal warning signals. In that context, he later found himself involved in a sexual relationship.

"When I came to my senses, I couldn't believe what had happened. I felt as if I was monitoring the behavior of someone else. I can't describe how totally I hate myself. I literally shiver every time I think about it."

Naturally my friend is shaken. What has this all meant? What will it do to his marriage and family if his wife finds out? "I really love my wife," he says. "Can you imagine what this will do to our relationship if this thing is exposed?"

What does it say about his character, his years of Christian living? "I know it sounds stupid in light of what I'm telling you. But I'm really not that kind of a guy. I thought this sort of thing only happened to other men."

And, assuming he can resolve this, what about the future? "I'm actually terrified each time I reenact in my mind what occurred. Could this happen again? Am I that weak?"

And then he'd like to know where he stands with God. "I really am committed to my Christian life; I thought I'd been a believer long enough to avoid these kinds of temptations."

As we try to analyze his experience, I point out that he will never get anywhere in understanding this thing he now so thoroughly detests unless he begins with an acceptance of his own responsibility.

"You have to face the fact that before God you're liable for the choice you made that evening. The core issue is sin, and the acts of that night spring from an inner being that, left to its own instincts, will usually swing away from the laws of God and the personal covenants you have made to those around you.

"But then you have to go on from there to understand that you put yourself into an environment that made it easier for you to make a bad choice, a choice you probably wouldn't have made on another occasion. That's not an excuse I've provided for you, but it does describe the context for a bad choice."

"Explain what you mean," he says.

"Well, let's put it as simply as possible. If you had been at home on a normal workday, what would you have done at the end of the afternoon?"

"Gone home."

"Exactly. And, assuming that you and your wife are on the good terms you describe, you would have had some sort of an evening together that would have reenergized you in terms of your needs for intimacy, for sharing the 'goods' and 'bads' of the day, for relaxation among people you love. Right?"

"Of course."

"And let's throw one more thing in. Suppose that there in your own home community you had indeed been going through some form of sexual temptation. Is it reasonable to say that you probably wouldn't have gotten past the fantasy line because, first of all, within a short time you would have been with your family and, second, you would fear being exposed if you did something wrong?"

"Sure. A guy would be pretty dumb to fool around with anyone where he works or in his community. I wouldn't do that anyway, but assuming your logic, it would be a stupid thing to do. There's too much that can go wrong that hurts everyone."

"So what you're saying," I respond, "is that our normal and routine home life is itself a reasonable restraint against what a lot of men and women might otherwise do if they were somewhere else."

"Yeah, that's what I'm saying."

We go on to discuss the environment in which my friend made his regrettable choice that night. Days of hard work in which he felt isolated. A hotel's strange surroundings that offered no accountability for untoward behavior. A person met at an unexpected moment who had acquired seductive skills in order to appeal to and stimulate the desires and weaknesses of a tired, lonely man.

"Tell me," I ask, "who was the first of the two of you to sit down in that restaurant?"

"I guess she was. She was sitting there when I came in."

"Could you have seated yourself any other place in the restaurant?"

He pauses and thinks for a moment. "Yeah, I could have."

"But you chose to sit there, near her. Level with me. Why?"

"Man to man?"

"Yes, man to man."

"Am I really sounding stupid when I say I thought she was beautiful, and I guess I just wanted to connect with some person who was attractive? But I had no intention of anything happening. I guess I would have been happy if she had just smiled at me. Isn't that the way a lot of men want it to be?"

"We all like the smile of an attractive person. It makes us feel valuable. And apparently you weren't feeling very valuable that evening, were you?"

"No, I wasn't. And I guess you're tempted to feel valuable if you can get a good-looking woman to notice you."

"So it started with a choice about where to sit and went on from the hope she might notice you to a few friendly words and then a longer conversation. By then some kind of line had been crossed. Is that the story?"

"That's the story."

"There is nothing in the world that excuses your behavior," I say again. "That has to be acknowledged before God and perhaps to your wife as your responsibility. You're going to have to take your lumps on that. But we can help each other if we examine that environment in which you made your choice and ask what could have been done to make your choice making different."

"So what could have been different?" he asks.

"The first thing is the most obvious. Before you left on that trip, you could have foreseen what those days were going to be like. The schedule was already there to tell you that the days would offer little more than fatigue and loneliness. So you could have prepared yourself spiritually and psychically for it and reminded yourself that this was an environment essentially hostile toward a man who wants his life to follow Christ's ways.

"Then you could have arranged some specific activities in the evening that would have crowded out negative opportunities. Frankly, you and your wife should have discussed the pressures you might be living with before you left. It would have been good to have a telephone date with each other at a certain time. It might have been prudent to think about altering the places where you ate each evening. One businessman I know takes all of his meals in his room to avoid the very thing that happened to you. He isn't interested in meeting strangers in public places. He doesn't go into the restaurant and deliberately pick a table right next to an appealing woman.

"You could have brought along some projects to work on during the evening. An engaging book or two, for example, that would have given you something to look forward to each evening. In other words, you have to know when an enviromnent is dangerous and how you're going to prepare for it.

"On any given day the best of us can cave in to a bad choice if we fool around in hostile environments. Frankly, it would have been wise to have sought out some Christian fellowship. In most cities these days one can find something going on that centers on a Christ-oriented activity. Perhaps you would have been too tired; but at least that would have been an option."

"I don't know that I could have done all that," he says. "I was awfully tired at the end of those days."

"Probably," I respond. "But you did want to know how you could have avoided what happened, and the only thing I know is that one has to avoid adverse environments and pursue healthy ones. Let me illustrate what I mean. My mother called me the other day and told me that she and her husband were going to have to move out of Denver. You'll never guess why."

He couldn't guess, and I told him my mother's uncomplimentary story about Denver . . . going all the way back to 1952. You might have known I would do that.

CHAPTER 9

O-Rings and Cold Temperatures

When the space shuttle Challenger lifted into the sky and blew up seventy-three seconds into its flight, the world was shocked. Most of us have seen the videotape of that terrible moment many times. And we can re-create the picture in our minds of a deep blue sky marked with twisted trails of smoke and large chunks of metal plummeting toward the ocean. And we know, as we recall the grim specter of the explosion, that among the falling pieces were the bodies of some of America's finest men and women.

Most of us also know that the investigations into the cause of the tragedy pointed out some serious shortfalls in human judgment and materials management. The *New York Times* put it frankly: the ulti-mate cause of the space shuttle disaster was pride. A group of top managers failed to listen care-fully to the warnings of those down the line who were concerned about the operational reliability of certain parts of the booster rocket under conditions of abnormal stress. The people in charge were confident that they knew best and that they should not change the launch schedules. They were wrong.

If the ultimate cause of the explosion was *pride*, the specific cause had something to do with O-rings, circular rubber seals that were supposed to fit snugly into the joints of the sections of the booster engines. Their function was to prevent gases from leaking at the joints during the launch phase when the rocket was under the great strain of lifting the shuttle into orbit.

The O-rings performed adequately on all the flights previous to the day of the tragedy. But on that day something was different. The environment. The temperature had dropped below the freezing mark, and under such conditions, some engineers warned, O-rings were apt to become brittle, inflexible, and therefore unreliable. Either that warning was not heard, or it went unheeded. And thus when the go-ahead to launch was given, pressurized fuel did leak past the O-rings, and there was a disaster.

Again, the story is one about environments, the conditions that can affect the performance of objects *or* people. As it is with O-rings in cold temperatures, so it can be with human life. History includes many stories of reliable men and women who suddenly seem to have reversed course and engaged in a personal scenario totally out of keeping with what they said they believed, what they might have done in the past, or what their stated goals and objectives in life have been.

Why such a break? Why such a choice? We've already established as firmly as possible that the ultimate answer to those questions focuses on the evil in the human heart. Not one of us, in the past or the present, can shirk our responsibility for the dark side within our private worlds. Unmanaged and unrestrained, evil can run amok, confuse and distort thinking, and affect our choices.

But there is the follow-up question of environments that we looked at in the previous chapter. What part do they play in the process of broken-world choices and consequences? A lot, I believe, and I feel strongly that most of us probably do not pay enough attention to these conditions surrounding us and affecting us. *If we did, we might be able to predict those times in which we ourselves as well as others are more likely to struggle and face the full onslaught of battles of the spirit.*

The friend who shares with me his grievous experience in a far-off hotel clearly understands in the aftermath of his terrible moral choice that the chances of his misbehavior happening in "home" territory would have been considerably lessened. He would have been on much more solid ground if he had been sensitive to the fact that the restraints and accountabilities of home were absent while he was away, that he would have to take care to monitor his thoughts and needs to make sure they were not susceptible to untoward influences. He didn't, and his world broke.

On the day of the space shuttle tragedy someone should have said (and somebody probably did but was ignored), "It's cold enough at the launch site to jeopardize the reliability of the O-rings. We can't be sure what might happen, but the margin of risk is too high. Abort the launch!"

Cain made his choice to kill his brother in a time of great anger. Abraham made a choice to impregnate a servant-woman, Hagar, in a time of anxiety as he considered the aging process of his wife, Sarah. In a mood of righteous indignation Moses killed a man. Saul, the first king of Israel, made his choice to disobey God when he was in an agitated state of impatience.

A fascinating successor to Saul a few generations later, King Uzziah, made a broken-world choice when he resisted the warnings of the priests in the temple that he was not qualified to approach the altar. He became a leper and died in disgrace. I can only assume that he made his choice in an environment of boredom and pride.

Study the tragic moments in many lives, and you will often discover that a secondary set of conditions was right behind the reality of embedded evil. Those conditions weakened the resolve of a man or woman to resist temptation and make decisions that were not right or true.

Later on I'll briefly note some more positive environments, the kind that protect personal worlds and provide opportunity for growth and development. But because our theme centers on broken worlds, my objective is to point out samples of negative environments, the kind that contribute to disasters.

Why should we highlight what some will certainly see as the pessimistic side of these milestones in life? I can think of five reasons:

1. We should become more sensitive to the reality of environments so that we can acquire the habit of internally asking questions such as, what are the conditions inside and around me today that are liable to play havoc with my thinking processes, my values, my responses, my choices?

2. We can make decisions about environments we'd like to avoid and ones we'd like to enhance whenever possible.

3. Knowing something about environments may help us to surround ourselves with various forms of resolve and defense when we know we are in an environment we cannot change.

4. An awareness of environments will make us more sensitive to others around us: what they are facing and whether or not we can, as Christian brothers and sisters should, offer protection and mutual accountability for superior performance.

5. Finally, if we think through environments, we may be able to understand more compassionately what has led to the failure of others and give the sort of mercy and encouragement that might make the rebuilding of their broken world possible.

So I offer some sample environments. Five of them. There are doubtlessly many more. And as I write about these environments, I write with the pen of a Christian man taking a look at life through my own experience and those I've shared with others. There is nothing new here; only the familiar described as succinctly as possible so that we can take a fresh look at ourselves.

The point is simple. If the people at NASA need to know how their O-rings will operate in various temperatures, we need to know how our spiritual and mental systems are liable to operate in the various environments we are likely to face.

THE ENVIRONMENTS OF OUR AGE GROUPS

1. The Environment of Infancy

Gail and I sit on an airplane for the six-hour flight from Los Angeles to Boston. The computer, bless it, has assigned us seats near the bulkhead, as they call it, and that means the odds have increased that we will be near young families with babies. On this flight we have three of them. Now, we like young families; we used to be one. But young families mean babies who cry. Frankly, I don't remember (although Gail strongly disagrees) that our children ever cried in public.

Predictably, soon after the plane takes off, a baby begins to cry—no, scream would be a better description. Perhaps rage might be even better.

Whatever it is, it continues across Nevada, Utah, Colorado, and well into Nebraska. I have sensitive ears, and after 1,050 frequent-flyer miles of screaming, my ability to ignore the matter wanes considerably. I know my question isn't going to gain a satisfying answer, but something in me just needs to ask Gail, "Why doesn't that mother do something for that child?"

Gail knows the answer and says exactly what I knew she would say, "Honey, the child is obviously overtired. They had to get the child up unusually early this morning to make it to the airport, and now the poor thing is simply saying that this is not a pleasant place to be." That explanation settles the matter for Gail; I try to pretend that it settles it for me. And the baby goes on affirming Gail's interpretation of its behavior.

Over Illinois, Indiana, and most of Ohio, another child begins to make its presence known. I look at Gail, and before I can even pose the question, she answers, "You can see, can't you, that the child is hungry? The mother is out of milk, and the flight attendants don't have anything to offer her." Again, Gail is satisfied with her analysis. I am rattled but manage to hide it.

Over Albany, New York, the plane begins to descend toward Boston. A third baby notes this and begins to outscream the other two. Now Gail doesn't even wait for my signal. "Can you imagine how that child is feeling?" she says. "She's got a cold, and her ears are reacting to the changes in altitude. She's probably going to cry all the way down to the ground. I hope her mother and someone sitting beside me realize the problem. You'd cry too if you had those ears."

We may not like the sound or the performance of a screaming child, but we try (at least Gail does) to understand what might contribute to such behavior. *Environments* of course: fatigue, hunger, altitude changes. And if we believe that, we suddenly become merciful.

I don't wish to belabor this matter, but the very simplicity of the problem of a crying baby may help when the issues later become more complex. On one or two occasions I've watched angry parents spank a toddler for violent crying in public. They seek to end what they perceive to be a misbehavior caused by pain or discomfort, and they do this by causing more pain. They are not happy with the misbehavior, but neither is the child. Wise parents in the airplane situation make a decision: when to be tough and disciplinary and when to be merciful and comforting. They know which alternative to choose not because of some all-encompassing rule about how to treat crying or misbehaving children but because they are there at the moment and sense something of the conditions the children are facing.

2. The Environment of Adolescence

Just as babies do, *adolescents* face the issue of environments. Years ago when our son, Mark, was entering his teen years, he would often sit on the edge of his bed on a Saturday morning and stare out the window for hours if I would permit him to. I would pass by his room several times and wring my hands at the apparent waste of time. "Son," I wanted to ask and frequently did, "how can you squander so much valuable time? What are you doing?"

"Oh, I don't know . . . thinking, I guess."

"What are you thinking about?"

"Oh, ah, I dunno . . . just thinking."

My physician friend, also the father of teenaged boys, tells me that Mark at twelve and thirteen was like any other boy his age. He was the victim of overdosages and underdosages of valuable hormones that were just becoming activated in his body. "That's one of the major reasons why he could be so active one moment and so frustratingly inactive at another moment. Hormones!"

At the time I gained this insight about teenaged boys, I saw my need to be more understanding of my son. I realized that his choices were often influenced by things going on in his body that he knew little or nothing about. Could he control them? How could he listen to them, monitor them, know when to say no to them? That's in part what fathers and mothers are for: to back off when their children are in good control and managing life responsibly and to assert authority when they are not. I had to be sensitive, for example, when Mark's choices were being influenced by energies inside himself that he could barely manage. And sometimes I wasn't.

When she was a teenager, our daughter, Kristy, had more than her share of friends, all of whom seemed to have great plans for her life. Come here with us; go there; do this; do that. More than once I saw her eyes tearful under the weight of trying to be everything and do everything that the group wanted. It was a social environment that could be hazardous at times, a context of life and action in which she could much more easily make bad choices that she might not make if she was around individuals with stronger and sounder judgment.

As I watched our teenagers grow up, I realized and took into account the fact that they were often affected by environmental factors within their bodies and in their social connections. Knowing that caused me to respond differently from ways I might have otherwise responded when their behavior was not what I wanted or expected. It wasn't that their mother or I ever compromised the standards in which we believed; rather, we tempered our reactions with an understanding of their pressurized environments.

If teenagers have made choices that shattered their personal worlds, it's likely that they made their choices when peer pressure was at its highest, when they felt unloved by significant people in their lives, or when their inner drives and passions were stirred up and they were in situations with others where there was minimal restraint. The choices

were theirs, of course, but the choices were more easily made to the destructive side in certain environments than in others.

Knowing that our young son and daughter would be vulnerable like all others at the ages of thirteen and fourteen, I sat down with them when they were eleven and said, "You need to know that your mom and I believe that boy-girl dating should not begin until your sixteenth year. Now you're going to find it hard to accept this at times, but we believe that we should not permit you to date until then. It would be wise if you didn't accept any invitations or extend them without remembering this rule. I'm not going to compromise it when you come home and say you'll be humiliated if I don't change my mind. I won't."

And I didn't. Well, perhaps I did compromise at fifteen and a half. It wasn't that I mistrusted our children; rather, I felt I understood that some environments offer options and pressures that young teenagers are not ready to handle. Better for our kids to be a bit frustrated with their father and mother for a short while than to be crippled for years to come with consequences of choices they weren't yet prepared to make.

The point is this: adolescence offers a whole array of possibilities for misbehavior. But those can be effectively checked in most cases if proper loving authority and accountability exist between family members. If what I am saying is true, by the way, then one has much to think about in terms of the consequences when families adopt separate lifestyles where there is no influence whatsoever across the generations.

3. The Environment of Young Adulthood

A *young adult* is not as likely to be controlled by physiological hormones as by emotional needs. *Intimacy,* for example, is the need to enter a circle of personal relationships where there will be the chance to give and receive love. *Identity,* the need to fit in as a useful person in one's society, and *functional value,* the need to prove oneself in a vocation or career, become critically important.

Frequently, young adults will make decisions and choices that seem to make little sense as they try to meet these needs or drives. Broken-world consequences can be just around the corner, and the onlooker wonders how a vibrant young person with a whole future ahead can jeopardize it all with so little wisdom or restraint.

I visit with a woman in her forties who has come to discuss a marriage that has exploded after fifteen years, leaving two people with worlds so broken that they will probably take years to recover. She speaks of a relationship that soured almost before the end of the honeymoon. Of two people who seemed adept at inflicting maximum emotional damage on each other.

"Didn't you see this sort of thing coming before you walked the aisle?"

"Perhaps I did," she answers. "I remember my parents expressing strong reservations about the wisdom of the relationship even up to the week of the wedding. They pressed me pretty hard, but I didn't listen."

When I ask why, she says, "I had a terrible fear of loneliness and couldn't bear the thought that I might go through adult life as a single person. And even though I realized that he wasn't the perfect man, I told myself we could solve some of these problems after we settled into the relationship. You can do that, you know. But maybe I've discovered that there's a set of problems between two people that can't be solved. I wish I'd listened to my parents."

Why the poor choice? The overwhelming emotional environment of the need for intimacy. It spoke louder than wisdom. It should have been controlled, but it wasn't. As you ponder the loss of a marriage, the years of domestic strife, you wonder why there wasn't a stronger opportunity for better decision making.

The fear of living an unmarried life may be the very emotional environment capable of leading a young woman to compromise her moral standards in order to attract the attentions of a man she likes.

In the environment of ambition, the desire to establish oneself and one's dreams, there is the greater likelihood of compromise. The desire to establish a career, get a foothold in an organization, might make it easier for one to turn one's head in the moment of an unethical decision or to ignore an injustice being done to a fellow worker. "Making waves," as some put it, is not the most judicious thing when you're young and vulnerable in the marketplace. There's always someone ready to step in and take your place, one hears. Pressure mounts, and a person finds it much easier to take the first steps toward choices and decisions never before thought possible.

These are just a few reasons why young adults badly need mentors or sponsors, older couples who come alongside and offer supportive wisdom, encouragement, and models of godly behavior. Young adults can thrive in these difficult environments when they renounce the youthful tendency to want to go it alone and seek relationships providing guidance and accountability. In no other phase of life is it more important to establish clear, routine spiritual disciplines than in young

adulthood. The temptation to rely on abundant energy, youthful cha-
risma, and inner enthusiasm will lead many to ignore the necessity of
quiet, solitude, reflection, and listening. And that temptation has to be
checked and countered with the prayerful and receptive life-style. In
these ways the danger points in the environment are all but neutralized.

4. *The Environment of Mid-life*

The *mid-life person* is in a time of life in which the feelings of gradual
and inexorable loss can become very real: loss of time, of opportunities,
of energy, of youthfulness. And the person may be sensitive to the fact
that a large part of the world gears itself to the values and tastes of a
younger generation.

Relationships are changing for the mid-lifer. His parents are aging,
his children are leaving, and his peers may seem to be passing him by in
their various pursuits of success. His marriage may have lost some of its
charm if he hasn't been vigilant in its maintenance; his body may be
letting him down because he hasn't taken good care of it. It's a scary
time because it suggests that more than half of life is ended and the last
half is not as likely to be as kind as the first.

The mid-lifer may experience the pressurized environment of having
major responsibility for parents and children. How is he going to handle his kids' college tuition, the needs of his aging parents, and the
monthly bills he has to pay? Then one day he has the choice to enter an
elaborate kickback scheme that promises to ease the burden. This person would never have thought to do such a thing. *But*, he thinks, *times
are different now. Everyone seems to be doing it; I'm not fairly treated by the
organization anyway.* The choice, once very clear in its rightness and
wrongness, is now not so easy to make.

There may be a great temptation to slow life down by trying to return
to young adulthood and all of its perceived glamour. Or there may be a
temptation to speed life up and grasp for things that have great promise
on the surface but rarely deliver.

"I like you a lot, but I have to tell you that you look awful," I say to a
man I know when we bump into each other at a gas station.

"I have a right to look awful," he says. "Everything is coming unglued."

We go for coffee, and I learn that he is deeply in debt and that an
unexpected government cut in a weapons systems program on which he
has been working is going to cost him his job.

"Carrie (not her real name) and I went way out on a limb this past year. We put an addition on the house, bought a much nicer car than we should have, and credit-carded our way into a lot of stupid debts for clothes and trips we shouldn't have accumulated. I've used up all our savings, and we're broke. The job market stinks—at least in my specialty."

Knowing this man as I've known him, I'm surprised. It's out of character, it seems, for him to have taken such financial risks.

"We got tired of controlling ourselves so tightly, I guess. We saw all our friends taking skiing trips to Switzerland and said to ourselves, 'Why don't we go too?' I got fed up with driving a Chevy when all our friends were into BMW's and Audis. Do I sound unspiritual when I say that I think we were bored? So . . . it seemed rather easy to sign for all that stuff. A lot harder to pay for it later on. Especially when they call you in on a Friday afternoon and tell you that nine years of a good job are over."

After further conversation, I leave my friend and think about bad choices we mid-lifers make when we panic at the passing of our lives. I think about his attempts to cope with perceived boredom by acquiring glittering, expensive things. I'd like to think I wouldn't do what he has done, and I find little reason to excuse his choices. But I do understand his age-group all too well, and I remind myself that the environment makes it quite easy for a man or a woman to do some strange things out of character with previous performance. It's easy to reason that you're missing out on things. And the temptation becomes rather large for some to take risks and make decisions that have great broken-world possibilities.

Mid-life is a time for the building of peer relationships, friends who covenant to walk through the remainder of life together. Their relationship needs to be built on the mutual sharing and exploration of their faith in God, what it means to support one another as the challenge of change comes their way, and what it means to protect one another from foolish choices based on false premises.

Mid-life is a time to dream new dreams, determine to invest oneself in the younger generation as a mentor, and press for quality of life rather than quantity of things or experiences. In athletic terminology that means taking the offensive and not settling for the defensive decisions my friend at the gas station made that cost him so dearly.

5. The Environment of Senior Adulthood

Even our *senior generation* is quite capable of misbehavior. And when one asks what might be behind certain poor choices, it becomes important again to ask contextual questions about how aging people think and act.

For example, the senior person may be tempted to think that he is losing his value as a person. Rightly or wrongly, he perceives that younger people are more than willing to take his place and often even more capable. He struggles with self-esteem when he discovers that it takes longer to do simple things, and that the mind may not always be hospitable to change although everyone seems to be calling for change. An aging man or woman is tempted to anxiety about sicknesses and diseases, broken limbs, and systems of health care that seem very impersonal and increasingly expensive.

The possibility of bitterness also arises. One finds it very easy to get angry at a world that seems bent on shoving older people aside and not caring that they have feelings too. Add to this the difficulty in covering up negative feelings that used to be "suppressible": words slip out that one used to be able to control; sharp emotional reactions may show themselves before one is able to put a cover over them.

The aging person is frequently reminded of death. Good friends and loved ones slip away, and funerals are frequent occurrences. Children may hardly ever be seen, and young people aren't interested in hearing another's memories or even in finding out what wisdom the aged might have to offer.

It's a difficult time for many senior people. It's easy to sink into despair, and the environment of the senior makes it too easy to choose selfishness as a way of life. One sees it happen with increasing frequency. Good men and women decide that they have given enough and it's time to live only for themselves. They rather easily make a choice that they might have formerly called ungodly because their feelings and needs have ascended over convictions. This is no excuse, mind you, but something that needs our sensitivity.

A Florida man in his seventies watches as his wife slowly succumbs to the effects of Alzheimer's disease. The lovely woman to whom he has given himself all of his adult years, with whom he has shared the raising of a family and a volume of memories, seems no longer to be the person he once married. He sees her suffer and lose her dignity, and when he perceives that he can do nothing more to help her, he murders her, thinking it to be an act of mercy.

His terrible act represents in the extreme the misbehavior that can happen when one has reached a lonely and confused end of the rope. What support systems for him might have prevented what happened?

If babies and adolescents need parents, and young adults need mentors, and mid-lifers need friends, aging persons need almost everyone. We could say that they deserve everyone. They do not deserve what so many aging people get: isolation. And when we permit our aging generation to step out of the mainstream of daily life, we leave them vulnerable to broken-world choices, and we who are young lose a major asset to our lives also. When we understand that our elderly brothers and sisters need to be touched, thanked, respected, and consulted, we will have neutralized some of the negative effects of their environment of age-group.

Put simply, there are five environments of age-groups: infancy, adolescence, young adulthood, mid-life, and the elder years. Each one offers opportunities for people to make choices leading to broken worlds, choices opposed to God's laws and their best interests. But each environment properly understood provides rich opportunity for growth and wholeness. When we explore the upsides and downsides of each, we know how to act, what to choose, and where to be wary of the evil that can come from within or without.

And that kind of wariness is what you wish might have happened the morning the space shuttle lifted off. You wish that the people in the launch control center had asked a few more questions about how the parts of the rocket might act in an unprecedented climatic condition of coldness. But, as the *New York Times* says, there was too much pride in the space agency. Too many self-assured people thought that since they'd already put fifty-five people into space without a mishap, nothing would go wrong that day.

And perhaps nothing would have if it hadn't been for a unique environment. Would that we all knew that about life. Broken worlds might be less in number if we did.

CHAPTER 10

When Mud Slides and Floods Take Their Toll

> BOTTOM LINE #10:
> *When the body and the emotions and the mind are stretched to the limit, the risk of sinful choices climbs out of sight.*

Friends of ours recently took us on a tour of famous Catalina Island off the coast of California. As we walked one of the island's many valleys, they noted the seasonal danger of serious mud slides and fast runoffs of water if there is a prolonged rainy period.

"What makes it happen?" I asked.

"The ground can absorb only so much water," someone said, "and then there comes a moment of total saturation when the hills become destabilized. You can't ever tell when that moment is going to come. But when the soil is saturated and the hills are destabilized, the next rain, no matter how light it is, will set off a slide of mud and a raging flood down through the valley that will destroy everything in its path: buildings, livestock, and roads."

Saturated and destabilized! That could be a description of an inner life-style down deep where the emotions, the mind, the heart, the instincts, and the appetites vie for control of one's values and choices. As I stood there imagining the devastation of a mud slide and flood, I could see some personal worlds breaking up in the same way I had seen imploding buildings, exploding booster rockets, and meteors hitting the earth.

I began to imagine the pressures, stresses, and sensations of the marketplace, the conflict-ridden home, and anxiety-producing events beating on a person like an endless rain. Suddenly, saturation and destabilization; slides, floods, destruction. A broken world. Everyone in the path affected in one way or another as hearts are wounded, reputations are jeopardized, trust is shattered, and security is lost.

I found myself in a pensive mood that day as I tried to visualize the effects of slides and floods. Here and there in the valley I could see the signs of such damage from former years. *It completes my word picture,* I thought. *The destruction caused by slides and floods doesn't go away in a short time.* The effects can remain for a lifetime whether we're talking about a valley or a personal world.

On that day I came up with a name for an environment of choice making that many of us frequently share. I simply called it the *Saturated and Destabilized Environment.* It includes many possible components, and I couldn't begin to list them all. They would probably not be scientifically or psychologically (let alone, theologically) defined anyway, for we're talking about experiences that can differ from person to person. And what affects one may not even touch another.

Perhaps that's one reason we do not spot saturation and destabilization in others so easily. And it may be why we're sometimes unsympathetic when someone else is struggling with an issue in the personal world that seems rather uncomplicated and quite manageable to us.

The saturated and destabilized environment describes those times in our lives when events and their results have tumbled in upon us to such an extent that we are in overload (as they like to say in our high-tech times). These are the periods of life when we feel that we have lost the initiative, that we no longer control the events around us. We feel as if we are spending all our time responding to the issues and problems other people create. And we sense that our effectiveness is quickly diminishing.

My physician friends tell me that this is exactly what they are testing for when teaching hospitals make medical students work thirty-six-hour shifts. They wish to induce overload, an experience of saturation and destabilization, so that they can see how a man or woman is going to perform under duress. They are anxious to see if the student's ability for diagnosis and treatment is as good at the end of the shift as it may have been at the beginning.

Gail and I know the saturated and destabilized environment well. Individuals who deal in temperament types and know us personally frequently warn us that this environment is our greatest personal threat to well-being.

Like many others, I've spent a large part of my adulthood in a vocation that knows no hourly bounds, no seeming limit to the number of things to do, no point where one can walk away and refuse to see another person. I'm not complaining; I've always liked my work. But I've grown increasingly aware that it can exact an enormous toll on spiritual and physical energy reserves.

Add to this that I am by nature a feeler and an "absorber"; I feel the struggles, the pain, and the aspirations of people around me, and I tend to absorb the anger of others and reveal none of my own. I am likely to accept more responsibility that I can adequately handle because I do not wish to hurt or disappoint people. I find it hard to erect protective fences around myself, assuming that there will be time and strength enough to get everything done that people expect of me. That's why the disciplines described in *Ordering Your Private World* were and are so important to me. They are my "fence" against saturation and destabilization.

Not long ago a young man expressed frustration with *OPW,* as we call the book, saying that he was not as organized as I was and therefore couldn't live up to its standards. I think I surprised him when I said that I wasn't naturally organized or disciplined either and that the book generally described what I found necessary to make my private world work.

Sometimes traits like the ones I've just described appear to look like virtues to some people. But they may not be virtues at all. They are simply facts of temperament and personality. I hope God has seen fit to baptize them into usefulness on occasion. But if these tendencies aren't properly managed, they backfire and lead me and those like me into the saturated and destabilized condition.

One obvious result can be weariness; another can be the feeling that I cannot please people enough. Sometimes having said yes to too many people, I'm liable to let someone down and seem not to have kept my word or followed through.

That's one of the many reasons why I thank God for a wife like Gail who, knowing this temperament of mine, will often say to me as she listens to me make one more commitment or promise, "Now I know you want to do this; but are you being realistic? Can you possibly meet that deadline?" Or make that call? Or have that appointment? Or write that article? Or travel to that meeting? She, more than anyone, knows the signals when I'm headed toward saturation and destabilization.

I sit one night with a friend at a National Hockey League game. The teams are warming up, and I watch the Boston Bruins stand on the blue line and shoot dozens of hockey pucks at the goalie. They shoot them one after another in machine-gun fashion. The goalie must spot each one instantly as it skims the ice or cuts through the air, and then he must catch it or deflect it with his stick, his pads, or the back of his glove.

I watch him respond to every hockey puck and then say to my friend, "I think I know exactly how he feels; I've just had a day like that. Pucks coming at me every minute. If he and I aren't alert, one of those things is going to get past and into the net or in the face, his or mine." Many people in our busy world know what I'm describing.

What sort of conditions might make up the saturated and destabilized environment? Let me name and comment on a few as samples. If we learn to be sensitive to their existence, perhaps we can do a better job of containing and managing them. And if we cannot, we must understand that here we are likely to open the door to the work of evil.

WEARINESS

Weariness, like the relentless seasonal rains on Catalina, certainly leads to saturation and destabilization. Weariness is that deadening fatigue of the body, the mind, and the spirit.

We can assume the presence of weariness when we do our work from obligation and not from challenge, when we seek to escape every time we see another person coming toward us, when cynicism, negativism, and the low fever of bitterness possess our minds. In a check for weariness we might want to look for irritability, the inability to quickly renew energy, the feeling that life no longer includes fun, or the panicky feeling that nothing we do is ever good enough.

Why be overly concerned about weariness? Aren't all busy, productive people always tired to some extent? Of course. But the wise person knows a danger zone when it appears on the screen of life, and he acts accordingly.

My father taught me to ski when I was a young boy. I recall one of his first pieces of advice on the slope: "Remember, Son, that more accidents happen in the final hour of the day than at any other time." I now know that he was correct.

Trying to get one more downhill run in before the ski tow closes, some skiers will rush down the slope forgetting that their bodies are tired and that their reflexes are no longer sharp. Shadows are long; icy and bare spots are hidden. The combination of a depleted body and obstacles not easily seen creates conditions (environments, if you please) in which accidents are far more likely to happen.

My dad was right; at the end of the day one should ski much more cautiously because the good skier knows himself and he doesn't trust the terrain.

Many men and women trying to follow the Lord make their world-breaking choices in similar times of extreme fatigue. Again, not necessarily the physical fatigue after a long day's work; but the fatigue of the spirit and the emotions that occurs after a lengthy period of time when frustration and difficulties have increased to an intense pitch.

I spoke of weariness when I wrote *Restoring Your Spiritual Passion* because I had experienced firsthand what it was all about, and I had become sensitive to the number of people who were signaling that they had the same problem. I did not say in that book what I might have: in the context of weariness I made a series of very bad choices that led to falling flat on my face into sin and hurting many people. Weariness is never to be construed as an excuse. It simply suggests that a person may make certain choices in one environment that he would probably never make in another.

Weariness often leads to something called burnout. One simply loses the will to pursue dreams and senses of mission. I'm reminded of the comments of a champion boxer who described the other day how he had worn down his opponent and positioned him for the winning blow. "I just kept pounding on his arms and body until he became tireder and tireder. Then when he lowered his arms in fatigue, I put him away with a left to the side of the head." I can identify with the fellow he hit.

It's not a delicate description, but it's an accurate one for a boxer as well as for a man or woman with a broken world. More Christians than any of us know have made decisions that they will regret for the remainder of their lives under the influence of fatigue.

And what do we learn from this? How to monitor the times and circumstances in which such weariness and its ultimate product, burnout, are likely to occur. And then we learn either to avoid that extreme condition or to ask others to help us. In relationships of accountability others can protect us so that we are less prone to hurt ourselves with actions or attitudes leading to broken worlds.

In 1982 we bought a car that included a device that actually speaks to us when something is amiss or needs to be checked. We came to call the computer-generated voice Hilda because it is female in sound.

Hilda says, "Your right door is open" when the door is not properly shut, "Your parking brake is on" when I forget to release it, "Your keys are in the ignition" when I try to get out of the car without taking my keys, and "Your lights are on" when I forget to turn the headlights off.

Hilda's most helpful reminder comes when we have less than fifty miles of gas left in the fuel tank. "Your fuel level is low," she announces, and we begin to search for a service station. Hilda has saved us from some inconvenient moments: from dead batteries, from possible theft, and from being out of gas.

Some of us need to ponder where the "Hildas" are in our lives—the external Hildas, people with enough insight and courage to acknowledge that they see evidences that our tanks are running dry, and the internal Hildas, who send up unavoidable signals that we are suffering from a weariness that is abnormal and potentially destructive.

Weariness may have been a key to the poor performance of Jesus' disciples in the garden. It had been a grueling week, the tension high on every one of the holy days. Debates, accusations, threats, and the ups and downs of the public's response to their Master's message must have worn them down. When they got to the garden that night, their only thought was to sleep. And when Jesus was arrested, they tried to get their wits about them but could not emerge from that fog of weariness. Thus "all the disciples forsook Him and fled" (Matt 26:56 NKJV).

I've written in other places that I believe weariness is a spiritual and physical plague of our time. Modern men and women are choosing to live in constant emotional and spiritual deficit. Most of us are expending more energy than we are taking in. Only a certain number with unusual resilience can maintain such a pace. The rest of us try to measure ourselves against these superperformers and then wonder why we lapse back again and again into weariness and guilt because we cannot keep up with them.

We must be candid with one another that this is a reality of not only the marketplace but also the church and nonprofit institutions of our times. Expectations are increasingly raised, glittering programs and opportunities promoted, and in the excitement of it all, we try to go one more round. In the aftermath of such processes we are most likely to make the initial choices that lead to a broken world.

We may need to be sensitive to how some of us inadvertently create conditions that bring weariness to others. An older woman, now childless, may unwittingly intimidate a young mother absorbed in child raising by making her feel guilty that she is not as active as someone thinks she should be in a community or church program. One man may be coaxed into more and more public activities by another man whose temperament or flexibility of time makes it possible for him to be more active.

I see Jesus dealing with weariness. He appears to have kept long hours, and He frequently went the second mile to meet the needs of people. But we cannot miss the fact that sooner or later He always broke free of the crowds and withdrew into the refreshment of quiet. And He did it without the paralyzing "guilt" that so many of us carry today. When He was alone, He looked heavenward, inward, and only then outward to the world. We never see the Son of God operating from a prolonged environment of weariness.

ADVERSITY AND FRUSTRATION

At other times I have written of a short period of our lives when we lived in western Kansas. Then it was necessary for me to drive our inexpensive Volkswagen "beetle" to Denver twice a week for classes in graduate school. The 176-mile trip was straight westward, and I often encountered powerful headwinds that swooped across the plains from the Rocky Mountains.

Headwinds meant a very slow trip to Denver, and they meant, of course, a relatively fast trip back home. If the winds were powerful enough, I often had to drive most of the trip in second or third gear rather than the fourth gear normally used for cruising. The car was blown all over the road, but I always reached my destination.

Naturally, one could drive the distance in second or third gear, but it meant much slower speed, poor gasoline economy, and some wear and tear on the engine. And the wind gusts often came as a surprise and created dangerous driving conditions.

I came to see that we can begin to encounter certain headwinds in life that offer the same kind of challenges I experienced on the road to Denver. Instead of living in fourth gear, with an economy of motion and emotion, we find ourselves living in second or third gear: working harder to accomplish less. We can do it, but like my Volkswagen, the wear and tear and the slower speed of achievement will be our lot.

I think of such headwinds when I think of *adversity* and *frustration,* great sources of saturation and destabilization. When I use the word *adversity,* I'm thinking of our dealings with abrasive, unlikable, or unpleasant people. And when I speak of *frustration,* I'm thinking of tasks that seem to offer no fulfillment or satisfaction. These are second- and third-gear conditions: dangerous and time consuming headwinds. I meet a lot of people who are living in second or third gear.

These will be no problem at all for those of us who do not let people get inside our skin or for those who enjoy a challenge and remain unflappable no matter what the degree of difficulty on the job.

People who are sympathetic toward the brilliant title of Harvey McKay's book, *Swim with the Sharks without Being Eaten Alive,* will be able to name some adversity-producing "sharks." A shark can be a boss or manager in the workplace whose leadership style (if there is one at all) runs counter to the way we like to be motivated and evaluated. A shark can be a family member who makes our lives absolutely miserable: a mother who cannot be pleased or an uncle who incessantly whines and complains. Sharks can be nasty students if we are teachers or grouchy teachers if we are students. The list of potential sharks is long and scary.

The sharks wear us down. They consume large amounts of our mental time as we try to think through ways to defend ourselves, maybe even how to get back at them. Even if we get up every morning determined that they will not get the best of us, it's likely that the sharks may break through our defenses more times than we would like to admit. We pray for patience, wisdom, and even supernatural love. And we feel good about ourselves when they come. We feel ill about ourselves when they don't.

A long-time friend of mine works every day with a man whose managerial style creates confusion, mistrust, and joylessness. My friend comes home on the majority of workdays with an intense dislike of his job. When I'm with him, I'm very much aware of how wearing this is on him. Realistically, my friend can do nothing about his situation. And knowing his pain causes me to pray for him regularly because I know that he is often near the point of saturation and destabilization because of that adversity.

I'm reminded of the Greek myth of Sisyphus who was condemned by the gods to the endless job of pushing a gigantic boulder up a steep hill. Every time he reached the top with his stone, it rolled back down to the bottom and had to be pushed back up again. Sisyphus, the Greeks said, was compelled to perform his task for an eternity.

Many people share Sisyphus's imposed vocation. The young mother with two or more preschool children who rarely hears from anyone that her work with them has immense value. The salesperson in a slump who gets only what-have-you-done-for-me-lately questions from his manager. The clergyman who leads a church where no one in the congregation seems to cooperate except in maintaining the status quo.

Frustration is a common experience for the people who face long-distance commutes or heavy traffic jams every day, the individuals who encounter problems getting things done in a massive bureaucracy, and the vast military establishment if one is assigned to a post where a supervisor seems not to care about excellence or development. You'll find frustrated people in the marketplace, the church, the school, and the home. In their frustration as well as their adversity, there is usually the possibility of saturation and destabilization. And that is an environment for broken-world choices.

GRIEF, LOSS, AND ANGER

Recently a well-dressed, middle-aged man walked into the offices of a New England brokerage house and shot his boss. Police and reporters quickly discovered that the previous day the assailant had been dismissed from his stockbroker's job by the man he killed.

Everyone who knew the two men was in a state of disbelief. Fellow employees observed that the suspect had not been a productive worker, but on the other hand, he had been likable, gentle and, as far as they could see, incapable of such violence.

Something obviously snapped; thinking became confused; feelings exploded; all normal restraint was neutralized. The loss of a job, the humiliation of a personal failure, was apparently more than the man was able to accept. Thus, he made a choice to punish the symbol of all that had happened to him.

What happened? Evil in the heart conspired with a saturated and destabilized environment of the mind. We're not talking about a man with a lifelong record of violence. We're not looking at a man who had a history of temper tantrums or vindictiveness. We're looking at a man who slowly came to a breaking point. And environment and evil conspired to make possible a choice entirely out of line with what others might have expected.

The incident of the man who shot his boss reminds me of a dramatic moment in the movie *Network* when a saturated and destabilized newsman suggested to his TV audience that they should open their windows and shout to no one in particular, "I'm mad as hell, and I'm not going to take it any longer." It would make them feel better, he said.

My first reaction was to laugh as people in the movie began to shout as they'd been told. But then I realized that the film was probably only a short distance from reality. In their grief, loss, or anger, many people are often on the edge of making broken-world choices.

We see this anger in traffic jams when people often exhibit enormous rage at being cut off. We hear of occasional shootings on freeways. We witness anger in supermarket lines and at professional athletic events. And at town hearings when planning and zoning decisions are made that cost someone some money, anger is a prevalent mood.

A common kind of grief is that of losing a loved one in death. As a pastor I've had the responsibility of walking through part or all of the grief process with many men and women. I quickly realized that many of them in their sadness were capable of enormous errors of judgment as they lived in a formidable amount of death-induced confusion.

Grief is a strange inner energy of the mind. We were never created to grieve since we were not made to die or sustain great loss. So grief happens, as far as I can see, when all of the internal systems of the mind and heart scream out, run amok, and try to make sense out of something that seems to have no meaning.

In a state of deep grief and loss, some will withdraw, become almost antisocial. Others will become angry and unconsolable, blaming God or even themselves for the death of a loved one.

Some widows and widowers have fallen into immorality in the aftermath of the loss of someone they have loved and with whom they've shared life. Their loneliness and emptiness seem greater than they can bear. And when friends do not understand the extent of their anguish, they are tempted to turn in whatever direction there is an offer of intimacy.

I've seen good people make unsound financial decisions, choices to move to different parts of the country, and unwise job changes because they were in an environment of loss and grief that led to saturation and destabilization.

Having visited Third World countries on several occasions, I've watched people of more primitive cultures go through loss and grief when a family member has died. I am impressed with the fact that they understand this environment far better than most of us. They take time to grieve, time to think about and resolve their losses. I've heard their wailing and groans. Some people have criticized this process as pagan and bereft of hope. Perhaps there can be an element of that. But more important, these people understand that if we do not give vent to our grief in healthy, acceptable ways, we are quite likely to channel that grief toward the creation of an environment where world-breaking choices will be made.

SUBSTANCE ABUSE AND PHYSIOLOGICAL STRESS

Not long ago three young Boston medical doctors were found guilty in the rape of a nurse. As one might expect, with their convictions and sentences also came the loss of their reputations and their careers. Four worlds were quickly broken in one night. Four lives marked by excellent educations, extraordinary skills, and optimistic futures were destroyed.

The environment? Alcohol. All four had attended a party earlier in the evening, and the heavy drinking while they were there had exacted its toll. Minds were clouded; restraints were cast aside; and animalistic behavior took over. The result? Destabilization and bad choices. Broken personal worlds.

An Amtrak train derails sending a number of people to the hospital with serious injuries. An engineer is killed. Subsequent investigations reveal that half the railroad men involved in the accident showed traces of illegal drugs in their blood.

A small commercial plane crashes in southeastern Colorado. The FAA reports that the pilot tests positive for cocaine use.

A star basketball athlete headed for a professional career dies from a cocaine overdose the night after signing a multimillion dollar contract.

What's happening here? Why are the best and the brightest destroying themselves and others with these broken-world choices? What are individuals who use drugs and alcohol seeking? Psychic liberation? Pleasure? Relaxation? Escape? Social acceptance? Is the risk really worth it?

Most of us are used to identifying these problems with the inner city, with the poor and the undereducated. But if we do, we stick our heads in the sand. It is probable that 10 percent of the people sitting in a suburban church congregation on a Sunday morning have drinking problems. It is also likely that more than a few in the pews have dabbled in the use of drugs that the government has declared dangerous and illegal. And it is frighteningly possible that on the way home from church we will pass and be passed by more than a few whose level of drunkenness or drug-induced state makes them a serious threat to us and our families.

The Bible recounts a somewhat obscure story in the life of Lot in which alcohol played a dominant role.

One day the older daughter said to the younger, "Our father is old, and there is no man around here to lie with us, as is the custom all over the earth. Let's get our father to drink wine and then lie with him to preserve our family line through our father" (Gen. 19:31–32).

Their plan succeeded. Lot in his drunken state lost management of himself, and his two daughters were impregnated. With that incident Lot's biography ends, and we get the picture of a beaten man whose personal world had broken to pieces. The choices to go to Sodom and to intertwine his fortunes with the people of that city had been bad ones. And this is one more bad moment like the others. This time the choice was made "under the influence."

What can we learn from all that we see going on around us today? The murders, the gang warfare, the arrests, the violence. We can at least learn that men and women jeopardize the last inner restraints against the evil in their hearts when they turn their minds over to substances that alter the perception of reality. A lack of concern for this problem probably creates as much possibility for broken worlds as anything we can think about.

Gail and I walk with our friends through that beautiful Catalina Island valley, and I listen to the frightening descriptions of mud slides and floods that level everything in their path. When does it happen? When the soil becomes saturated and destabilized.

When are men and women liable to get themselves into trouble big enough to break apart a personal world? The same kind of answer applies: when life becomes saturated and destabilized. When the weariness is numbing, the frustration and adversity intolerable, the grief and anger unconsolable, and the mind uncontrollable. In the accumulation of draining experiences like these comes the increasing danger of broken-world choices.

CHAPTER 11

Carrying the Baggage

BOTTOM LINE #11:
Misbehavior may often be rooted in the undisclosed things of our pasts.

It has been ten years since I had the conversation, but I never forgot it. He was a young man, a relatively new follower of Christ, hardly in his twenties. The subject matter of our talk: the struggle he said he was having finding success in his commitment to Christ.

As we visited, I read resistance and hardness, even anger, in his words and in his face. I sensed these things also in his physical posture and in the angular nature of his gestures. But even though I read those signals, I wasn't quite sure I understood exactly what they meant.

When he said he'd come to discuss the dwindling vitality of his young spiritual life, I responded by trying to provide an academic sort of response for each of the problems and objections he raised. It was kind of like a tennis game: he would serve up a question or a difficult situation he was facing, and I would try to react with the right answer. But the conversation was going nowhere. His "serves" seemed amateurish and my "returns" were no better.

The breakthrough to the real issue came during an interlude of small talk. "What do you like to do for fun?" I asked.

"Sing" came the answer.

"Sing?" I said. "Are you good?"

"Yeah, I have a very good voice."

"Well, why aren't you in the choir?"

"I can't stand the director."

"What's wrong with the director?"

"Nothing as far as I know. I just don't like choir directors."

I'd heard critiques of choir directors before, but nothing as sweeping as this. So I urged him to go on.

"I get angry anytime someone up in front waves an arm and tells me when and when not to sing. I tried singing in two or three choirs but usually ended up so agitated that I just walked out in the middle of rehearsals."

I couldn't believe what I was hearing; but he went on, and I listened.

"Singing in a choir is the least of my problems, really. I have those sorts of feelings every time someone tells me what to do or expresses an opinion about me. I get mad at cops, at signs that tell me what I can and can't do; I even get mad at you."

"At me? What would you get mad at me for?"

"I get mad at you when you're preaching along and start telling me where I'm wrong and how I need to get my act together. I even walked out on you one time. Hey, I know it's probably weird, but I fight these feelings all the time."

What was supposed to be an interlude, small talk, to get us unglued from our conversational impasse suddenly became the real agenda. My visitor may have had a spiritual problem in his relationship with God, but the solutions did not lie in a serve and return-serve volley of questions and answers.

"Tell me about your dad and mom," I said.

"Not much to tell. What do you want to know?"

"I'm interested in knowing something about your relationship with them. Did you feel close to your dad? Do you have good memories of your childhood? Was your mother a warm person? Stuff like that."

"So what we're really talking about here is a lifelong struggle with anyone in authority. Someone tells you what you should or shouldn't do, and you hear your father all over again."

"Exactly."

"Has it ever occurred to you that you might have the same problem with God? If you don't like your father and therefore all choir directors, cops, and sometimes people like me, why should you like God? Doesn't He present an authority problem too?"

"I'd never thought of that. Are you saying that every time I think about the place of Christianity in my life I'm coming up against those feelings?"

That's exactly what I was planning to say to him. But I was glad that he said it first.

I re-create that conversation as I remember it because it describes a psychic environment in which evil is very likely to exert itself with diabolic power sooner or later. My visitor of more than ten years ago may have expressed himself in a rather interesting way, but his problem was not unique to him.

He carried what I like to call *heavy baggage from the past*. Baggage that had never been properly identified, sorted, and discarded, but should have been. Now, because he had waited so long to enter into the process of handling his baggage from the past, he had a difficult challenge on the journey ahead of him. But he made it, and within a reasonable amount of time he was a free man, able to "travel" lightly.

What I have likened to a journey, the writer of Hebrews likened to a race, and in his encouragement to men and women to run as Christ did, he said, "Let us throw off everything that hinders . . . and let us run with perseverance the race marked out for us" (Heb. 12:1). Throwing off everything includes the luggage from the past that bogs down our present and jeopardizes our future. Our inner private worlds are capable of storing up enormous amounts of these unfortunate pieces and permitting them to become influences in present attitudes and motives that can easily produce broken-world performances. Thus, a vigorous identification and disposal of these pieces is an important personal exercise.

There is such a large assortment of this baggage from people's pasts. Much of it is heavy and bulky. It takes a lot of energy to carry it, and the fatigue of carrying it brings out the worst in many of the baggage handlers. I'd like to name three pieces of luggage of the past as examples. They are the "suitbag" of *unresolved relationships*, the "overnighter" of *unaddressed guilt*, and the "attache case" of *untreated pain*.

By giving each a name and identifying it, perhaps we can see some of those areas of one's personal world where there are likely to be seeds of potential brokenness.

THE "SUITBAG" OF UNRESOLVED RELATIONSHIPS

My young visitor of ten years ago had come to hate his father. And neither he nor his father had ever done anything to address the issues between them and bring them to peace. We call that an *unresolved relationship*. Two sisters carry on a lifelong feud; they are filled with resentment toward each other and seldom speak. That's also an unresolved relationship. Two men have a business partnership that dissolves in conflict and acrimony. Each feels cheated by the other and inwardly seethes at every thought of the former association. That's obviously an unresolved relationship too.

Unresolved relationships are most often connected with family situations, for it is within the matrix of family experiences that we are given some of the most important "gifts" that help us form our sense of personhood. If those gifts are not given in a timely and orderly fashion, relationships will be injured. And if we receive something other than those gifts, the injury may be even worse.

What kind of gifts am I talking about?

There is a gift of *well-being* that comes from being loved. God has created us with a hunger to be loved, and if that hunger is correctly satisfied, we will go on in life to love and give self-value to others. We receive this gift through physical affection, verbal affirmation, and a tenderness of contact that stands out in contrast to most other social contacts.

There is a gift of *competence*. Our parents and family are the first people to build into us a confidence that we can learn, create, serve, and make a difference in our generation if we want to. They give it by assigning positive value to things we do.

There is the gift of *security*. As vulnerable children, we must receive security, and if we do, we will learn to produce it later on for ourselves with God's help. We receive this gift IF we live in a home where a mother and father openly love and respect each other; IF we live in a home without destructive conflict; and IF we live in a home where there are the assurances of a set of restraints and routines that give life order and consistency concerning what is expected and allowed. As a result, we learn to feel safe.

Then there is the gift of *becoming*, the gradual freedom that wise mothers and fathers provide so that children might learn how to make choices and determine directions in life. Under ideal conditions we are not overshielded from challenges nor are we unprotected from things too big for us to take on.

Finally, there is the gift of *modeling*, the exemplary life that provides a vision for a boy as to what it means to be a man; that provides a vision for a girl as to what it means to be a woman. It wasn't long ago that most boys hoped to grow up and be like their fathers and most girls like their mothers. It may be different now.

In times past, these gifts could be given to children not only by their parents but also by members of their extended families: grandparents,

uncles and aunts, and others who usually lived nearby and who inter-
sected regularly. What one parent might not be able to provide, another
individual in the larger family could.

But recent decades have brought the dissolution of the *extended* family as mobility has become a way of life. And in more recent times most
children had only the *nuclear* family (parents and children) from which
to receive their necessary gifts. Today more than half of America's children grow up in *single-parent* families, and 60 percent of mothers of
preschool children have joined the work force. Perhaps this trend suggests the era of the *nonfamily* is just around the corner.

What happens when children do not receive these necessary gifts? Or
what happens if they live in homes where the gifts are decidedly
hurtful? Instead of the gift of *well-being* there are constant assertions of
worthlessness. Instead of the gift of *competence* there are put-downs or
reminders that their efforts are futile and noncontributive. And instead
of the gift of *security* there is a sense of never knowing what is going to
happen next. Children of alcoholics know this experience well.

Instead of the gift of *becoming* there is smothering or its opposite,
apathetic freedom. And instead of the gift of *modeling* there is an absence of anything for which to aspire.

When these gifts are not given, inner anger and resentment will grow.
And they are liable to surface again and again in adult experiences that
are faintly reminiscent of childhood disappointments.

In Brazil a radioactive isotope from a medical laboratory was carried
to a public dump and discarded. Some poor people found the dangerous substance, and not knowing what it was, they handed it around.
One child spread some of it on her body; another even tasted it. Before
anyone discovered what had happened, a significant number of people
in the town were contaminated with radiation.

The anger that some of us carry from childhood is like a dosage of
radiation. It will not go away until it is named and properly disposed of.
Anger is like nuclear energy; it can have useful purposes, or it can
become destructive. We must know the difference.

The Scriptures are not critical of all anger—only of unresolved anger
in relationships. Jacob had an unresolved relationship with his brother
Esau, and it brought the worst out in both of them until they dealt with
it. Absalom was angry with his brother Amnon, and because their father, David, did not force a resolution of the relationship, Absalom
killed his brother.

We can begin to deal with our anger only when we acknowledge its existence, find its source, and engage in whatever forgiveness is necessary in both directions between the giver and the receiver of bad gifts. In families where there is anger, some of us have a lot of forgiving to do with our parents, and the longer we wait to do it, the more we are injured and the more we permit an environment that makes misbehavior more possible in our present and future lives.

THE "OVERNIGHTER" OF UNADDRESSED GUILT

Similarly, we encourage negative environments when we live with *unaddressed guilt* from the past. Now we are talking not of what others may have done but of what we have done that has generated shame and regret.

By using the word *unaddressed*, I'm thinking of those occasions when a significant wrong or harm has been done, and the offender has refused to acknowledge the misdeed and to make whatever restitution is necessary: perhaps a confession and an apology, an untangling of the unfortunate events, or a return or replacement of something taken.

Guilt is usually experienced as a feeling, but it is actually spiritual pain. Real guilt is the result of the inner spirit, created in God's image, crying "foul." God's laws have been violated; His honor diminished. Something deep within us shouts in protest. We feel the shout as guilt.

Guilt can be constant or intermittent. Sometimes it can lie dormant for long periods of time only to surface when we talk with someone who shares a similar situation to ours or when we see something with which we can identify on the movie screen or in a news report. Or as we shall see in a moment, unaddressed guilt may resurface when there is a later pressure or stress that seems somehow mysteriously related to an earlier incident.

It's hard to quantify the full effect of guilt from person to person. Some seem more sensitive to it, actually driven by it. Others appear to have a higher threshold and seem able to ignore the messages. We do know that it is possible to squelch the entire guilt-producing mechanism. That can happen if a young person's conscience is not sharpened by adults who maintain discipline and order, and it can happen when one simply refuses to listen to the inner voice long enough so that the voice gets drowned out by other noises. The biblical writers referred to this as "searing the conscience." Apparently one can turn off the immediate consequences of guilt, but it will take lots of emotional or psychic energy.

Jacob's sons, the brothers of the Older Testament Joseph, seem to have wrestled with unaddressed guilt for more than fifteen years. If you know the story, you'll remember that they were incited to rage by their young upstart sibling, Joseph, and plotted his murder. But just before they implemented their plan, they were appeased by Reuben, the eldest. Relenting, they sold Joseph as a slave to a passing caravan. Out of sight; out of mind. Problem solved.

They covered the disposal of Joseph with a lie to their father. Joseph was dead, they said, killed apparently by a wild animal. The old man accepted the story and lapsed into grief.

It appeared as if the secret of their conspiracy was safe for at least fifteen years. But the guilt lay unaddressed deep in the private world of each brother. And when they later journeyed to Egypt to purchase food during a famine, they trotted out their lie once more.

It came when they bowed before the governor of Egypt not knowing that he was actually Joseph. But he recognized them and put them off balance with harsh interrogation. To his accusation that they had come to Egypt as spies, they said: "Your servants were twelve brothers, the sons of one man, who lives in the land of Canaan. The youngest is now with our father, *and one is no more*" (Gen. 42:13, emphasis mine). In other words, Joseph is dead. A believable story, perhaps, if it wasn't for the fact that Joseph himself was standing right in front of them.

The not-so-dead brother, Joseph, increased the pressure, and the brothers felt it immediately. The interface between the past murder plot and the present sticky situation in Egypt was established in their minds. And even though they were still unaware of who they were dealing with, they replayed the crime of years ago. Unaddressed guilt suddenly was corkscrewing its way back to the surface. It wasn't out of sight or out of mind after all.

They said to one another, "Surely we are being punished because of our brother. We saw how distressed he was when he pleaded with us for his life, but we would not listen; that's why this distress has come upon us."

Reuben replied, "Didn't I tell you not to sin against the boy? But you wouldn't listen! Now we must give an accounting for his blood" (Gen. 42:21–22).

Joseph overheard these words. In their ignorance, the brothers remained unaware that he, the governor, could understand their language. And while they panicked, Joseph secretly wept.

Even after the brothers reconciled with Joseph and were assured of his grace and forgiveness, they lived the entirety of their lives waiting for the roof to fall in. They couldn't quite believe that Joseph wouldn't seek vengeance for what they had done. And their fear of retribution was only exacerbated when Jacob died. Then they were sure that in the wake of his death, Joseph would have his revenge. But Joseph's forgiveness was authentic and unwavering. The brothers' long-lived fear was an example of how powerful guilt unaddressed for long periods of time can actually be.

Unaddressed guilt makes for unstable choice making. It distorts perspectives, twists meanings, and undermines the confidence we need to press forward in the present. We cannot expect to live healthily in the future when the baggage of the past keeps banging away at the trapdoor of our minds demanding attention.

Stanley Jones was thinking of the awfulness of unaddressed guilt when he wrote:

> In the book of Revelation are these words: "It was in my mouth sweet as honey: and as soon as I had eaten it my belly was bitter" (Rev 10:10). Is that the total picture of sin? In the mouth it is sweet as honey, in the beginning sin tastes good, seems good; but when life tries to assimilate it, it can't—it turns bitter. For life does not and cannot assimilate or digest sin; sin and the body are not made for each other—they are allergic to each other. A Hindu youth said to me: "After committing adultery with that woman I went up the mountainside trembling." Trembling at what? At the sourness in his stomach. "I was a ninny to do it," said a woman to me in America. Her stomach turned sour.
>
> Everybody who sins, east or west, begins to turn sour. They sour against this, that, and the other; everything and everybody is wrong. They are soured on life because life within has soured. They are trying to assimilate the unassimilatable. Sin is sour business. *(Song of Ascents)*

Our own unaddressed guilt often creates suspicion of others' behavior. It makes us struggle to like ourselves. We wallow in self-accusation. And in this environment of suspicion, self-perceived cheapness, and general bad feelings we are apt to make commitments and choices that will further break our worlds.

Guilt is dispelled only when the truth is told, when the cover-up is exploded away, confession made, and restitution accomplished. Only then will guilt like a block of ice melt away.

Perhaps you've seen an ice sculpture in an elegant restaurant. Once I had an occasion to remain in one of those restaurants for several hours while a meeting was in progress. It gave me time enough to watch the ice figure slowly melt into formlessness and then disappear.

If anger is like a piece of radiated material in a dump, poorly identified and improperly shielded, unaddressed guilt is like a huge block of ice. Kept in a dark, cold place, it remains hard. But brought into the light, identified, and confessed, it begins to melt, and soon it is gone. And free is the soul that no longer is frozen by unaddressed guilt.

Thus, the man or woman who wishes to prevent broken-world choices monitors the inner self for the signals of guilt. These people seek to prevent the choices that lead to a broken world, and they will not carry the heavy baggage of guilt. They leave it at the Cross where Christ affirmed that He would handle it in His grace.

THE "ATTACHE CASE" OF UNTREATED PAIN

Among the other things that hinder us as we seek to keep our personal worlds strong is the problem of *untreated pain*. These are the open wounds created and sometimes perpetuated by others in our worlds.

When I was a pastor, I often talked with young couples who wanted to be married. Like many other pastors, I always required a series of conversations with a bride and groom as a condition of my participation in the wedding.

One of the first questions I usually asked was: would both of you like your marriage to be like the one your parents have? I remember well the answer of one bride, "If I could have a marriage like the one my parents have, I'd be the most fortunate woman in the world."

Unfortunately, I didn't often hear such an enthusiastic and positive response. More often the answer came in the negative. But one negative sticks in my memory more than any of the others. When I asked that question of one couple, the soon-to-be-bride seemed to freeze. It was as if death (or was it hatred) swept across her face. I was sure I'd said something that was completely misunderstood and taken badly. But I could produce nothing in my memory to suggest that possibility.

"You're very disturbed about my question," I probed.

"Why do you say that?" she said with a distant stare.

"I read it in your eyes, your facial expression. You're telling me in every way possible, except with words, that you're angry."

"Let's just drop it," she said. And I did, for the moment.

A few days passed, and then a call came with a request for another appointment. This time the woman came to see me by herself.

It was my first acquaintance with child molestation. As she unfolded her story, it included details with which most of us are now familiar: a father who had made sexual advances to which she had yielded, a mother who had been aware of what was happening but lived in denial of it all. Having nowhere to turn—"who would believe me?"—the now-adult bride-to-be had endured what she had to until she was old enough to leave the home.

"Now do you see what your question meant to me? You brought back a memory I thought I'd buried. It took me a day or two to be willing to face it myself. Why would I want a marriage like that of my parents?"

A later visit with her and her fiancé resulted in a postponement of the wedding for a few months until some counseling could take place. It was a case of untreated pain, which had engendered hatred, a distaste for sexual intimacy, and a hidden resentment for men in general. All of that might have exploded, broken-worldlike, in the subsequent marriage.

Untreated pain can exist far below the surface of our conscious minds. Smoldering like an underground coal fire seeking oxygen, it simply awaits a distant moment when it can explode.

We are living in a time when the issue of child molestation and abuse is receiving heavy attention. We are learning that many men and women are walking about with the pain of exploitation and humiliation deep within. And as that pain surfaces, it leads to unhealthy present relationships and decisions in which the wisdom and value are not solid.

Untended pain may include failures and humiliations that have never been properly understood. Romances that dissolved so suddenly that one of the parties was left with a lifelong scar of rejection. A death in which one has never fully grieved or faced the loss. A betrayal in a marriage that is never worked through to forgiveness and reconciliation, just swept under the rug.

Again, as with guilt, some of us feel pain longer and deeper than others. The threshold of psychic or emotional pain seems very high for some individuals; they find it easy to forget moments when they've been slighted and embarrassed, when they've been exploited or badly defeated. For others, the threshold is low, and they remember almost everything: a slap in the face, a forgotten line in a school play at which everyone laughed, being stood up for a teenaged date, or being fired from a summer job. For some, these seemingly trivial incidents can be as devastating as a Fortune 500 company CEO being fired by a board of directors or the breakup of a marriage. The pain is measured by the one experiencing it, not by an objective observer.

What does untended pain leave us with? Sometimes a struggle with self-confidence. Sometimes an inability to trust others, especially anyone who reminds us of the one who may have caused hurt in the past. Or we can be left with an expectation that we will be mistreated again, so we resist participating in a relationship or a task that might raise the risk of a repeat experience.

Our memories are deep, seemingly bottomless. And unless we search them in a time of dis-ease, they are liable to betray us when unresolved relationships or unaddressed guilt or untreated pain tap into our spiritual circuitry.

Gail and I enter a hotel carrying our suitbags and our attache cases. We're worn out, my back is sore, and I'm getting tired of traveling. A uniformed attendant comes alongside.

"Let me take those things for you," he says.

"No," I answer. "We can handle them by ourselves." As much as I'd like to give them to the young man, we do not have any cash in our pockets (only credit cards), and I'm ashamed to admit the real reason.

"You sure? I'd like to help," he says.

"I'm sure. Thank you," I say back.

We reach the hotel desk, register, and turn toward our rooms. "Let the bellman bring your bags up in a little while," the desk clerk says.

"No thanks," I respond, again ashamed to admit that I'm short on tipping change.

"Please let him do it," she says. "All the gratuities are added to your bill anyway. You don't have to tip him."

Has she read my mind? Have I carried these bags for fifty yards when someone was there, already paid in effect, to handle them for me? I have the brain of a bird.

Carrying bags when someone is there, paid to carry them for me, is almost as incomprehensible as carrying baggage from the past, be it unresolved relationships, unaddressed guilt, or untreated pain, when Someone *has already paid* to lift it off me. And that's exactly what happened at the Cross. As the hymn writer put it so well: "Jesus paid it all."

CHAPTER 12

Tiptoeing on the Spiderweb

> BOTTOM LINE #12:
> *A disrespect for the power of evil is a major step toward a broken personal world.*

While I was in graduate school, Gail and I moved to St. Francis, Kansas, where I became the weekend pastor of a small country congregation. The pastor's study was located in the basement of the church building. It was a rather damp and musty room, and that meant bugs.

That's why I wasn't surprised one day when I discovered a large, magnificently designed spiderweb on one end of a bookcase. I was about to brush it away when my curiosity took control and caused me to sit back and watch what happened if and when some creeping thing got caught in the web.

For several days, I permitted the spider to enlarge his web (I assume it was a male spider), and soon he had managed to take over half a shelf of church history books: all the way from the first-century church fathers to Martin Luther.

When I wasn't concentrating on my studies, I found a certain amount of amusement locating insects and depositing them in the center circle of the spider's silken prison. They were instantly trapped, of course, and a huge black spider would emerge from behind a copy of LaTourette's *History of the Christian Church* and make a quick end to the insect's resistance. I never detected any hint that the spider was thankful for my meals.

One day I became annoyed by a large fly buzzing around the study. Occasionally, he would land near the spiderweb, and each time

140

he wandered closer and closer, even venturing onto some of the outer strands much like someone might test the ice of a frozen pond in the early days of winter. But always after a few tentative steps, the fly would dart away, returning again a few minutes later.

I had the impression that the fly was driven by curiosity about the spider's web. Or perhaps he was playing I-dare-you games with the spider or with something within himself. Did the fly have something to prove?

If he did, the fly didn't get the job done. He made one visit too many to the edges of the web. This time the fly tiptoed too far out on the strands and suddenly became entangled. He struggled mightily but unsuccessfully. The well-built web held its prey, and soon the spider was out of his hiding place behind LaTourette pouncing upon the hapless fly. The contest was over swiftly, and the study was silent; no buzzing any longer.

I think of the spider and the fly every time I reread the Older Testament story of Samson. A man of unusual strength, he had known the favor of God as he had led the oft-beleaguered Hebrews out from under the domination of the Philistines. The enemy blanched, then ran, whenever Samson took to the field because they came to know by experience that it was no contest when he was there.

But Samson liked "spiderwebs," one could say. For him, the spiderwebs were the women of Philistia. And despite the warnings of his father not to get involved, he chose to do so. On both occasions—he consorted with a woman of Timnah and with a woman of Gaza—he made a fool of himself. He never learned from one bad experience to another that while there might be pleasure, there was no love to be found. Only entrapment; only ultimate disaster. It was a matter of tiptoeing one time too many out on the Philistine spiderweb. And finally he became entangled.

It's a strange but instructive story about God's acts in a person's life. In spite of Samson's stupidity a first, a second, and even a third time, God kept giving him the necessary strength to fight battles. We might think that one mistake would have been too many for God. But divine patience and kindness lasted for a longer period than human patience and kindness might have.

What drives a Samson? Is it the love of danger? The unique and the unusual? Does a Samson get a thrill out of testing the outer limits? Or does he simply assume that there is no situation he cannot handle? Is his physical strength to him like the words of a smooth talker? Like the money of one who thinks he can buy his way out of any tight spot? Like the brains of a thinker who presumes he can outwit all competitors?

When men and women get drawn into Samson's game, thinking they can take on anything or anybody, they usually do not think seriously enough about three things: the strange *curiosity within* that draws one toward the web, the *entangling potential* of the web itself, and the *spider* who uses the web for its own selfish designs.

We've been looking at the environments in which evil is most likely to break forth in human behavior. We've looked at the vulnerable moments in our age-groups, observed those times when people become saturated and destabilized, and glanced at the past and how it can affect the present.

But no discussion of the environments in which evil is most likely to show itself would be complete, no matter how cursory the treatment, if we did not take a look at something the Christian church has traditionally called spiritual warfare. This controversial topic cannot be discussed at any length without considerable disagreement and diverse opinion. But I need to take a deep breath and venture into the subject because I believe that a biblical understanding of broken worlds would be incomplete if we did not ask what it has to teach us about ourselves and our human vulnerabilities.

Temptation is a key word at this point. Temptation suggests the notion of a seduction of sorts, a drawing of the fly to the spiderweb through whatever means necessary. The purpose: neutralization and then destruction.

Sin, of course, is another key word. It is usually used in two different ways. A sin can be an act or an attitude that is incompatible with God's standards of right. Or sin can refer to the spiritual disease of the innermost being. Some have likened that disease to cancer, for left unchecked it grows and chokes off what is good. I prefer to use the word *evil* in this second definition because the overuse of the word *sin* has led to a tendency to disregard its destructive nature. It's reasonable to observe that sin isn't taken very seriously by most of us until it has a clear effect in some part of our lives.

The Bible is clear in its teaching from beginning to end that people live in an environment of temptation that seeks to draw them away from the pleasure of the Creator and toward the condition of sin, which is alien and antithetical to Him.

The first temptation and the first sinful acts occurred in the garden, which the Genesis account describes. A being in the form of a serpent approached Eve and proposed that she reconsider the Creator's prohibition on eating the fruit from a certain tree.

Temptation came first from the serpent and then, second, from within. All the serpent did was get the ball rolling. Eve's reasoning process took over from there.

The serpent did his job through deception. He distorted the words of God until he had effectively lowered Eve's concerns about disobedience. Then the writer says:

> When the woman saw that the fruit of the tree was good for food and pleasing to the eye, and also desirable for gaining wisdom, she took some and ate it. She also gave some to her husband, who was with her, and he ate it (Gen. 3:6).

Eve's broken-world choice was built on an evaluation of the issue as seen through her eye, her appetite, and her intellect. Somehow she turned off the deeper part of herself, the spiritual, where she might have measured her choice against the word of God. And that's why it all went wrong. The biblical writers clearly trace the emergence of evil in the world from this one simple but very profound act.

A study of this interesting and tragic encounter might suggest that temptation can come from at least two sources: from without and from within. And so it has ever been.

Why do men and women commit sins, acts that singularly or in clusters can break a personal world into pieces? Perhaps for the same reasons that Samson headed for the women of Philistia. Apparently we aren't perceptive enough to realize that we cannot beat the system that evil has targeted against us. Like Samson, we keep thinking that we possess the capability to do what history says cannot be done: overcome sin and evil on our own.

The temptation to sin can come, most Christians believe, from one of four sources.

SATAN

The first might be a temptation that comes from the devil, or Satan as he is known in the Bible. Among the nouns used in Scripture to identify this strange creature are *deceiver* and *slanderer*. The words themselves tell us that the principal strategy of this evil enemy is a distortion of the truth.

We have a number of biblical references to Satan as a distinct personality. Christian theology has drawn from biblical sources the insight that
Satan, once named Lucifer, was an angel of the highest order who chose
to rebel against God and, as a result, was expelled from heaven.

We read of a strange Older Testament conversation between Satan
and God regarding the integrity of Job. From that conversation came a
puzzling agreement that Job's faithfulness would be exposed to a series
of "stress tests," including illness, tragedy, and material and human
loss. What tests they were! One inference in the story of Job is that
Satan is sometimes permitted to initiate a certain amount of suffering in
the world. But the follow-up inference is always that it is a limited freedom and will not exceed bounds determined by God. These truths are
hazy, at best, to our finite minds. But one thing rings clear and true: the
God of Job is not limited in His power, and He can act when He chooses
to do so.

In the New Testament we hear of Satan attempting to draw Jesus into
impulsive decisions by making Him promises that he wasn't equipped
to keep. It was almost as if Satan was saying to Jesus, "You're on my
turf; let's play by my rules." But our Lord powerfully resisted Satan's
enticements.

Later we are told that "Satan entered Judas" (Luke 22:3 NKJV), and
this becomes a curious observation to ponder. What is the connection
between Judas's responsibility for his choice to betray Jesus and Satan's
apparent commandeering of Judas for his own designs? We aren't given
a clear answer to this question. We can only assume that Judas reached
a point in his life when he was so much in personal rebellion against
Jesus that, without realizing it, he made himself available as an agent
for Satan's designs.

Both Paul and Peter warned the early Christians that Satan plots to
neutralize Christians and congregations. They pointed out his
shrewdness and aggressiveness. He is like a lion, Peter wrote, roaring
about, searching for someone to devour. He masquerades as an angel of
light, Paul observed. In another place Paul noted Satan to be a schemer
and affirmed, "We are not ignorant of his devices" (2 Cor. 2:11 NKJV).

Will most of us be directly tempted by Satan? My own opinion is,
probably not. Satan is not omnipresent, as the theologian likes to use
the word to signify someone who is everywhere at all times. Only God is
omnipresent. Thus, Satan's activities have a primary limitation in that
he can be in only one place at one time.

The Bible seems to suggest that Satan's favorite place is somewhere near the throne of God so that he can level accusations at the heavenly family. I take that to mean that Satan rather enjoys trying to spoil God's pleasure in His children.

Perhaps there are occasional moments when Satan directly controls a person. A Hitler? A Genghis Khan? But is it always a mass killer? Could Satan have other disguises should he tempt a person? To outrageous materialism? Sensualism? Nihilism?

A few years ago a comedian employed the line "the devil made me do it" in a set of humorous characterizations. As with most humor, the laughs came because most of us would indeed like to put the blame for our actions on someone else, and the devil is an excellent candidate. He's bad anyway, and a bit more blame won't tarnish his image.

But the biblical truth is that the devil enjoys no control at all over anyone under God's care. He may be permitted to cast his most powerful seductions in our direction; he may be permitted to whisper his most convincing lies; he may be permitted to order certain events so that they seem in the present to be adverse to our interests. But at no time will he ever be permitted to make us do anything. As W. L. Watkinson once wrote: "Hell does its worst with the saints. The rarest souls have been tested with high pressures and temperatures, but Heaven will not desert them" (*Streams*).

THE DEMONIC HORDES

The Bible proposes a second source of temptation: demonic beings. Christian theology suggests that there are large numbers of demons who are invisible, destructive, and aggressive. They too are fallen angels. We are made quite aware of their existence during Jesus' public ministry.

In a dramatic passage in Bunyan's *Pilgrim's Progress* the traveling Christian is faced with enormous despair over his sinfulness. He is besieged by temptation that seems to come from without, perhaps from the very demons we mention in these paragraphs.

I took notice that now poor Christian was so confounded that he did not know his own voice; and thus I perceived, just when he was come over against the mouth of the burning pit, one of the wicked ones got behind him, and stepped up softly to him, and whisperingly suggested many grievous blasphemies to him, which he verily thought had proceeded from his own mind. This put Christian more to it than anything that he had met with before, even to think that he should now blaspheme Him that he loved so much before. Yet if he could have helped it, he would not have done it; but he had not the discretion either to stop his ears, or to know from whence these blasphemies came.

What we know of demons in Scripture suggests that they may affect people physically, mentally, and spiritually. We have descriptions of men and women possessed or controlled by demons.

The man of Gadara is a prime example. Filled with a legion (more than a thousand) of demons, he was said to be supernaturally strong, a serious nuisance to the community. Every day he ran naked about the countryside, screaming and making himself a general menace. We can imagine that he had parents, a wife, and children who watched this process of human degradation and could only remember what once had been.

Did this thing called demon possession happen all at once in this man's life? Or was it the product of a life-style always positioned on the edge of moral risk? Did he consciously or unconsciously open himself to darknesses deep within? Was there a discernible moment when powers deeper than he'd ever known simply seized control of his psychological and physiological processes? And what of the attitude of the people in the community as they had to find a way to restrain him? He is the ultimate broken-world person. He is a picture of environments and evil at their very worst.

In a newspaper report on the thousands of American students who go to Florida for their spring break from classes, one young man commented on why there was so much drunkenness associated with the event: "There's a time to be serious and a time to be out of control. Spring break is my time to be out of control." You get the feeling that he may have described the worldview of the man named Legion who ultimately became controlled by demons.

Whatever happened, we have the picture of a spiritually captive man the day Jesus encountered him. Half-crazed, he approached the Son of God, and almost immediately he was freed from his captivity. When Jesus expelled the demons, they are said to have entered a herd of two thousand swine that self-destructed by running into the lake.

We learn something of the man's transformation when we are told of his healed condition: he was "sitting there, dressed and in his right mind" (Mark 5:15). "Sitting there" suggests a new tranquillity;

"dressed," a new dignity; and "in his right mind," an ability to reason and feel.

I am forced to take the issue of demon activity seriously, first, because I take the Bible seriously. I think I have seen evidences of demon activity in some I've helped as a pastor, but I am not comfortable with those who find demon instigation behind virtually every broken-world failure. This is a matter for us to treat with caution and respect.

It should not go unnoticed that Christians in the non-Western world regularly testify to demon activity, and the stories are so consistent from culture to culture that they have credibility. In the more developed countries, it's possible that demon activity takes on different, seemingly sophisticated, forms. In many instances, we may not be aware that violent and antisocial behavior of people is directly tied to this kind of supernatural evil possession.

The value of the tragic and then beautiful story of the man of Gadara lies in its candid description of what demon activity is all about. But the key to the story is the fact that demons are always impotent in the presence of Christ's power. "Even evil spirits obey his orders!" (Mark 1:27, TLB) was the observation of the disciples when Jesus demonstrated absolute control over the world of evil. And that trust is as sound today as it was then.

The message is clear: demon activity, even possession, may be a real matter, but the overwhelming power of Christ is just as real. No one who has made a personal commitment to Christ need fear being destroyed by this source of evil. Perhaps some people have felt the oppression of demonic attacks, but they can never be possessed as long as their lives have been placed under Christ's Lordship.

SYSTEMS OF EVIL

If evil has been generated in terms of temptation by Satan and in terms of a possible possession by demons, then according to the biblical writers, a more generalized form of evil energy pervades the systems of our times.

St. Paul warned the Ephesians that the Christian's struggle is not against human beings but "against the rulers, against the authorities, against the powers of this dark world and against the spiritual forces of evil in the heavenly realms" (Eph. 6:12). Paul wasn't more specific in identifying this "enemy," but he obviously wanted people to be alert to such oppression. He seemed to be saying that creation is temporarily sated with the spiritual force of evil and that it would be totally devastating were it not for the restraining hand of God. Be alert, he advised. Be constantly in a state of armored vigilance. Do not take this enemy for granted, he begged.

One does not have to look across our civilized world for very long to believe that Paul was absolutely correct. The evil that seems to pervade the machinations of nations and peoples today defies credulity. In his book *Modern Times* Paul Johnson records and analyzes the history of the twentieth century and the multimillions of people killed by the violence of political action. He finally asks, "What has gone wrong with humanity?"

A spiritual plague fills the air, St. Paul might answer. And only the power of God holds back the full potential of its devastating effects.

Does this form of evil play a role in the spawning of racism, nationalism, and materialism? Do institutions like governments and multinational companies become so driven with self-interest that they slowly become corporate versions of the demon-possessed man at Gadara? Does this form of evil often account for the breakdown of communication in organizations and the failure of people in disparate places such as Northern Ireland, the Middle East, and central Africa to solve their conflicts? Does this evil infect the mind of the terrorist who coldly goes about blowing up people in the name of political goals?

Does this evil affect you and me as we walk the streets of our towns and cities? Is it beating upon us through the news and entertainment media, through the pressure of society's trends? Does this evil even enter the church and cause it to become bogged down with property acquisition, organizationalism, and fund raising? Maybe.

The answer? Paul's warnings to the Ephesians. Be alert. Be armored. Be prayerful. This environment is most dangerous, and it can bring out the worst in us just when we didn't know that it was possible.

THE HUMAN HEART

The final source of temptation comes from within the human heart. But this is not an attractive thing to think about. Nevertheless, the Scriptures are quite clear that inner spiritual sicknesses can plague us all and will always, given a chance, draw us away from intimacy with God.

We human beings are paradoxes. We love the fruits of commitment, love, and order. Yet a dark side of us is often anticommitment, antilove, and antiorder. We would prefer to receive these things; we have to be taught and we have to deliberately choose to give these things. This is a fundamental testimony to the evil within.

One could say that a barbarian is in each of us. To some extent the barbarian can be temporarily tamed in the best situations. And one needs only look at the deteriorating moral situation in many parts of the Western world to understand that the barbarian in us is very much alive. That man loves darkness rather than light.

Many of the temptations to sin first come from this source within. Paul had several lists of these, which included "sexual immorality, impurity and debauchery; idolatry and witchcraft; hatred, discord, jealousy, fits of rage, selfish ambition, dissensions, factions and envy; drunkenness" (this one from Gal. 58:19–20). Jesus of course noted that the motives and designs for man's worst behavior come from within the heart and often find a receptive climate in the public world (see Matt. 15:16ff).

We are on safe ground when we listen to this carefully, when we conclude that each of us is capable of the worst sort of behavior that will eventually break a personal world to pieces. No environment is more vicious, none more dangerous, than the dark side of the human heart and its capacity to promote evil.

Alexander Whyte quotes John Bunyan:

> Sin and corruption would bubble up out of my heart as naturally as water bubbles up out of a fountain. I thought now that everyone had a better heart than I had. I could have changed heart with anybody. I thought none but the devil himself could equalize me for inward wickedness and pollution of mind. I fell, therefore, at the sight of my own vileness, deeply into despair, for I concluded that this condition in which I was in could not stand with a life of grace. Sure, thought I, I am forsaken of God; sure I am given up to the devil, and to a reprobate mind.

Even as I write these words, something within me wishes I could delete this chapter from the computer disk upon which it is recorded. The subject is depressing, and were it left without the hope of preventing and rebuilding in the chapters to come, it would deflate the spirit. But sometimes there is good news amidst the bad news. If the conditions of evil around us and in us are bad news, the good news is that we can be alert to them and appropriate the power of God to defend against them. Christianity is not a gloomy faith; it is a brilliant and powerful strategy against all else that is gloomy.

This warfare in the spiritual realm is real; it must be recognized and prepared for. But before we look away from this environment, we might be wise to ask ourselves this: when is spiritual warfare most likely to make itself felt?

There are occasions when spiritual warfare is most likely to be at its peak in our personal worlds. For example, I call one of these occasions "Going Beyond the Fences."

GOING BEYOND THE FENCES

In early 1988 Charles and Diana, Prince and Princess of Wales, and some friends took a skiing trip to Switzerland. The shocking news came one afternoon of a terrible accident caused by an avalanche in which one of the prince's lifelong friends was killed and another seriously injured. It seemed sheer chance that the prince himself was not killed or hurt.

How did it happen? A day or two later the press reported that the prince's group had chosen to ski out on slopes that were closed to the public. The avalanche warnings had been posted, but they had chosen to go beyond the fences because, as one of them observed, that's where the optimum fun and excitement were to be found. Most likely, they found a brand of pleasure that was indeed more than attractive. But it went beyond the margins of what was wise and prudent. And the avalanche exacted its price among those who went beyond the fences. The result? Several broken worlds.

Like the prince and his party who could not stay inside the fences, all of us become curious enough at times to edge out to the fences and see what's on the other side. Perhaps we become curious to see how far we can sneak away from God and not suffer the consequences.

Going beyond the fences has to do with outright disobeying the will of Christ and neglecting the spiritual disciplines given to us for our maximum protection. When we cross the fence line, we open the gate to increasing possibilities for broken-world choices. We invite more intense spiritual warfare. And we are likely to have insufficient "weaponry" to handle the oppression.

Our God takes no pleasure in the disobedience of His people or in the consequences that often result. Rather, He mourns this errant self-confidence that will not bend to the lesson of history: those who go beyond the fences are at the mercy of temptation and will inevitably be overcome by the energy that lies deep within or the spiritual enemy without.

DOUBT

I'm a doubter by nature. And so I speak from personal experience when I say that spiritual warfare increases to a feverish pitch when people like me find it hard to trust.

Asking questions and admitting confusion are not necessarily wrong things for Christians to do when we are trying to grow. Nor does our God expect us to have all the answers sorted and defined.

There are understandable moments when, from the human perspective, events do not make sense and we wonder what these things mean. At times we are keenly disappointed when something does not happen according to our expectations. Suffering, death, loss: they can smash our resolve and our confidence for a time. And in their path some of us might doubt that we are grounded in truth.

I see no place where God condemns doubt. Gracious Father that He is, He seems not to be offended when we speak out in momentary anger to Him, when we frankly disagree with Him, or when we acknowledge that somewhere along the line we've missed His signals altogether and wonder if there were any signals.

But we must remember that while there may be nothing wrong with doubt, it is a dangerous time in which spiritual warfare can increase. At such a time our resolve to be alert to the evil in and around us can be diminished. When you see a Christian make a choice that leads to a broken world, you may be seeing a person who was in a time of great doubt and was caught in spiritual impoverishment.

THE COUNSEL OF THE WICKED

You could be rather blunt in the days when the psalmist wrote what we call the First Psalm. And he was blunt when he noted the tendency of some to walk "in the counsel of the wicked." That's not a complimentary description of some people in our world, but the psalmist was aware that there is no "blessedness" when we continually expose ourselves to the influences of people who have little or no use for God or for spiritual orientation.

Earlier we spoke of Lot, and his misfortunes again provide us with a powerful lesson. He was always being influenced by people around him.

As long as he was under the influence of his uncle, Abraham, his life and choices seem to have been exemplary. But somehow he one day assumed that he could get along without his uncle and so purposed to move to Sodom. Lot learned a sad lesson in that city: you cannot expect to be spiritually strong if your fellowship is constantly with those whose values and commitments are anti-God.

Lot's personal world and those of his family suffered total catastrophe because Lot didn't know this. He lost his wife, his extended family, his assets, and his dignity. The explanation is simple. Lot could not expect to be successful in spiritual warfare when he surrounded himself with people who had no use for his relationship with God.

This is a precedent for Christians to consider. Can we expect to acquire and maintain the spiritual strength and ardor that we want if the predominant influences in our lives are people who are alien to the faith? This is why the Scriptures urge the Christian on to supportive fellowship and accountability with men and women of like commitment.

The fact is that we increase the chances of succumbing to the spiritual offenses of the enemy within and without when we place ourselves in these situations: disobedience, doubt, and a pervasive non-Christian influence.

This subject of spiritual warfare is an awesome one. The thinking person is uncomfortable with it. The emotional person is frightened by it. The activist is sure that there is a conspiracy against him.

But that spider does spin his web. We are by our very nature tempted to explore the outer edges of the web, sure that we can handle at least that part. But every once in a while, someone wanders too far toward the middle. The result? A world breaks. And one again wonders why we did not learn history's lessons.

CHAPTER 13

Freeing the Bound-Up Heart

> BOTTOM LINE #13:
> *The freest person in the world is one with an open heart, a broken spirit, and a new direction in which to travel.*

In past centuries, it was a custom in many parts of China to keep the feet of young girls tightly wrapped. Small feet and short steps were considered a mark of feminine physical attractiveness in the Chinese culture. Only in modern times has this discomforting and deforming practice been scuttled.

I have the principle of bound feet in mind when I ponder how we get on with the process of rebuilding a broken world. How do we take the pieces of life and begin the process of putting them back together again?

We've looked at myths and case studies and environments of choice in an attempt to trace the origins and consequences when worlds break into pieces. That is an important foundation for the most important part of this book. How are broken worlds rebuilt? WHERE DO ANY OF US BEGIN?

My initial thought is to go back to the starting point of all broken-world choices: the inner being; the private world; the heart, the core of the person that Jeremiah said was deceitful and beyond full comprehension. But why go there?

Because the biblical writers almost always start there. They assess the performance of a person or a people by saying something first about the condition of the heart when they record and analyze the broken-world choices of individuals and nations. Favorite adjectives for describing the heart when personal worlds are breaking are *stiff-necked; resistant; darkened; blinded; afflicted; rebellious.* The Bible speaks of the hardened heart of the Egyptian Pharaoh, the cold hearts of the people of Israel, and the violated or penetrated heart of Judas.

On the other hand, when the writers speak of one who has moved into the rebuilding phase, the adjectives describing the heart turn to *broken; turned back; clean; undivided; contrite; new.*

David, the man who constantly struggled with deceit and personal integrity, said to his son, Solomon, as he pointed him to the future:

> And you, my son Solomon, acknowledge the God of your father, and serve him with wholehearted devotion and with a willing mind, for the LORD searches every heart and understands every motive behind the thoughts (1 Chron. 28:9).

In a few words David put the issues of faith into a capsule. We have a God whose view of us begins with the heart, and we are called to serve Him beginning from the heart. The heart is behind the mind; it produces the motives behind the thoughts. And out of all that come the actions that break a personal world or rebuild it.

Two extreme "heart conditions" are a distinct displeasure to God. Both attract His anger and judgment. In their extremes these hearts are bound by evil just like the feet of a nineteenth-century Chinese girl, and they therefore suffer from discomfort and deformity.

One extreme is typified by the personal worlds of the people of the earliest civilization in the Bible: "The LORD saw how great man's wickedness on the earth had become, and that every inclination of the thoughts of his heart was only evil all the time" (Gen. 6:5). This is a brief description of people whose hearts had become so oriented toward the production of evil that nothing of any value could be seen in them. These people apparently made no attempt at even a pretense of good. This unbelievably bad condition was the prelude to the flood of judgment from which only Noah and his family escaped.

At the other extreme is the heart absorbed in organized religion with the hope of mounting an impressive performance of human goodness designed to placate God and intimidate people. No one seems to have known this condition better than Paul. Once a Pharisee, he had been numbered among those for whom outward appearance was almost everything. Robes, gestures, routines, verbiage, intellectual life: from the tiniest detail to the most flamboyant ceremonies, the Pharisee's life was one big attempt to make an impression for God, for one another, and for the world in general. But in what order?

I think one of the sources of Paul's overwhelming joy in Christian faith was his sense of being freed from a formerly bound heart. In earlier days, impression making had meant at least three things. First, always living with the inner realization that he wasn't MEASURING UP to what he set as external standards. And, second, COVERING UP substandard feelings, thoughts, and desires when he was with others so that he wouldn't be found to be the imperfect person that he really was. And, finally, the Pharisees' style must have meant LOOKING OUT in suspicion and accusation to pinpoint what was wrong with other people. Only in that way could some sense of superiority and false security be maintained.

And when he chose to follow Christ, all of that discomfort and deformity in his bound-up heart was suddenly gone. No wonder he was exasperated with the Galatians when they showed signs of wanting to go back to the bound-up life: "It is for freedom that Christ has set us free. Stand firm, then, and do not let yourselves be burdened again by a yoke of slavery" (Gal. 5:1).

George Regas has provided a marvelous illustration of the repentant man:

There is a moment in Leonard Bernstein's modern opera, MASS, with which I identify in the most profound way. The priest celebrating the mass puts on one priestly vestment after another, one elegant robe on top of another. Then the priest staggers under the weight of all that tradition. There is a sense of violence in the scene, as if all that religiosity is about to destroy him. Finally the priest tears off all the vestments and stands in his blue jeans and a T-shirt before the altar. He sings, "Look at me. There is nothing but me under this." *(Kiss Yourself and Hug the World)*

And that's what happened to Paul when he found the key to an unbound heart on the road to Damascus. He could never understand why anyone in his right mind would want to go back to the old ways any more than a modern Chinese woman would wish to return to the tradition of bound feet and their discomfort and deformity.

A broken world will never be rebuilt until we learn this principle of the unbound heart. It must be unwrapped and exposed to the light. The light will show some unattractive evil, but then something wonderful will happen. The love of God will be free to flood into the dark recesses, and rebuilding will begin.

The Bible calls this unbinding process REPENTANCE. It is an old word, usually associated with revivalistic religion. And so, frankly, many people find the word repugnant. But as some say, they throw the baby out with the bathwater. They do not understand that behind an oft-misunderstood word is an action that must precede all attempts at rebuilding.

Repentance is a Middle Eastern word. It describes the act of turning around when people realize that they have been going in the wrong direction. It was most likely used in nonreligious settings, such as when a traveler asked directions of someone who knew the countryside and was informed that he'd taken the wrong road and was moving away and not toward his destination. In such a conversation, it would be appropriate for the one to say to the other, "You're going to have to repent and head for that road."

And so the practical word *repent* became useful to describe a moral and spiritual act also. Used by Older Testament prophets, then John the Baptizer, Jesus, and finally the apostles, it meant to change the direction in which the heart was inclined.

John the Baptizer made repentance the theme of every public talk. He spoke of a repentance that took place first in the heart and then in the moral performance patterns of the individual. The latter he called "the fruits of repentance."

When repentant men and women stepped forward and said, "What kind of fruits are you talking about?" he would speak to them about their clear concern for the poor, their renunciation of violence, and their commitment to justice. These things, he said, would clearly indicate that something in the freed-up heart was different.

When the people heard St. Peter's famous sermon on the street in Jerusalem, they "were cut to the heart," a graphic description of people coming to insight about their bound-up private worlds. "What shall we do?" they asked the preacher. "Repent," he told them. They needed to change directions. (See Acts 2:14–40.)

The act of repentance is actually a gift from God in at least two ways. First, repentance is a gift in the sense that insight into our own broken-world need and awareness that something has to change is undoubtedly initiated by God's Spirit. Need and change are issues we simply would not see or appreciate on our own. Jesus said that was the task of the Holy Spirit, who would convict and point out sin, stimulating insight and the desire to change. (See John 16:8.)

This is not a pleasant aspect of God's activity in us, but it is a necessary one. Similarly, physical pain is not pleasant when it sends messages concerning our bodily affairs. But without pain signaling danger or without God's Spirit convicting when evil is on the loose within, we would be vulnerable to every hostile element there is: physical and spiritual. When pain speaks, we stop doing what we're doing, or we immediately seek to rectify whatever it is that is causing the discomfort. When the Spirit of God speaks, we repent: we renounce what we are doing or thinking and choose to replace the evil behavior with a godly one.

Second, repentance is also a gift in the sense that God has made it possible for us to turn back from broken-world directions. He didn't have to.

In a sermon at Harvard University Chapel, David H. C. Read told of his World War II experience as a POW. Standing next to a German guard as a destructive allied air raid took place nearby, they commiserated over the horror of war. "Die menscheit ist verrueckt!" the guard said, "Mankind is mad." And he went on, "The good God should destroy us all and begin again."

But God did not destroy us all. He set in motion the act of repentance: the way back, the way of rebuilding a broken world. I have never forgotten the words of the chief of a small Brazilian jungle tribe who told me of his view of God before he ever heard of Jesus Christ. "We always assumed that our Maker was so disappointed with us that He went off and left us. Now we know that He came to us and made a way for us to come back to Him."

It is relatively easy for us to see this principle of repentance when someone has made a broken-world choice demanding confession and accountability. "If only Nixon had said he was sorry," many used to say, "the country (or most of it) would have most likely forgiven him and let him get on with his presidency." We look for people who have made terrible errors to repent, to acknowledge a change of directions, and we are sad, sometimes even angry, when they do not.

It is more difficult to understand that repentance is not a one-time act; it is actually a spiritual life-style. To live in a constant state of repentance is to acknowledge that the heart is always ready to drift into wrong directions and must constantly be jerked back to control. This is not a call to a morbid kind of introspection that is always on a sin-search, putting ourselves down. But it is an honest recognition that the inward part of us is inclined toward rebellion and disobedience against our Maker. And it will always be that way until the end of time. That's why the hymn writer, Robert Robinson, observed:

Prone to wander, Lord, I feel it,
Prone to leave the God I love;

Here's my heart, O take and seal it;
Seal it for thy courts above.

And it's why Isaac of Nineveh, an ancient mystic, said,

He who knows his sins is much greater than he who makes someone rise from the dead. He who can really cry one hour about
himself is greater than he who teaches the whole world; he who
knows his own weaknesses is greater than he who sees the angels.

The act of repentance can be broken down into several steps. The
first was something referred to in earlier chapters: INSIGHT. It usually
comes, as we saw in the experience of the prodigal son, when there is a
revelation of the state of the acts of evil either by consequence or by
confrontation. The prodigal came to insight through CON-
SEQUENCE; David came to insight through CONFRONTATION.

It would be helpful to recognize a third possibility for initiating insight, and that would be the experience of the prophet Isaiah who came
to insight through an EXPOSURE to God in a vision of heavenly glory.
What he saw and attempted to record exceeds the mind's ability to comprehend. All we know is that the man was overwhelmed by what happened. And rather than use it as a pretext for religious power grabbing
or as something to boost his notoriety, he tells us frankly that the whole
thing broke him. In the contrast to God's glory, he came to insight
about himself: he was a broken-world person in need of rebuilding, and
he lived among lots of other broken-world persons who had a similar
need.

If insight has done its work, the result will be something that can be
described only as BROKENNESS. As I noted before, variations of this
experience are presented throughout the Bible. Broken men in the
Older Testament could become very dramatic about their display of
sorrow. They might tear their clothes in tatters, daub themselves with
ashes or wail loudly. All of these were outward expressions of deep remorse over their own sins or those of their families and people. We
might find such public displays rather amusing to think about, but they
were serious matters in those days.

One king of Israel reflected brokenness as he moved among the people of his city and saw them starving to death and so desperate that
some were even eating their children. After an encounter with a woman
who had cooked her own child, "he tore his robes. As he went along the

wall, the people looked, and there, underneath, he had sackcloth on his body" (2 Kings 6:30).

Nehemiah expressed what one might call a macro-brokenness when he, like others, confessed not only his sins but those of previous generations. He represented thinking somewhat unknown to people in Western culture that people shared a mutual responsibility for evil in their own generations and in those of their forefathers.

Job also seems to have understood this mutual responsibility for repentance from the other generational direction when, as the Scripture says, he offered sacrifices on behalf of his children saying, "Perhaps my children have sinned and cursed God in their hearts." The writer added: "This was Job's regular custom" (Job 1:5).

Brokenness implies an acceptance of full responsibility for what has happened, a genuine sorrow reflecting an awareness that one has grieved God and those who have been affected by the broken-world choices. We see indications of that kind of emotion and grief in the prostitute who kneeled at Jesus' feet and washed them with her tears. Simon, Jesus' host that day, took one look at the weeping woman and said to himself: "If this man were a prophet, he would know who is touching him and what kind of woman she is—that she is a sinner" (Luke 7:39).

The irony is that Jesus knew exactly who and what kind of person she was. Simon didn't realize that Jesus was most drawn to that kind of person: THE BROKEN KIND. A study of the people with whom Jesus spent His time and gave His compassion might suggest that He was not as concerned about what one had done in the past as about whether or not there was expressed brokenness in the present.

The woman had apparently committed all sorts of immoral acts, but she was broken. Simon had committed nothing in life that his generation thought worthy of an accusation, but his heart was proud and stiffened. He received a stunning, a rather embarrassing, rebuke; she received forgiveness for her sins.

The gospel writers seem to highlight two kinds of people as representing the worst sin in the times: immoral women and tax-collecting men. The former represent a corruption of personal life; the latter a corruption that gouges and exploits others. We have at least three specific encounters with immoral women and three with tax collectors (one is a fictional encounter in the parable of the tax collector and the Pharisee). On each occasion the writers point up the scorn, the judgmentalism, and the feelings of superiority of the upper class. And on each occasion, the grace and the tenderness of Christ are revealed as He reaches out to give hope for a rebuilt broken world.

This is significant. It is not that the Bible is in any way diminishing the seriousness of the sins of immorality and greed; rather, it is pointing out to us that Christ looks past the sin to the point of potential brokenness. And when He sees it, an immediate rebuilding process begins. But when He does not see brokenness, rebuke, anger, and frequent confrontation result.

Resistance to brokenness caused Paul to be harsh in his critique of the Corinthian church. Paul's own cry of brokenness—"What a wretched man I am! Who will rescue me from this body of death?" (Rom. 7:24)—modeled what individuals do as they come to insight and realize that their performance is beneath the standards of God.

Most outstanding men and women in the Bible seem to have had some sort of experience with brokenness. In fact, it seems to be the absolute essential before God is willing to work with any of them. Having read and reread their biographies, I've come to the conclusion that we might have disqualified the majority of them from ever holding appointed Christian leadership.

Had we lived in Joseph's lifetime, we would have seen him as a convicted attempted rapist. Jacob would have been set aside as having a serious character defect in the area of truthfulness. David would have been considered a poor manager of his home, an adulterer, and a murderer; Moses, a murderer; Simon Peter, a coward; and Paul, a volatile enemy of the church probably not to be trusted, let alone listened to.

St. Augustine never forgot the broken-world performance of his past and how it drove him to confess faith in Christ. In his *Confessions* he wrote often of the constant life of brokenness:

> For what am I without thee, but a guide to mine own downfall? Or what am I even at the best, but an infant seeking milk, and feeding upon thee, the Food incorruptible? But what kind of thing is any man, seeing that he is but a man? *Let now the strong and the mighty laugh at me, but let us weak and needy souls ever confess unto thee.* (Emphasis mine)

Like Augustine, we must live as perpetually broken people. Those who are broken only in the crisis will soon grow cold, and other kinds of broken worlds are liable to follow. Brokenness is a way of life, the realization that the recovering alcoholic carries all the time: I'm licked if I think I can beat this alcoholic enemy alone. And so the man or woman broken before God lives.

Not long ago one of the world's greatest violinists, Isaac Stern, was playing Mozart's Violin Concerto no. 3 in G with Zubin Mehta and the New York Philharmonic Orchestra. Midway in the first movement, Mr. Stern had a lapse of memory and forgot his music. Immediately he ceased playing, walked over to Mehta, the conductor, and asked him and the orchestra if they would prepare to begin the concerto again. Then turning to the audience, this remarkable musician apologized for his mistake and started from the beginning.

Donal Henahan, writing of the incident in the *New York Times*, noted that "the performance began again from the beginning, allowing the audience to hear Mozart unmaimed. Though Mr. Stern could have vamped for a while until memory got back on track, his was surely a more honest and more musically satisfactory solution."

Indeed, a professional like Isaac Stern could have fooled his audience and covered his mistakes. But his fidelity to Mozart and his music demanded of him a clear accounting of his error and a desire to start over. A simple and straightforward way of doing things, something all of us—beginning with me—need to remember. In the spiritual realm, we'd call what Stern did brokenness and repentance, admission of error and desire to start over.

The final phase of repentance, the UNBINDING OF THE HEART, is that of the specific change of direction. *Behavior must not only change; it must be renounced, repudiated.*

R. T. Kendall in an inspiring book on the life of Joseph has a fascinating insight on the relationship between the governor of Egypt and his brothers. They had become broken men through their confrontations with Joseph and had made their initial repentance quite clear.

He instructed his assistant to hide his personal cup in the baggage of Benjamin, the youngest and most beloved of the brothers. Then soon after the brothers had headed homeward to their father, Joseph's men caught up with them and insisted that the cup had been stolen by one of them.

The brothers were horrified and quickly offered their baggage for a search. Soon the cup was discovered in Benjamin's bags. This would have been the time, Kendall observes, for the brothers to revert to type if there was no brokenness. Just as they once discarded Joseph, they might have said to the governor's assistants, "Take him back to face his penalties; we are innocent."

But they didn't. They insisted on returning with Benjamin to face the situation. Kendall writes:

> They all loaded their donkeys and returned to the city. All of them. They didn't say, "Goodbye, Benjamin. Tough luck, but goodbye." No. They all went back. Repentance had truly taken place. *(God Meant It for Good)*

In so doing they proved beyond a shadow of a doubt that they were different men on this side of repentance from what they had been on the other side.

On my bookshelf is an old book of stories D. L. Moody loved to tell. Most of them are outdated now, but one has caught my attention and affection. Moody writes:

> Dr. Andrew Bonar told me how, in the Highlands of Scotland, a sheep would often wander off into the rocks and get into places that they couldn't get out of. The grass on these mountains is very sweet and the sheep like it, and they will jump down ten or twelve feet, and then they can't jump back again and the shepherd hears them bleating in distress. They may be there for days, until they have eaten all the grass. The shepherd will wait until they are so faint that they cannot stand, and then they will put a rope around him, and he will go over and pull that sheep up out of the jaws of death.
>
> "Why don't they go down there when the sheep first gets there?" I asked.
>
> "Ah!" he said, "they are so very foolish they would dash right over the precipice and be killed if they did."

Moody concludes his story by saying:

> And that is the way with men; they won't go back to God till they have no friends and have lost everything. If you are a wanderer I tell you that the Good Shepherd will bring you back the moment you have given up trying to save yourself and are willing to let Him save you His own way.

Bound-up feet create discomfort and deformity. It is no different with hearts that have never been unwrapped by repentance.

CHAPTER 14

The Peace Ledge Principles

> BOTTOM LINE #14:
> *The process of rebuilding requires some temporary operating principles by which to navigate through the dark times.*

When my world broke, it happened in three painful stages. The first stage was contained deep within myself as I came to the experience of insight of what I had done. There are no words to describe the inner anguish of knowing that you have disappointed and offended God, that you have violated your own integrity, and that you have betrayed people you really love and care for. There are moments in the life of one whose world is so broken when death would seem a merciful experience. Like others with broken worlds, I lived with that stage for a long time, secret carrying, hoping that I could contain the consequences within my inner life.

Strangely enough, while it was a time of inward anguish, it was also a time in which I became increasingly sensitive to the needs of others. I didn't need many words from men and women who visited with me to know what they were going through; it wasn't hard to identify. And if I gave a public talk during that time, it wasn't unusual for people to speak privately to me and remark about my seeming sensitivity to personal weaknesses. Of course when I would respond by saying that we were all sinners, that we all had weaknesses, they would smile. It was clear that they were thinking how nice it was of me to be so gracious and kind when in fact (as far as they were concerned) I had my own "act all put together."

The second stage of my broken-world experience began when I

came to the conclusion that I had to open my troubled inner being to my wife, Gail, and to a few trusted spiritual advisors. The good news was that there was someone with whom to share the grief over what I'd done; the bad news was in hurting those who had trusted me so completely.

Others knew and shared the burden of the grievously heavy baggage. And there was a period of time when they had to catch their breath and wonder how to react to what I had told them. In each case the ultimate reaction was one of remarkable grace and the beginning of the extension of forgiveness.

Gail had spent the better part of a year studying the Bible and the available Christian literature on the subject of grace and forgiveness, and when I opened the dark side of my heart and shared my secret, she knew that her study process had been something more than an academic or a theological exercise. The material she had accumulated on paper and in her heart from the year's study was quickly put to work in a magnificent way. It wasn't done euphorically or automatically. Sometimes it was hard going because our lives were lived in heavy public activity; but the progress was always forward. Both of us embarked on a partnership of giving and receiving grace and discovered that our marriage relationship was rugged enough to stand the shock of a major injury.

The key friends—we came to call them the (ministering) angels— were likewise gracious, but firm! The story of their involvement will be told later. But what should be said now is something about the way they poured their lives and love into Gail and me. We were limping people, the result of my self-inflicted wounds. They came alongside to assist in the process of rebuilding. Our son and our daughter and her husband were drawn into the loop of knowledge, and their support and encouragement brought strength to us that we never thought possible.

Many months later the third stage of the broken-world experience came. And that happened when the secret of what we had hoped was a resolved past became a public piece of information in some parts of the Christian church. Gail and I and our "angels" had faced the possibility of that moment, although we had hoped it would not happen. But when it did, we were prepared to accept the moment as a directive from the hand of God, and we knew what we had to do.

Our worlds were broken. A dream had turned into a nightmare of loss, humiliation, anger, and a sense of a very dark future. There was the terrible realization that many who had trusted me were now disillusioned. There was the knowledge that some people were talking, with or without a knowledge of the facts.

At each of the three stages I had to wrestle with a decision. Would I become defensive, hardened, or resistant? Would I run, quit, or try to rationalize? All of these were tempting, and a part of me—not made of God—would like to have experimented in each category. But I had several things going for me that prevented me from doing so: the partnership of Gail; the encouragement of our children; the pastoral oversight of those we called the angels; and the constant prodding and poking that came from my readings in the Scripture. God clearly used each of these to rebuke me and restrain me.

That's when we withdrew to Peace Ledge, a simple home we'd built years ago in New Hampshire. I will never forget those first days. It was almost impossible to ward off the feeling that life was over, that all the brightness and joy that we had known for more than forty-five years had come to a screeching halt. But those are feelings, and they move quickly into one of the most dangerous moods: self-pity. We had made an early decision to renounce self-pity at all costs.

As the days became weeks, the rebuilding process picked up speed. I began to discover that a set of principles had come into play. We had not devised them; they were a gift to us from God, and they had been mediated to us through our reading, through our friends, and through the dynamics of our personal discoveries. I came to call them the Peace Ledge Principles because they surfaced here on the hill where I write today.

The principles appear over and over again in our journals. Each morning we would arise very early and ponder what God might say to us that day. Who might call? What would the mail bring? Was a visitor coming? Would there be something in the Scriptures or in the spiritual classics we were reading?

In some ways I began to appreciate the alcoholic's view of life. Make it for one more day. Don't think in terms of months and years ahead. Just brood on today and what tiny thing God may have as He orchestrates the rebuilding process.

Now as I study the journal that carries the record of each of those days, these are the principles I see that we followed. They are simple and workable.

BE SILENT; WITHDRAW

The broken-world person who lives with self-inflicted damage faces a heavy temptation to defend himself and his "territory." If he cannot escape responsibility for his misbehavior, he is tempted to do at least three things to ease the embarrassment.

First, he is tempted to spread the blame for his deed. The mind sharpened by this pain of humiliation is adept at looking at all involved in the tragic events and trying to see what they did and did not do. Second, the person with the broken world may try to complain about how poorly he perceives he is being treated by his accusers and critics. And third, he is liable to diminish the seriousness of his own choices by concentrating on the sins of others. *This way,* he thinks, *I don't have to feel so badly about myself. They're as bad as I am.*

Such thinking never brings rebuilding. It retards and usually defeats the process.

In a sermon on the parable of the Pharisee and the publican Helmut Thielicke said,

> When a man really turns to God with a burdened conscience he doesn't think of other people at all. There he is utterly alone with God. It would never have occurred to the publican to say, "Sure, this Pharisee is a man of a different stripe from me, but he too has plenty of blots on his scutcheon; he's a sinner too." This would have been true, of course. But when a man is utterly alone with God and dealing solely with him, then many things that are true are completely immaterial to him. He has something else to think about. And that's why the publican's attitude is completely genuine and radically honest. He measures himself "upward." God *himself* is his standard.

Thielicke went on to remind his congregation that the German people had "had some conception of our guilt after the collapse at the end of the last war and many of us had uttered the prayer of the publican, 'God be merciful to me a sinner! Remove not thy grace from our sunken people.'"

> But then came one of the most dreadful moments in the spiritual history of our nation when suddenly we began to say, "Others are just as bad as we." Then suddenly our aloneness with God vanished, then repentance and spiritual renewal were gone, then began that fateful measuring of ourselves by looking downward and comparing ourselves with the hypocritical democratic Pharisees among the victors. (*The Waiting Father*)

St. Paul made it clear that there is only one useful posture when we come to insight about ungodly choices in life: the posture of silence before God and before the world. We may lessen the impact of the sorrow for ourselves in the short term if we try to avoid the full effect of the responsibility. But we do nothing for the rebuilding the Bible says God wants to make happen if we do not become silent so that we can listen.

Gail and I learned not only that silence implied no defense, but that it meant withdrawing into quiet places. For us, that was Peace Ledge. I am not so much thinking, however, of a *place* as I am of activity. When the broken-world person is living with great wounds he has brought on himself and perhaps also inflicted on others, a season for slipping into a quiet place is necessary. This is no hour for plotting what the politicians call a comeback.

The deeper and wider the hurt, the more important this withdrawal. It is a time to take stock of what happened and why; a time to realign and recharge spiritual resources; a time to probe deep within the inner world to understand where the blind spots were. This cannot normally be done in a matter of weeks. If it is unwisely hastened, there may possibly be a recurrence of misbehavior later on.

Oswald Chambers wrote, and we took his words seriously:

At times God puts us through the discipline of darkness to teach us to heed Him. Song birds are taught to sing in the dark, and we are put into the shadow of God's hand until we learn to hear Him. "What I tell you in darkness," —watch where God puts you into darkness, and when you are there keep your mouth shut. Are you in the dark just now in your circumstances, or in your life with God? Then remain quiet. If you open your mouth in the dark, you will talk in the wrong mood: darkness is the time to listen. Don't talk to other people about it; don't read books to find out the reason of the darkness, but listen and heed. If you talk to other people, you cannot hear what God is saying. When you are in the dark, listen, and God will give you a very precious message for someone else when you get into the light. (*My Utmost for His Highest*)

DON'T DEFEND YOURSELF

The second Peace Ledge Principle was a difficult one to handle. And I had to learn to submit to its charge on almost a daily basis.

When the broken-world person hears of a rumor concerning him that some have not bothered to check out, he has a desire to find every possible medium of communication that might be used to squelch it. When some people think they can explain the broken-world person's behavior on the basis of generalizations that work fine for them, there's a temptation to sound out and let people know of the exceptions.

I have studied Jesus' defensive strategies. They only operate when the issue is truth or the rights and needs of another person. But Jesus never defended Himself. The corollary to this principle, of course, is the mandate we all carry to defend one another. This seems to have been the instruction of the Spirit of God when I looked for direction. If there is to be any defense or advocacy, let it come from others, from friends and colleagues, not from me or from my family. The friends were there, and the principle vindicated itself.

ENJOY THE AMUSEMENT OF GOD'S MESSENGERS

Peace Ledge is a beautiful place to Gail and me. It is our home. But in another sense it became a wilderness when my world broke. A lovely, quiet wilderness. In the past other men like Moses, Elijah, John the Baptizer, Jesus, and Paul went to the wildernesses of their day when they were hunted, when they had something to learn, when it was time to be tested. And when a busy life comes to a screeching halt, broken persons suddenly find themselves in "wildernesses." That's where we were.

In such places you become aware of little things, things that aren't immediately noticeable when schedules are complicated and crowded. For us, the little things were birds, chipmunks, squirrels, deer, raccoons, and even skunks. The flowers, trees, and forest trails all furnished the theater and the scenery for their antics.

The living things at Peace Ledge became our friends, close friends in a strange way. We laughed at the chipmunks who chased one another mercilessly back and forth across the stone walls that lace the Peace Ledge property. The birds with their glorious colors and their individual personalities delighted us with their visits to the feeder. The dignified mourning doves always arrived in pairs. The hyperactive chickadees flew together as if in an airlift grabbing one seed at a time. And the arrogant woodpeckers and the stealthy hummingbirds put on a grand show as they came to Peace Ledge to pay respects.

The squirrels spent literally hours trying to invade the birdfeeder and usually succeeded until we daubed the pole with Vaseline. The raccoons visited regularly and insensitively at 3:30 A.M. All of them, our friends, were God's messengers.

We call them God's messengers because one day at the peak of their performances for us, Gail recalled a description of Jesus' time in the wilderness of temptation. "He was with the wild animals, and angels attended him," Mark wrote (1:13). Did they amuse Jesus also?

We lost all interest in television, world news, professional sports, and scandals. Strength came from everywhere around us. It was as if God had chosen the impersonal elements of His creation to form a fortress about us, a place where we could think and pray, talk and share.

The living things, the trees and flowers, the sky, all became God's messengers of endurance and empowerment. They were our amusement, our inspiration, our reminders of His presence. Each day we offered up thanks to God for the special gift of Peace Ledge and the "messengers" He sent to us.

ASSUME THE MINISTRY OF THE INTERIOR

Sometimes the most stunning reality to hit the broken-world person can be the loss of primary function. *What value do I have to anyone any longer?* one might ask. *What can I do?* These were burning questions to me, ones that I probably asked God several times each day. Soon He provided a preliminary and very significant answer.

It came one morning as Gail and I read Oswald Chambers's *My Utmost for His Highest:*

> Enter into the ministry of the interior. The Lord turned the captivity of Job *when he prayed for his friends.* The real business of your life as a saved soul is intercessory prayer. Wherever God puts you in circumstances, pray immediately, pray that His atonement may be realized in other lives, as it has been in yours. Pray for your friends *now;* pray for those with whom you come in contact *now.*

Would you be surprised if I told you that we were astounded by this challenge? It was as if God had prepared a word specifically for us seventy-five years ago, and we were ready to hear it in its fullest force. We felt as if we had lost every opportunity to serve people in the exterior world. But here was a ministry that can never be lost, "the ministry of the interior," Chambers called it. It's a work that can be performed if one is banished to a desert isle or a prison cell. It cannot be stripped away.

That morning I wrote in my journal:

Chambers challenges us to enter into the ministry of the interior. He points out that the work of intercession is the highest work. Only after Job prayed for his friends was he restored. The Lord seems to be saying to me this morning that I should focus on the ministry of the interior: intercession for my friends. If there is ever again to be a ministry of the exterior, that will come later and in His good time.

I went on in my journal:

A ministry of the interior, it seems to me:
    a. Worships in God's presence
    b. Roots out personal impurity
    c. Broods upon eternal truths
    d. Offers thanksgiving
    e. Prays for the world
    f. Intercedes for friends

Gail and I made a commitment to each other that day that we would accept God's call to the ministry of the interior, a ministry we had merely dabbled in by contrast up until that time. If we find no other way to serve the Lord in the coming years, we determined, we will do the one thing no one can take away from us. We will learn the discipline of intercession.

And so we started. We were fascinated with how quickly our intercession list grew. Each morning it became a habit to go to our knees in the living room of our Peace Ledge home and lift friends to the throne of God. When people shared their personal concerns and challenges with us, we immediately took it upon ourselves to make them daily issues of prayer.

Intercession became a marvelous instrument of ministry. And we gained the conviction that we just might accomplish more for people on our knees than all the speaking and writing we might have ever done.

Intercession doesn't come easily to most of us. Many husbands and wives do not find it easy to pray together. Although we had learned to do that long ago, the extended intercessory discipline taxed our willpower. But we were determined to seek God's rebuilding of our broken worlds the way Job had sought it—by getting our minds off ourselves and praying for our friends.

Today it would be an uncompleted day if we did not make our appearance—as it were—before the seat of our Father where we can pray for our friends. Our prayer list includes many pastors, especially younger ones who are carrying the responsibility for large congregations and need much wisdom and protection. It includes our children, our parents, and our brothers and their families. The list includes many friends across the world; some of them we do not know personally but God has laid them upon our minds.

It became my activity on the many nights when I couldn't find sleep after midnight. Tempted to lie awake and worry about the past and the future, I learned to dismiss the anxiety by entering into intercession from a global perspective. Putting my junior-high-school geography class to good use, I would start around the world beginning with Argentina to the deep south of Peace Ledge, praying my way through the countries of Latin America, seeing how many cities in each country I could remember and pray for. I'd pray for national church leaders I'd met or heard of. After Latin America came the island countries of the Caribbean and the nations of the Central American isthmus. Through the states and provinces of Mexico, the USA, and Canada. Over to Europe, down to Africa, then to the subcontinent and on to Asia and down through the Pacific. I rarely made it past Egypt before the Lord provided a quiet sleep.

I have no doubt that this Peace Ledge Principle of intercession has played a key role in the rebuilding process of our lives. Now we know what it is like to be prayed for and to pray for others and to be trusted with their prayer needs.

CHAPTER 15

More Peace Ledge Principles

At Peace Ledge we were alone with our heavenly messengers and our questions. "When a man is to be hanged in a fortnight, it concentrates his mind wonderfully," Samuel Johnson said more than two centuries ago. Although I wasn't due for a hanging, I sometimes felt like it was what I deserved. And in that prevailing mood the mind was concentrated. It was time to search for more substantial truths about God and about self than we ever had before. We determined to do it.

Out of that came a fifth Peace Ledge Principle:

LISTEN TO THE DEEP THINGS

Somewhere in those early days we equated the principle of being silent with listening. We wished to be listeners to the deep sources where certain kinds of heavenly truth are tapped only by those who have a heart to be attentive. Usually those are the hearts of the suffering or the hearts of broken-world people in search of a rebuilding effort.

We wanted to look at pain the way Joseph looked at it when he scanned the many years of slavery, imprisonment, and ill-treatment and said, "You meant evil against me; but God meant it for good" (Gen. 50:20, NKJV). Our questions were another version of that. How do you take an evil event and its consequences and squeeze good out of it? Is that really possible? Can the worst that human

172

beings do be forced to render something good? Can God play a trick on evil?

For answers to those questions we turned to the Scriptures and browsed through both Testaments. We searched out the biblical biographies of every man and woman whose world had broken for one reason or another. As I've noted elsewhere, we discovered that almost everyone in the Bible was conversant with some kind of broken-world experience. And we came to understand that in almost every case the broken-world moments were the turning points to great spiritual insight, development, and godly performance. That was both a comfort and a marvelous promise.

We also turned to the spiritual classics. Here, our friends became women and men such as Amy Carmichael whose personal world broke through no fault of her own when she suffered a series of accidents and spent the last twenty years of life bedridden. Oswald Chambers whose life was probably shortened through his enormous intensity and physical exertion in serving the Lord during the World War I period. William and Catherine Booth who plowed through powerful ridicule and discouragement to establish the work of the Salvation Army.

I twice read the *Confessions* of St. Augustine and gained insight into the deep struggle of this early church father as he learned what it might mean to give his life to God. John Bunyan, an early Puritan pastor, opened up his life to us in his spiritual autobiography *Grace Abounding*. Only after reading Bunyan's account of his battle with evil did I come to appreciate what I read as I later went through *Pilgrim's Progress* and Alexander Whyte's two-volume *Bunyan's Characters*.

Mrs. Charles Cowman's *Streams in the Desert* and Chambers's *My Utmost for His Highest* became a daily spiritual feeding trough, never failing to provide a word from God to nourish our hearts. The prayers of Quoist, Baillie, and François Fénelon, the words of Tozer, and the liturgical worship of the Book of Common Prayer became our spiritual lines to the deep. And out of them all, words came from heaven itself each day to help in the rebuilding process.

Because we had more time here at Peace Ledge, we read more. And both of us came to a similar conclusion as we discussed the books we were reading. Books written by people who had sustained some sort of a broken-world experience—debilitating illness, humiliating failure, intense persecution, conflict with evil, numbing disappointment—were powerful in their ability to reach into our inner spirits. But books written by people who had little to offer but advice and pithy stories were no more nourishing than cotton candy. Genuine Christianity is a faith of the suffering, we learned. In the broken-world moments, deep calls to deep; pain reaches out to pain; failure searches out failure. And Christianity talks of better, more hopeful days when night ends.

Listening to the deep things also meant spending time in quiet meditation and thought. Our journals filled more quickly than ever as we tried to record everything God was whispering into our spirits through the Scriptures, the classics, and the impulses entering our hearts. There were the early evening conversations as we compared notes from our quiet moments and taught each other what we were hearing.

The themes? The ugliness of *sin*, not only in terms of its sad consequences but also in terms of offensiveness to God and His church. The *grace* of Christ, the *tenderness* of the heavenly Father. The *hope* held out for all who come with the broken pieces of their broken worlds asking to be put back together again. A growing *sensitivity to the fact that scores upon scores of people are seeking hope and rebuilding all the time and that many are not finding the grace and compassion they need.*

And what were we learning personally? How insignificant in God's eyes is the applause that comes with organizational leadership and public recognition. How relatively empty the overly busy life no matter how good the goals and objectives. How cheap the mountains of words we pile up in public talk after public talk. Not that these are bad or inconsequential things. But they are fruitless if one operates from a spiritual baseline that is not richly fed and nourished in communion with the deep where God speaks.

Gail had often wondered aloud in earlier days what it would be like if we were driven to a point of no resources but those God provided. Although financial resources and a place to live were not the problems of those dark days, encouragement, meaning, and security were. And we began to learn as we listened to the deep things that when you are on the bottom, God does indeed speak in ways that would have been otherwise incomprehensible.

Peace Ledge provided a place to listen carefully. Soon we became aware that God has much to say that we had not been hearing. We were usually too busy and in places where the noise levels were too high. God will not shout; He whispers in the deep. Only those who stop long enough or who are STOPPED long enough hear the text of the message from the deep.

RECEIVE THE MERCY; LIVE LIKE A FORGIVEN PERSON

This may have been the most difficult of all the Peace Ledge Principles. It was difficult because I came to see that the greatest accuser of the person with a broken world is the broken-world person himself.

With alarming frequency, the circuitry of accusation activated somewhere deep within. It would replay the past and remind me of past feelings: cheapness, failure, wreckage. There was no way back, the "accuser" would say.

It was actually a challenge sometimes to be among a few select friends and loved ones who were trying as hard as they could to give grace and kindness. The tempter might occasionally suggest that their affection was not genuine; that they were patronizing me; that sooner or later they would have done with me. Their very success seemed to accentuate my failure.

But then a stronger voice would emerge from the deep and say: you never were valuable on those terms anyway. You said you were a sinner; and now you've proved it to everyone. The truth about you used to be subsurface. Now you are what you are, and the evidence is clear for people to see. But you've been to the Cross, and it's time to put your performance where your mouth is. Either you believe in the capacity of Christ's atonement to make you a new person, or you don't. If you do, then start living like a forgiven person should live.

And how is that done? By being a lot more quiet, humble, thankful, sensitive, and anxious to serve than you ever were before. Forgiven people basically live like that.

I listed a series of short-burst guidelines that I thought sounded like what a forgiven person might be and then committed to them, with God's help, one day at a time:

- Be quiet, don't push yourself.
- Don't be defensive; keep your fists unclenched.
- Serve every chance you get.
- Be as thankful as you possibly can be.
- Affirm everyone you can; build in their lives.
- Keep your new acquisitions to a minimum.
- Be the first to repent.
- Be quick to pray with others.
- Be orderly and dependable about your life.

- Accept and learn from defeats.
- Leave each place a bit better than when you first arrived.
- Watch for addictions to busyness and excitement.
- Don't enslave yourself to people's approval; say the appropriate noes.

DON'T DODGE THE PAIN; WALK RIGHT THROUGH IT

That was the seventh principle we learned at Peace Ledge.

When I was an athlete in track and cross-country, I learned that the champions spend a large amount of time dealing with the matter of pain. Mediocre runners like myself made pain the termination point of our performance. But champions made pain the threshold of performance. They knew what the rest of us resisted: you are only beginning to move into the possibilities of your best performance when you refuse to let pain become your termination point.

I had resisted pain as an athlete. For me it was the signal to stop or slow down. At Peace Ledge, we determined not to repeat that principle of mediocrity. We were going to face every ounce of the pain: whether it came from the rebukes, rumors, harsh criticism, or silence; the hurt that we had to face together; or the pain of inactivity.

What are the options in handling the pain of a broken world? Some turn off the emotional and spiritual nerve endings. Some stave off the pain with return anger or self-defense. We came to believe that the best response was to accept the pain, to permit the hurtful consequences to have their effect on us. This is not masochism; it is a process that purifies and calls one to greater alertness. It also resensitizes one to the awfulness of evil and creates a reaction toward sin much like antabuse causes a physical reaction in a problem drinker should he be tempted to take a drink.

The rebuilding process demands that one accept the pain. The bulk of the pain has an ending point, although I am presently convinced that the broken-world person may live with a certain amount of heartache for the rest of his life. That's part of the consequence of sin.

LOOK FOR THOSE WHO NEED GRACE AND AREN'T GETTING IT

Within a short period of time at Peace Ledge, Gail and I realized that we were receiving enormous amounts of understanding and affection from our friends and from many with whom we had never been acquainted. They made themselves known through the mail and through other forms of communication. We came to see that the Christian church is capable of pouring out grace in great quantities. And this is frequently not noted. It's much easier for all of us to talk about Christians *not* being forgiving or compassionate. But that was not to be our experience. Rather, we were startled at how powerful are the winds of encouragement that come from followers of the Lord.

But we were aware that here and there were people who had not experienced the affection and kindness shown to us. And we determined that even though we were in quiet, we would find ways to give grace whenever our spirits witnessed to someone who was suffering from a broken world.

Who might it be? The man who sells us our newspaper? The service manager where our car is maintenanced? The pastor who has been removed from his church in a controversial manner? The person struggling with homosexuality? The one whose business has failed? The mid-lifer suffering under a load of temptation he can hardly bear? The couple whose marriage totters on the brink of disaster?

Where could we send a letter of encouragement? When could we make a phone call that would lift spirits? Were there chances to invite someone to Peace Ledge for an overnight visit and turn our home into what we came to wish it to be: a home of grace?

Of all the Peace Ledge Principles, this became the most creative. We can step aside from positions of leadership that are offered in the Christian community, for those are offices in organizations. But we need never step aside from the actions of grace giving. To serve, that is true biblical leadership anyway. There is always someone in more trouble than I am; always someone who can profit from a probing question that will bring frustration or feelings of failure to the surface. There is always a chance to press a bit of value into the life of someone who perceives himself to be worthless. There is always a way to give if we want to get our minds off ourselves.

Grace giving and intercession began to go together. Those for whom we pray often become those to whom we give.

JOIN WITH THOSE WHO KNOW HOW TO PRAISE GOD

Some would say that we are meant to praise our Maker just as the stars in the heavens are meant to honor Him by their brilliance. It's possible that human beings reach a point of nobility when we gaze heavenward and direct our thanksgivings and affirmations to the God of Jesus Christ. But it's also quite possible that when Christians enter into praise, we set in motion a healing process for broken-world people.

In one of the darkest hours of my broken-world condition, I found myself one day in the front row of a Dallas church where I had been asked to give a talk. I had made a long-term commitment to be there, but had it not been for my hosts' hard work of preparation, I would have tried to cancel my participation. Frankly, I was in no mood to speak to anyone. But I felt constrained not to cancel, and so there I was.

When the service began, a group of young men and women took places at the front of the congregation and began to lead with instruments and voices in a chain of songs and hymns: some contemporary, others centuries old. As we moved freely from melody to melody, I became aware of a transformation in my inner world. I was being strangely lifted by the music and its content of thankfulness and celebration. If my heart had been heavy, the hearts of others about me were apparently light because, together, we seemed to rise in spirit, the music acting much like the thermal air currents that lift an eagle or a hawk high above the earth.

I not only felt myself rising out of the darkness of my spirit, but I felt as if I were being bathed, washed clean. And as the gloom melted away, a quiet joy and a sense of cleansing swept in and took its place. I felt free to express my turbulent emotions with tears. The congregation's praise was a therapy of the spirit: indescribable in its power. It was a day I shall never forget. No one in that sanctuary knew how high they had lifted one troubled man far above his broken-world anguish. Were there others there that day feeling as I did? Perhaps they would have affirmed as I did: *God was there.*

During that period in my life, I had similar experiences on many occasions in a small Episcopal chapel when I attended what is called Morning Prayer. Unlike in Dallas, praise was highly structured liturgy: written prayers, spoken creeds, the reading of much Scripture, the Eucharist offered at the altar. But there was something else I looked forward to each time I went. High above the altar was a cross upon which hung the figure of the suffering Christ. In my broken-world hours, I found it consoling to sit beneath that cross and look up at the face of the dying Savior. While there was trauma in that visage, there was also an affection and kindness that could be visualized and absorbed but not described. Somehow I gained a remarkable sense of Jesus' presence. If in the free-form worship in Dallas I had been spiritually bathed, there in the liturgical worship I came to peace, order, and healing. Simply put: *Jesus was there.*

Then there were my black friends who know how to praise with their hands, their marvelous gospel rhythms, and their unrestrained expressions of unspeakable joy. Probably no group knows more about a tradition of pain and bondage and the healing message of liberty than our black brothers and sisters. They have learned the hard way that if there can't be liberty in the circumstances of one's public world, nothing can stop the acquisition of liberty in one's private world. Sadness simply cannot endure for very long when music and testimony emanates from the soul tradition. When my black friends included me, I felt free to love and be loved. Rarely have I ever left a time of praise in the black community that I didn't affirm to myself: *the Spirit was there.*

All three traditions of praise—free-form, liturgical, and soul— taught me there is a place of rest and wholeness in the congregation that praises God. It is a place for a broken-world person to be. There is no place like it.

Who knows how many broken-world people enter a sanctuary on a Sunday morning? My guess is that there are a lot more than anyone could guess. And what might they find? Do they find a lifeless liturgy of empty prayers, tired singing, and endless announcements? Or do they find men and women with hearts open to God's Spirit, thankful for God's blessings, and compassionate in the face of human pain? If they have found the latter, they will have discovered one of the principal elements of rebuilding.

Here at Peace Ledge Gail has captured much of the music of those traditions on stereo tape. Often on a Lord's Day morning before we leave for worship, we have sat for a couple of hours listening to the voices and the instruments of praise. And when the time of reflection ends, we know that praise has once again done its great work. Where God is honored, the broken and tired spirit is rebuilt.

LOOK FOR NEW THEMES

That was the tenth and last of the Peace Ledge Principles.

As one seeks to rebuild a broken world, one is tempted to move quickly to the question of future function.

"What are you going to do?" friends frequently have asked. And there was a time when that question rattled about in our minds. I wanted badly to give an answer. Not because I wanted to satisfy their curiosity but because I was tempted to want to make myself feel and sound important again. And in such a temptation I realized that we often want to establish our identity and value on the basis of some defined function.

I wonder what John the Baptizer said that he did for a living. Would his business card have said, "A voice crying in the wilderness"?

Slowly I understood that to worry about what I was going to do was to worry about the wrong thing. The better issue was: what have I learned that I didn't know before, and how am I going to manage the information and the experience for the glory of God and the serving of others?

When there has been a broken-world experience and the rebuilding process is under way, one should take an inventory of what God has been saying. Paul told the Corinthians that when comfort came their way, they should study it carefully because it would most likely be a kind of comfort that they could give away to others. (See 2 Cor. 1:3–4.)

For us, nothing that God said became more important than what He said about hope and rebuilding. Day after day I heard my heart say: think hope; talk about hope; give hope wherever you can. And we determined to take that from Peace Ledge wherever we went in this world. Find the hopeless and tell them that rebuilding is possible.

Recently, a Texas man was painting the bulbous side of an extraordinarily high water tower. When the scaffolding on which he was standing collapsed, he fell fifty feet before the safety rope broke his fall and left him suspended 150 feet in the air.

Television cameras recorded the drama as rescue workers ascended to the top of the tower and one man was lowered to the dangling painter. Finally, the rescuer and the painter were lowered to the ground. As I watched the rescue process take place, I saw one more picture of how we give hope and value to another who has lost it, who dangles, as it were, helplessly in space. And I knew that giving hope and value to others had to be an important part of any future function of mine. Having been given hope, it might be my chance to give it to others.

Peace Ledge became the wilderness where God spoke to us. For other broken-world people the wilderness may be somewhere in the middle of a city or a desert or a jungle village. God knows where He wishes to place us broken-world people during the time of our rebuilding. And He makes no mistakes.

When we are in the wilderness, it is time to make sure we know how to act. That's why principles like these were so important for us.

A deacon in Alexander Whyte's Edinburgh church came to the pastor's office one Sunday morning to tell him of a visiting evangelist who had preached the night before in another part of town.

"Dr. Whyte, the man said that Robert Hood Wilson is not a converted man."

Robert Hood Wilson was at that time the pastor of the Barclay Church and a friend of Whyte. Whyte was outraged at such a false accusation. For several minutes he spoke in Wilson's defense out of his personal knowledge of the minister's deep spiritual life.

When he was through, the deacon said, "Dr. Whyte, the evangelist also said last night that you are not a converted man."

Suddenly the anger left Alexander Whyte. He became silent and thoughtful. Finally he said to the deacon who waited for a response, "My brother, please leave me alone; I must examine my soul."

These are the reactions of a man who had principles of performance built into his soul for the difficult moments. When a brother was falsely accused, he sprang to his defense. When he was falsely accused, he became silent and searched for the kernel of truth that might be hidden in such unjust and unkind remarks.

Whether or not we have experienced a broken world that is our fault or someone else's, it may be a time for the wilderness. But it is not a time for fear. Even though the pain might be great, life on the other end will be full of hope.

CHAPTER 16

Giving a Summer Purse

> BOTTOM LINE #16:
> *The granting of
> restorative grace is among
> the greatest and most
> unique gifts one Christian
> can give another.*

I could not write two chapters in this book—this one and the concluding one—if a gift had not been given to me that I could not offer to myself. I regard these chapters as the most important ones. The gift is *restorative grace*, and its objective is TO REBUILD A ONCE BROKEN PERSONAL WORLD.

At one time I had the privilege of being a pastor at Grace Chapel in Lexington, Massachusetts. The church started as a small group of people meeting in weekly Bible study. Later it constituted itself as a regularly worshiping congregation and called a pastor. Many years later Gail and I spent twelve wonderful years with those remarkable men and women.

The founders of Grace Chapel chose to celebrate the Christian understanding and experience of grace in their selection of a public name. What's in a name—especially in a name like *grace?* Sometimes in the moments of a congregational struggle, I found myself wondering if we knew anything about how to live up to the name. Then in moments when blessings seemed to pile in on us, I was convinced that we did. But did we really understand the full implications of this heavenly quality with which we dared to identify ourselves? That's an important question.

One day soon after I had announced my resignation from Grace Chapel, a friend of ours, Ken Medema, a gifted poet and musician, sat at a piano and sang to the congregation about its wonderful name and the implications of living up to it:

Grace. . . .
I knew it would be this kind of place.
I knew the people I would face
Would be loving and full of grace.

Time. . . .
I haven't been here for a long, long time,
And I have missed the place.
It's different now from the days
When I was here before,
And it's going to be different more.

Frontier. . . .
You're on the edge of a new frontier.
I wonder what we'll hear;
About the things that go on here.

New. . . .
Some things in your life will be new.
What in the world are you going to do?
And how will you make it through?

It's my prayer that you will be
Open to the spirit-wind that blows
And it's my prayer that
You'll be open to the river of grace that flows.

Name. . . .
Grace is your name;
This is your claim,
Satan-chained,
Made new each day by grace.

Well, I pray that whatever happens in this place
Will be a wonder work of all-miraculous grace.

I'm not sure the surrounding community ever fully comprehended the meaning of our church name. That was apparent the day I handed my Grace Chapel credit card to a service station attendant, and he smiled and said, "Thank you, Mr. Chapel; please come again." I'm sure he wondered what my wife, "Grace," was like.

Our Catholic friends, familiar with churches named after saints, sometimes said, "How are things at St. Grace these days?" And our Jewish friends said, "It's a nice name; why did you name your church after a prayer?"

So you see, it was easy to permit our special name to become nothing more than just an identifying symbol on our signboard, our checks, and our membership applications. We probably even signaled our immunity to the significance of our name when, in our hurried-up language forms, we referred to our church not as Grace Chapel but simply as "G.C."

Most of us are liable to think deeply about grace only when we really need it. For example, I thought positively about grace the afternoon I was motioned to the side of the road by a policeman with a portable radar device. After studying my driver's license, he radioed its number to some central location and then turned to me and said, "Mr. MacDonald, you've got a clean driving record. I'd like to help keep it that way; you help too. Have a good day." I guess that was a form of grace.

I think about grace if the insurance premium payment is overdue. And I think about it when I mail my son's income tax in a day after the deadline: his grace and that of the IRS. Obviously, those of us not good with details may have a lot of thinking to do about grace.

But you think most about grace when it seems as if it is the only thing left that might provide a "tomorrow." When there's nothing else. And, rightly or wrongly, many of us have had times in life when we wondered if there was a tomorrow that would be of any value.

It came to me one day as I walked along to a New England beach that I'd seen life-saving rings hanging on poles before, but I never really paid serious attention to them *because I've never come close to drowning*. Assuming that I might have such a traumatic experience one day, I'm quite sure that I would take a much keener interest in the availability and performance standards of life-saving rings.

Let me tell you: grace to me is like a life-saving ring. It was thrown out to me in the darkest hours of my life when my world was breaking in tiny pieces, and I was sure I would never have an opportunity to rebuild.

The grace to rebuild came first from God. It was there all the time for the asking, ever since the Cross guaranteed its availability to anyone who sincerely asked. The challenge for me was in receiving it appropriately.

Grace also came from people close to me: family, friends, and a host of men and women I'd never met who found ways to say they wanted to be counted among the givers.

And then grace came from the church in the form of a congregation (the Grace Chapel congregation) whose spiritual leadership decided to extend it for the purposes of restoration. Grace indeed was their name. Probably a few did not wish to extend grace. It wasn't that they were antigrace; but they just weren't in a mood to give it. We who have broken our own worlds and have inflicted damage and hurt in the personal worlds of others must not ignore the fact that we disillusion and anger some people; that some are not going to recover from what has happened very easily.

On the occasions that I heard or thought about people who were not prepared to act in grace, I confess that I was tempted to nurse a defensive spirit. But then something inside would remind me rather pointedly that broken-world people are in no position to demand grace or even to deserve it. They must merely be appreciative receivers; and if some people do not wish to give it, broken-world individuals must accept that as part of the consequences of the situation. What some people may or may not do with the grace there is to give to others is between them and their God.

History records many ugly moments in which human beings have subjected one another to cruelty, exploitation, and vengeance. But history also records some brilliant moments when human beings have given grace to one another. Ah, what a difference!

Several such brilliant moments of grace giving are noted in the Scriptures. Take, for example, the grace that David gave to Saul. David's sins are so often pointed out that we forget he also was a man of grace. As many others have observed long before me, David had every reason to act vengefully toward Saul. The king of Israel cultivated a love-hate attitude toward the young shepherd boy. In his down moments Saul threw spears at David that the young man never threw back. Saul chased David into and through the wilderness on a number of occasions and would have gladly ended his life had he been smart enough to catch up with him. And Saul burned with jealousy toward David whenever he heard anyone praise him for anything. It did not help that Saul's own son felt more loyalty for David than he did for his own father.

But David never fought back. He never returned the thrown spears; he never took advantage of Saul's vulnerability when he could have killed him in the wilderness. And he never taunted Saul when he could have made him appear the fool. He responded by giving grace.

David's greatest moment in grace giving came at Saul's death on the battlefield. David's grievous lament for Saul is startling. I paraphrase his words when I quote David's cry to his troops at what must have been a memorial oration:

Don't talk about Saul's death, and don't gossip about what has happened. This is not news to be published among our enemies lest they use it as a pretext for laughing at God. Saul and Jonathan were loved . . . they were swift and strong men . . . how the mighty have fallen in battle (2 Sam. 1).

It would have been understandable for David to have said something like this:

I want you to take a hard look at how this man has died. He had a great start, and he failed miserably. This is a good example of what happens when you make serious mistakes. This is how you end up. Feel free to talk about it all you want to your kids. Maybe we will all learn a lesson from it.

One sees great models of grace giving at the time of St. Paul's conversion and almost three years later when he was introduced to the Jerusalem church. The grace was given by two men: first Ananias the prophet and later Barnabas.

Ananias of Damascus received a message from God that he should go to a particular house and call on the newly arrived Saul of Tarsus whom he would find blinded and praying. Ananias's reflex reaction was to protest, to inform God about the terrible reputation for killing and imprisoning Christians that Saul had. But God was already informed and urged Ananias on his way with the notice that He had great plans for Saul.

Ananias did as he was told. The Scripture says that he entered the house and placed his hands on Saul while he exclaimed:

"Brother Saul, the Lord . . . has sent me so that you may see again and be filled with the Holy Spirit." Immediately, something like scales fell from Saul's eyes, and he could see again. He got up and was baptized (Acts 9:17-18).

I've often wondered what it cost Ananias to reach out and touch the greatly feared man and address him as "Brother Saul." The laying on of hands, the familiar greeting, and the baptism were the gifts of grace from one member of the Christian family to another. Grace at great risk and at great cost.

The opposite of grace might be *retribution:* repayment in kind or punishment or the demand for reparations. It wouldn't have been sur-

prising to some if Ananias had refused to go to Saul and had instead
sent a note saying:

> We hear you may have had a change of heart about Christians. If
> that's true, get back to me in a couple of years. If there has been
> no further hostile action on your part between now and then, we
> might meet in a neutral location. In the meantime you might wish
> to think about repayment for all the damages you've caused be-
> cause if there is nothing done, we're going to sue your socks off.
> Our church's attorney's name is. . . .

Church history is different, of course, because Ananias chose the
grace option and eschewed the retributive one.

Barnabas entered the process of grace giving almost three years later
when he learned that no one in the Jerusalem church was in a mood to
receive Paul and give him a hearing. Barnabas became the giver of
grace, endorsing Paul and bringing him into fellowship with the
Jerusalem church leadership.

Ironically, some years later the same Barnabas would try to graciously
mediate in a moment when Paul—who should have known better—
rejected the notion of a second chance for John Mark, a previous failure
on a missionary venture (see Acts 15:36ff). There was no way Paul
would bend in giving grace to Mark; and there was no way Barnabas
was going to allow the young man to feel ungraced. So Barnabas became
graciously tough, splitting with Paul and heading out on a missions
project with Mark. Barnabas's advocacy of Mark is a powerful precedent for giving men and women who have failed a second chance. Many
years later Paul seemed to acknowledge that Barnabas had been the
more correct of the two of them. From that long-range perspective, he
wrote of John Mark, "He is helpful to me" (2 Tim. 4:11).

Like David and Ananias and Barnabas, the good Samaritan in one of
Jesus' stories was also a giver of grace. A nameless man, the victim of a
brutal mugging, lies in a ditch on the road to Jericho, Jesus told a
crowd. He is ignored by dignitaries with clerical and theological creden-
tials, and it appears that he will die alone in the ditch. But a Samaritan
(as far as the Jews were concerned, a good-for-nothing) comes along,
assesses the situation, and provides everything necessary to bring the
man to wholeness: food, bandages, clothing, and hospitality. Everything is given from the generous hand of grace. It was not a story designed to make Jews feel good; rather, it was to provoke them into

understanding that real neighbors are those who give grace, not those whose sole preoccupation is with right doctrine and impeccable theology.

Without restorative grace, broken worlds cannot be rebuilt according to God's standards. Unfortunately, there are many stories of men and women who in their distress felt so abandoned and so ostracized that they put their own worlds back together in whatever fashion was possible. But this kind of rebuilding process was fueled perhaps by anger or by the need to survive or by the energy that comes from wanting to stubbornly prove oneself. The results of such rebuilding are usually something like my attempts to rebuild an appliance. Several pieces are left over, and the thing doesn't work very well.

And usually such people have subsequently chosen to go elsewhere, lost to the Christian community where they perceived they were no longer welcome. I think that's a waste. It's also an indication that sometimes we misunderstand one of our central purposes: to rescue the perishing and grace the failing.

We might be startled by the large number of people in our world, now outside the active Christian community, who think of their earlier Christian experience as a bad dream. I know this is too simple an observation, for it does not always take into account those who were willful and seemingly unrepentant in broken-world days. But we must consider what might be possible if repentance and grace were retrieved as prominent activities in the modern church. What might be possible if we deliberately set out to challenge the sin that has captured too many people and snatch back those whose worlds are breaking?

Why do we talk about spiritual warfare and then show surprise when there are casualties? And why, when there are casualties, are we not more active in sending out the "medics" whose task is to apply the healing and restorative medicines of grace? If we are to find this healing and wholeness again INSIDE the church, it will be only because people believe that grace is a gift from God to be given.

In its primary sense, *grace* (literally meaning "gift") is the power of God in the form of forgiving and healing love; it comes to men and women despite the fact that they have done nothing to deserve it. Like the facets of a lovely diamond, grace seems to have many forms. For example, I've found it helpful to talk about RECLAIMING GRACE as the energy that brings a state of peace between a person and God. Traditionally, we may refer to this moment as being born again, accepting Jesus Christ as Savior, or confessing faith in God.

I've used the term REFORMING GRACE to describe the often slow but certain reshaping of one's life into what the Bible calls Christlikeness. This process also is a gift from God, and we are told that God sends His Spirit into the life of the follower of the Lord to make this possible. The gift of His Spirit is part of that grace.

Then there is RESTORATIVE GRACE, and that is what this chapter is about. This kind of grace comes to a broken-world person who comes to insight and acknowledges misbehavior in attitude or deed. Restorative grace is God's action to forgive the misbehavior and to draw the broken-world person back toward wholeness and usefulness again. It is God's response to the acts of repentance and brokenness. Restorative grace doesn't mean that all of the natural consequences of misbehavior vanish, but it does point toward a wholeness of relationship between God and the one who has returned in repentance.

Karen Mains, using beautiful language of her own choosing, is talking about the effects of restorative grace when she writes:

Nature shouts of this beginning-again-God, this God who can make all our failures regenerative, the One who is God of risings again, who never tires of fresh starts, nativities, renaissances in persons or in culture. God is a God of starting over, of genesis and regenesis. He composts life's sour fruits, moldering rank and decomposing; he applies the organic matter to our new day chances; he freshens the world with dew; he hydrates withered human hearts with his downpouring spirit. (*With My Whole Heart*)

How big must a sinful act be before restorative grace becomes an important matter? In principle, restorative grace is necessary EVERY time a misbehavior of attitude or action occurs. It would appear that on most occasions a person is dealing with the necessity of restorative grace every time he becomes aware of a personal offense against God and His law. That's what David was seeking when he called out, "Search me, O God, and know my heart; [and] . . . any offensive way" (Ps. 139:23–24).

But if the misbehavior is great enough in consequence that others are also greatly affected or offended, it may become necessary for restorative grace to be received also from those involved.

The father of the prodigal son gave restorative grace when the boy came home. Expecting to be received as a second-class citizen, he was instead received as an honored son with a robe, a ring, and a celebration. That's restorative grace.

One day our local newspaper carried this classified ad: "[Name]: I know you are in [city]. Please call your father (collect). I love you son." (Home and work phone numbers were included.) It was, as far as I could see, an offering of restorative grace.

Grace in any of these forms cannot be purchased; it can only be given and received. Grace is the "glue" that takes the pieces and bonds them into something new again. Grace is the "welcome mat" that lets a person know that having repented and demonstrated the fruits of brokenness, he or she is bid back to a privileged place in the family just as the father welcomed his lost prodigal son. Grace is the "scrubber" that cleans the blotched record and says that some things will be remembered no more. Grace is the "rubber stamp" that says CANCELED and acknowledges that the account is paid for. And (may I go around one more time) grace is the "electric current" that energizes virtually everything of value in the life of followers of the Lord.

An old gospel hymn says: "Mercy there was great, and grace was free." Four biblical words seem to come together when the subject of grace is under consideration. They are *grace, mercy, peace,* and *kindness.* We act out of grace; we give mercy; we extend peace; and we treat one another kindly.

The person receiving grace cannot be patronized. The granting of grace does not give one Christian an opportunity to "lord it over" another. It does not suggest that the grace giver is a first-class citizen of the kingdom and the grace receiver is a second-class citizen. In our human condition we all too frequently give off that sort of signal.

In truth, I was as much a sinner in need of *grace* before my sin as I was after. But that is not quite believable to many Christians, and unfortunately our treatment of one another shows it. The giving of grace merely extends from one sinner to another.

When we act in *mercy,* we are carrying out the feelings of grace. We have chosen not to belittle or demean the person in need. Jesus never looked down with disdain on the adulteress brought to Him by the religious leaders. He treated her with dignity and showed deep concern for her future.

When we act in *peace,* we show that although we may have been angry about or hurt by what the world breaker has done, a state of peace exists between us.

And when we act in *kindness,* we are going the second mile. We are generously giving to the broken-world person, doing the unexpected thing: giving encouragement, giving hope, giving generously whatever is needed.

Gail and I will never forget two visits on the day our world publicly broke apart. Each visit was from two people. The first visit was with a young man and a young woman who had worked as my assistants for the two previous years.

They sat and listened tearfully to what I had to tell them: how our lives were about to be abruptly changed and how—as a result—their lives would be changed. And when I was through, they instinctively came across the room, laid hands upon Gail and me, and struggled through a prayer for us. These two, in their early twenties, gave more grace and kindness than we could have ever imagined.

The second visit came from two much older people: also a man and a woman. Their gift came in their insistence in reflecting on a number of specific things they felt we had done for them and their colleagues. They insisted on going into detail so that we would not forget for a moment that, as far as they were concerned, history was not a black hole. Grace, mercy, peace, and kindness filled the room that day. And we lived off it for several days that followed.

Restorative grace came through scores of letters as people sat down to express not only their sorrow but also the promise of their prayers. Those with whom we had personal relationships usually tried to remember something positive that one or both of us had done that had made a difference in their lives. If the present sorrow could not bring much value, they seemed to be saying, let's look back into the bank of memories and remember days that did make a positive difference.

There were those who managed to gain our phone number and called to pray or to read Scripture, to assure us of their love and their certainty that God would exchange this time of pain and humiliation for something useful.

And some came to visit. Gail and I will long remember the day-long visit of a well-known pastor who flew across the country, sent by the board of directors of an evangelical organization to share their concern for our welfare. He sat and wept with us, prayed for us, and took us to dinner. A couple, long close to us, came to Peace Ledge for a day and insisted that we permit them just to share the routines of life on the hill: shopping, changing the oil in the car, answering the phone.

A special grace came from my father who flew across the country to meet us as we traveled to Peace Ledge. As we drove the endless miles, he sat and listened. He wept with us, and he made us laugh. After years of living very separate lives, grace drew a father and son into an intimacy that we had never known before.

And then there was the grace that came from a specific group of men I will describe later. They enveloped us as Styrofoam packaging might protect a breakable item being sent through the mail.

All of this was grace: restorative grace. Its eventual hope: restoration. A broken world rebuilt.

More than a hundred years ago D. L. Moody lashed out as a loving critic to certain parts of the church of his time for its misappropriation of energies. The church reminded him, he said, of firemen straightening pictures on the wall of a burning house. In a single sentence he drew a vivid picture of what any of us can become in any generation when we forget the basic activities given to us by the Lord of the church.

I can hardly think of a more important function than the giving of grace: to the man or woman who has never learned of the love of Christ and His reclaiming grace. To the young or struggling believer who seeks a Christlike faith and the joy of experiencing reforming grace. And to the broken-world person who has so disappointed his brothers and sisters in faith and needs restorative grace. Where there is grace, there is hope, hope for a broken world to be rebuilt.

In the *Journal of the American Medical Association* a few years ago Jane McAdams told the story of her sixty-nine-year-old mother who had lived a life deeply marked by the Great Depression of the 1930s. The evidence showed in her frugality and utterly practical perspective on all material things. The only extravagance she had ever permitted herself, McAdams wrote, was a frilly nightgown kept in a bottom drawer, "In case I should ever have to go into the hospital."

That day had come. All the symptoms that made her visit to the hospital necessary spoke of a serious cancer, and McAdams feared the moment when she would have to tell her mother that the prognosis for the future was very poor.

The daughter wondered, "Should I tell my mother? Did she already know? If not, did she suspect? . . . Could I give her any hope? Was there in fact any hope?"

As she wrestled with these questions, McAdams noted that her mother's birthday was approaching. Perhaps she could brighten her mother's days by purchasing a new nightgown because the one that had been in the bottom drawer was yellowed, limp, and unattractive. So she purchased and presented a new nightgown and matching robe. "If I could not hope to cure her disease, at least I could make her feel like the prettiest patient in the entire hospital."

McAdams described how her mother studied the gown after the package was opened. And after a while she pointed to the wrapping and the gown and said to her daughter, "'Would you mind returning it to the store? I don't really want it.' Then picking up the paper she pointed to a display advertisement and said, 'This is what I really want, if you could get that.' What she pointed to was a display advertisement of expensive designer summer purses."

My reaction was one of disbelief. Why would my mother, so careful about extravagances, want an expensive summer purse in January, one that she could not possibly use until June? She would not even live until spring, let alone summer. Almost immediately, I was ashamed and appalled at my clumsiness, ignorance, insensitivity, call it what you will. With a shock, I realized she was finally asking me what I thought about her illness. She was asking me how long she would live. She was, in fact, asking me if I thought she would live even six months. And she was telling me that if I showed I believed she would live until then, then she would do it. She would not let that expensive purse go unused. That day I returned the gown and robe and bought the summer purse.

That was many years ago. The purse is worn out and long gone, as are at least half a dozen others. And next week my mother flies to California to celebrate her 83rd birthday. My gift to her? The most expensive designer purse I could find. She'll use it well.

The gift of restorative grace to a broken-world person is the gift not of a nightgown that announces death but of a summer purse that says there is life after failure. That is the message of the Cross and the empty tomb. And it must be the message of the church to the broken-world person.

PART V

PREVENTING A PERSONAL WORLD FROM BREAKING

CHAPTER 17

The Bradley Tutorial

> BOTTOM LINE #17:
> *We must assume the inevitability of attacks by an enemy hostile to our spiritual interests and build our defenses in the places he is most likely to attack.*

In his autobiography, *A General's Life,* General Omar Bradley writes of the first time he met William Westmoreland, who many years later became commander of the American forces in Vietnam. On the occasion Bradley describes, Westmoreland was a cadet first captain in the West Point class of 1936.

The encounter between the two occurred during summer maneuvers: war games in which Westmoreland commanded a battalion defending a hill. The young captain and his men performed so poorly in the mock battle that the attackers succeeded in overrunning them.

General Bradley (then a major) had been an observer that day, and when the exercise on the hill was ended, he took the young field officer aside and said, "Mr. Westmoreland, look back at that hill. Look at it from the standpoint of the enemy."

"Turning," Westmoreland later wrote, "I became aware for the first time of a concealed route of approach that it was logical for an attacker to use. Because I had failed to cover it with my defense, he [Bradley] as umpire had ruled for the attacking force."

"It is fundamental," Major Bradley said firmly, "to put yourself always in the position of the enemy." He was speaking of course about those moments when the soldier plans for battle and determines how he will prevent the enemy from seizing positions that are his to defend.

I think Bradley's point is also useful for thinking through how broken-world experiences might be prevented. I'd like to call it the Bradley Tutorial: *put yourself in the position of the enemy.* It's a place to start when you ask the question: *how can broken-world misbehaviors be avoided?* During the past year, I've received many letters from young men and women who pose one form of this question or another. Letter writers are usually polite and respectful as they ask, "Can you tell me anything out of your experience that will help me to avoid major (misbehavior)?"

Although this is a worthy question, I'm not always comfortable being considered an expert on the subject. But pressed to answer, I usually begin with a version of the Bradley Tutorial. Take a look at yourself, I might say, and then put yourself in the position of the enemy: the source of evil that relentlessly comes at you from without and from within. Where will evil find the "crevices" in the defenses of your personal world that can be overrun? The answer is likely to be a different one for each of us.

When we face evil, it is as if we are facing a smart enemy. It is as if we are being carefully studied by a perceptive foe in order to discover the places where we are most likely to make broken-world choices. *The objective of this enemy is to deny God the pleasure of His glory being reflected in us and to deny us the pleasure of being what God created us to be.*

There is an obvious danger in becoming so obsessed with the possibilities of sin that we become morbidly introspective and defensive, adopting what some have called a fortress mentality. It is admirable to be deeply concerned lest we fail, but it can be just as dangerous to forget that *the Christian is called to enter the world and advance the authority of Christ's kingdom. That means the inevitable risk of wounds and casualties.* One would hope few need be self-inflicted wounds.

Everyone knows of the fortress mentality with which the French began World War II. Standing behind their Maginot Line, the French were convinced that their country was impregnable. But they had deluded themselves into a false security, and things didn't work out the way they'd planned. In short, they didn't put themselves in the position of the enemy and take note of its unprecedented mobility. What was needed was a mobile defense system to prevent the invasion of a very mobile army. The astounding part about the French failure to recognize this fact is that their enemy, the Germans, had made no secret of their strategy and capacity to move over the ground and through the air at blitzkrieg speed.

And that is what I have in mind when someone asks me how to defend against the possibility of a broken world. I want to talk about a defense that respects and notes the movements of the enemy, one that is flexible and imaginative enough because of the power of God.

My idea for a mobile and flexible defense of one's personal world comes in seven parts. None of the points are new, but they tend to indicate areas in which the possibility exists for broken-world kinds of failure. Each proposition is centered on what I'll call a PERSONAL DEFENSE INITIATIVE (PDI). This takeoff on a modern military defensive strategy suggests that an effective defense also requires initiative, an aggressive or positive element in our lives that just doesn't stand around waiting for something bad to happen.

PDI #1: ADOPT A REPENTANT LIFE-STYLE

When our son, Mark, was in his seventh and eighth years of life, Gail and I noticed that he often had a difficult time admitting that he had made a mistake or that he was wrong in a conclusion or an opinion. No matter how hard we tried to get him to admit to being wrong occasionally, we could see that a terrible battle in his inner being caused him to slip and slide out of such admissions with excuses or rationalizations.

This trait worried his mother and me because we believed that if he carried it into adulthood, it would adversely affect his personal relationships or his work with teams of people. On many occasions I tried to point this out but never seemed to succeed.

One day Gail and I seized upon a new approach to the problem. Whenever we made a mistake, we would exaggerate our statements and feelings of contrition. For example, when Gail pointed out that something I'd said or done was wrong, I would cry out in mock dismay: "WHAT? ARE YOU SURE? YES, BY GOLLY, YOU'RE RIGHT; I AM WRONG; I'VE MADE A TERRIBLE, HORRIBLE MISTAKE." And turning to Mark, I might say, "SON, DO YOU REALIZE WHAT HAS HAPPENED? YOUR DAD HAS MADE A MISTAKE. I'M WRONG, WRONG, WRONG!"

This reaction usually generated much laughter among all of us. But we were delighted when repetitions of this performance had a positive effect. Mark began to see that his parents had no trouble acknowledging mistakes and that it was OK to be less than perfect. And when he might quietly admit to an error, we made an effort to treat his admission in the same jovial manner. A dance. A song. A loud round of applause. Soon there was no need for the hilarity. We had a son who found that it was safe to be mistaken in his home with those who loved him. Today, many years later, Mark is a man I greatly admire for his skills in developing people. Now he's the one helping others to be more honest with themselves.

This is the pattern of the repentant life-style: the daily awareness and admission that misbehavior, small or large, is an unfortunate reality of our lives. It is probably unhelpful that many of us assume the first mark of growth in the Christian life to be better behavior. I would like to propose that the first mark of maturity is actually *the ability to identify and admit to bad behavior.* A consciousness of God's presence is much more likely to make us aware of things in need of renunciation than anything else.

Some veteran Christians who have shown healthy concern for holiness in their lives have shared with the rest of us the startling news that the closer one walks to the light, the darker the shadows become; the closer one draws to the presence of Christ, the greater the realization of one's indwelling evil.

Thus, the repentant life-style. Maturity, according to this PDI proposition, suggests not that we become more perfect but that we become more willing to face up to what we are within and without and name what is offensive to God and to others. In naming our misbehaviors, we begin to gain control over them. We have a handle with which we can renounce them and throw them away. We have an identifying symbol that we can carry to the Cross when we confess our sins and ask for forgiveness.

John wrote lovingly to relatively new Christians: "My little children, these things I write to you, so that you may not sin. And *if anyone sins, we have an Advocate with the Father*" (1 John 2:1 NKJV, emphasis mine). It is preferable, John acknowledged, not to engage in sinful misbehavior. But when it happens—and John clearly assumed that it will—there is advocacy available before the offended God in the person of Christ. But he would not advocate for those items in our lives that we will not name in repentance. He said at another point: "If we confess our sins, He is faithful and just to forgive" (1 John 1:9 NKJV).

Corrie Ten Boom suggested that the person with a repentant life-style has developed the habit of telling the Lord his sins five minutes before his accuser does. That makes sense. She also coached her listeners to "keep short accounts with God."

The repentant life-style means that I acknowledge my misbehavior to Christ and to others who need to know that I am not what my image or persona often tries to say I am. "In every Little Nell, there is a Lady MacBeth trying to get out," James Thurber wrote. We would do well to acknowledge that fact to God and to others whenever necesary and possible.

The phrase *repentant life-style* is simply another way of referring to brokenness or humility, which I've discussed throughout this book. Brokenness is not only an immediate experience when we come to insight about misbehavior; *it is a way of life.* It is an attitude of spirit, and it is built on the conviction that left to itself, evil is liable to break out in almost any form in our thought life, our words, or our actions. Therefore, we must be ready to name it, acknowledge it, and repudiate it. No excuses; no rationalizations; no denial.

Watchman Nee writes:

> Our spirit is released according to the degree of our brokenness. The one who has accepted the most discipline is the one who can best serve. The more one is broken, the more sensitive he is. The more desire to save ourselves, in that very thing we become spiritually useless. Whenever we preserve and excuse ourselves, at that point we are deprived of spiritual sensitivity and supply. Let no one imagine he can be effective and disregard this basic principle.

And a few sentences later, Nee remarks: "The way of service lies in brokenness, in accepting the discipline of the Holy Spirit. The measure of your service is determined by the degree of discipline and brokenness."

This most obvious of spiritual principles would hardly be debated by most evangelical Christians. Yet the practical failure to act the principle out privately and corporately is probably at the root of small and large choices ultimately leading to broken worlds.

It was his understanding of what I have called a PDI principle that made John Bunyan the great man of God we know him to be. In his spiritual autobiography he modeled the repentant life-style with these comments:

> I find to this day 7 abominations in my heart: 1) inclinings to unbelief; 2) suddenly to forget the love and mercy that Christ manifesteth; 3) a leaning to the works of the law; 4) wanderings and coldness in prayer; 5) to forget to watch for that I pray for; 6) apt to murmur because I have no more, and yet ready to abuse

what I have; 7) I can do none of these things which God com-
mands me, but my corruptions will thrust in themselves; when I
do good, evil is present with me. *(Grace Abounding)*

Although some of us may express great discomfort at such morbid
introspection, Bunyan understood that if we do not seek out and name
the impurities within while they are small and manageable, we can expect one or more of them to become oversized and, in a weak moment,
turn into the stuff of which broken-world choices are made.

PDI #2: PAY THE PRICE OF REGULAR SPIRITUAL DISCIPLINE

Some people have called it the quiet time; others, devotions; still
others, personal worship. But my favorite term is *spiritual discipline* because that's what it is. Spiritual discipline is to the inner spirit what
physical conditioning is to the body. The unconditioned athlete, no
matter how naturally talented, cannot win a world-class race.

John Sculley, CEO at Apple Computers, writes of the corporate
culture in which he once worked at Pepsi Cola. There the discipline of
the body was held in high esteem. Note the passion for discipline he
describes:

The culture demanded that each of us be in top condition, physically fit as well as mentally alert. At lunch time, the glass-walled
corporate fitness center was packed with the rising stars of the
corporation. Like me, they were the kind of people who would
rather be in the Marines than in the Army. Even our exercise
regimens became part of the competition. Placards on bulletin
boards charted each executive's progress against his colleagues.
(Odyssey)

It's not my intention to glorify this description of a rather driven life-
style. I simply want to point out that there are people who believe
enough in what they are doing to pay the price. These people understand that their bodies are part of the whole-person effort leading toward vocational and corporate success. *Thus, they see the importance of
taking the time to discipline and condition the body.* They may prefer to do
other things, but if it takes time to keep the body in shape, these people
will come up with the time.

My observation is that many men and women in the Christian community desire the blessings and maturities of the Christian life-style in much the same way as Sculley's associates desire success at their jobs. And they fervently desire that they will never fall prey to temptations or motivations leading to major misbehavior.

Interview them, and I'm sure they would confess that they desire the "well done" of the Master more than anything else. Call it a heavenly brand of success. But we need to ask ourselves sometimes, how badly is that "success" desired? There can often be a long way between confession of what we desire and performance of what we're willing to make happen. Do we want "success" quite as badly as Sculley and his friends appear to want theirs? One test might be the amount of time we put in disciplining the spirit, the core of our private worlds, the first line of defense when it comes to the enemy's attacks.

I'm convinced that paying the price for prevention probably means a substantial period of time set apart every day to condition the spirit. This was the burden of the book *Ordering Your Private World*, and I haven't changed my opinion at all about the principles set forth in that book.

Spiritual discipline means the cultivation of Scripture study, intercession, meditation, and general reading on spiritual subjects. That's easy for some of us, hard for others.

When we do this, we are stepping aside from all the noises of the public world that claw at our souls. We are asking for a "divine" noise, really a comforting whisper, to restore our sense of balance and guidance, to reaffirm our personal value in heavenly terms so that we will not have to seek value from other sources. And we are seeking empowerment to check evil and release the best we have so that we may give to those about us. The discipline of the spirit should result in putting us in touch with Jesus.

Again John Bunyan. In the most famous of all his writings, *Pilgrim's Progress*, Bunyan described a fierce battle that Christian fought against the lion Apollyon. Before and after the rugged contest, Christian was aware that his strength for battle came directly from God:

> When the battle was over, Christian said, "I will here give thanks to him that hath delivered me out of the mouth of the lion, to him that did help me against Apollyon." . . . Then there came to him a hand with some of the leaves of the Tree of Life, the which Christian took and applied to the wounds that he had received in the battle and was healed immediately. He also sat down in that

place to eat bread and to drink of the bottle that was given him a little before; so, being refreshed, he addressed himself to his journey with his sword drawn in his hand; *for he said, "I know not but some other enemy may be at hand."* (*Pilgrim's Progress*, emphasis mine)

Bunyan wrote much of Christian's journey from an autobiographical perspective, and he was clearly saying something about his own PDI program at this point. The discipline of the spirit was his only hope for preventing his own broken-world experiences.

The man or woman who is not taking a premium amount of time each day to look within and draw from the hand of heaven through the Scriptures and intercession takes great risks.

PDI #3: CULTIVATE KEY RELATIONSHIPS

If we are to successfully defend against bad choices resulting in broken-world experiences, it will also be because we have set out to develop some significant personal relationships that offer mutual accountability.

A glance at a major automobile race on television one day caused me to think of this issue of key relationships in a new way. In the middle of the race a car and its driver pulled off the track and into the place they call the pit. Instantly, a team of five men swarmed over the car. One poured gas into the tank; two others checked and replaced tires; one seemed to be checking engine fluids while another talked to the driver about racing strategy as he gave him water (or something) to drink.

The pit crew, the TV sportscaster said, is often the key to the driver's victory. If their work is speedy and complete, they can gain several seconds of advantage for their driver over the competition. They can send their driver and car back to the track with the energy, the strategy, and the capacity to win.

As I watched them work, I came to an appreciation of the fact that we all need to be part of one another's pit crew. I need those who will inspect the tires and the fuel in my life. I need others with whom to discuss "racing" strategy. And, just as badly, I need to join the pit crews of others. In each case the objective is simple: help one another win.

As we saw earlier, our modern world's way of life has all but stripped us of personal relationships where people provide balance, nourishment, and preventative maintenance for one another. Most of us live apart from our extended families, and we move at such a pace that hardly anyone knows the full breadth of our lives. The people in our church may see one side of us; our families another; our working associates still another. There is little pressure apart from what is inside ourselves to make sure that these three sides of ourselves (and there are probably other sides) coincide, that there is integrity in our personal performance.

We must keep reminding ourselves that the inner being is marked with a spirit of rebellion and deceit. Only the strongest of us is liable to maintain the sort of integrity we need by ourselves. Frankly, we need the help of others.

And that is what Christian fellowship is supposed to be. It's also why Paul wrote "love protects" (see 1 Cor. 13:7), a phrase scarcely acknowledged, let alone understood, by most of us. It suggests that we are called to stick close to one another much in the same way that a wingman flies close to his partner as they pilot their combat planes in an air battle. I am charged to protect you; you are charged to protect me.

This little phrase—"love protects"—sums up the meaning of accountability. We are accountable to look out for the spiritual interests and development of our brothers and sisters in the faith, and they are called to do the same for us. And how is it done?

By encouraging us and affirming us when we show growth. By rebuking us and holding us to the standard of godly character when we show the evidence of substandard performance. The friendship that stretches us to grow toward Christlikeness is perhaps one of the most valuable things we can ever have in life.

May I turn to Bunyan and his *Pilgrim's Progress* one more time to reflect on the companionship of Christian and his friend Hopeful? It isn't a coincidence that much of Christian's pilgrimage is in the company of others. Bunyan was anxious to point out, in the words of John Wesley's mentor, that Christianity is not a solitary religion.

In their mutual journey Hopeful is overtaken by a state of numbing fatigue and is in great danger of attack if he cannot be kept awake. Christian keeps him from sleeping, and when Hopeful realizes the danger he was in, he says in appreciation of his friend:

> I acknowledge myself in a fault; and had I been here alone, I had, by sleeping, run the danger of death. I see it is true that the wise man saith, 'two are better than one.' (Ecc 4.9) *Hitherto hath thy*

company been my mercy; and thou shalt have good reward for thy labour. (*Pilgrim's Progress,* emphasis mine)

I can think of certain friendships where I feel that I completely failed someone by avoiding the hard questions when I saw signs of stress. And, thank God, I can think of times when I sucked in my breath and, at the risk of losing a friend, made observations that cut to the heart and caused behavior to change. I would write endlessly if I were to record the times when friends have done the same for me.

I am often asked what sort of things friends in accountability might ask of one another. Having found little if any helpful literature on this subject, I put together a list of twenty-six questions, some of which friends might wish to consider if this personal defense initiative is to be effective.

1. How is your relationship with God right now?
2. What have you read in the Bible in the past week?
3. What has God said to you in this reading?
4. Where do you find yourself resisting Him these days?
5. What specific things are you praying for in regard to others?
6. What specific things are you praying for in regard to yourself?
7. What are the specific tasks facing you right now that you consider incomplete?
8. What habits intimidate you?
9. What have you read in the secular press this week?
10. What general reading are you doing?
11. What have you done to play?
12. How are you doing with your spouse? Kids?
13. If I were to ask your spouse about your state of mind, state of spirit, state of energy level, what would the response be?
14. Are you sensing any spiritual attacks from the enemy right now?
15. If Satan were to try to invalidate you as a person or as a servant of the Lord, how might he do it?
16. What is the state of your sexual perspective? Tempted? Dealing with fantasies? Entertainment?
17. Where are you financially right now? (things under control? under anxiety? in great debt?)
18. Are there any unresolved conflicts in your circle of relationships right now?

19. When was the last time you spent time with a good friend of your own gender?
20. What kind of time have you spent with anyone who is a non-Christian this past month?
21. What challenges do you think you're going to face in the coming week? Month?
22. What would you say are your fears at this present time?
23. Are you sleeping well?
24. What three things are you most thankful for?
25. Do you like yourself at this point in your pilgrimage?
26. What are your greatest confusions about your relationship with God?

Never before have I been more convinced that adult Christians need to form personal friendships with those sharing our commitments and values. And yet whenever I have talked about this, people—especially men—have acknowledged that they have no relationship quite as intimate as what I am describing.

One returns again and again to Jesus' forbearing statement to Simon Peter: "Simon, Satan has asked to sift you as wheat" (Luke 22:31). It was a warning that Simon did not heed, but it came from the lips of a Friend who knew what was likely to happen. The PDI principle was in motion; it simply wasn't heeded.

How do we protect one another? We watch a friend's eyes. Abnormal fatigue? Anger? Avoidance of truth? We listen to a friend's words to lovingly discern inconsistencies, attitudes, and negative criticisms of people. We watch spending patterns. Too excessive? Trying to prove something? We note the respect and affection with which he or she treats others. Loving toward a spouse and children? Too harsh? Disdainful? Disrespectful? Too familiar with others? We are sensitive to questionable habits. Substance abuse? Sleeplessness? Workaholism?

I'm not advocating the adoption of a KGB-like stance toward one another. But men and women who truly love one another protect one another from broken-world possibilities. I know of only one way I can protect my friend: stick close enough to him so that we are transparent to each other, so that we can spot the aberrant patterns before they get out of control.

Friends take time. And most of us do not have that time unless we make this cultivation of Christian fellowship a major priority.

PDI #4: RESIST THE "APPLAUSE" THAT BELONGS TO CHRIST

I am the LORD; that is my name!
I will not give my glory to another
or my praise to idols (Isa. 42:8).

The Lord spoke these words through the prophet Isaiah warning kings and religious leaders that it would be fatal for them to permit people to give them honor belonging only to God.

Of all the places where broken-world choices are likely to begin, this may be the most subtle and the one to which we are the most insensitive. Few things kill the soul faster than becoming addicted to the applause of people.

All of us are guilty of helping others fall into the clutches of the enemy when we offer praise that belongs only to the Son of God. We almost guarantee their fall when we do this. This is not to say that we should not express appropriate appreciation when someone has served us well; but it does suggest that we need to exercise greater care as to how we set out various leaders and praise them.

Perhaps we are in danger of permitting that today in the Christian community. Not just to those in the pulpit ministry or in organizational leadership, but in every sector of the church. Like the rest of the world, we always run the danger of creating our own heroes whether they are preachers with unusual communicative talents, musicians, business people, or artists.

We must not dare to ruin these people with undue praise. And we must not permit it to come to us. The temptation is too great to believe the nice things people tell us in the good moments. Such acclaim has a narcotic effect on our perception of the reality of our sinful predicament and our daily dependence on the operating grace of God. When we are praised, we are wise to accept it with graciousness, but to renounce it quickly in the heart lest it lodge there and become believable.

PDI #5: TAKE TIME TO HAVE FUN

Perhaps this personal defense initiative is more for people in leadership than anyone else. But I'm convinced that the enemy within and without uses this strange area of life as much as anything else. Some will grimace at my use of the word *fun;* perhaps they would prefer the word *diversion.*

Modern Christianity is often considered to possess a very serious view of life. Work seems never to be finished; the issues are perceived as too grave; the world is labeled as a dangerous place. These are some of the watchwords by which we approach life and do our work. Our sensitivity to criticism, sometimes our limited funds, and our perceived guilt are all likely to conspire to cause us to take a very serious view of life and feel uneasy about doing things purely for the pleasure of life.

Fun might be called the exercise of the mind and the emotions. It is diversion that takes us away from the pressure of the intense needs we are likely to encounter every day as we do our work in the church and in the marketplace. I'd be hard-pressed to give an instance of fun in the New Testament. The biblical writers were not writing to inform us of the private lives of the apostles, and so we are not likely to hear that they occasionally stopped somewhere for a refreshing beverage or that they enjoyed moments of humor. Is it possible that Paul was a player of practical jokes or that Barnabas occasionally enjoyed an afternoon of quiet reflection under a tree?

It is reasonable to assume that diversion came on long walking trips, on shipboard, and in the homes of people where the apostles stayed. With the pace of modern travel we have all but squeezed those kinds of relaxing moments out of our schedules and almost feel guilty if someone suggests that we take the time to relax and play.

The ambitious, hard-driving leader is quite likely to go weeks and weeks without ever taking the diversionary time off that renews the body and mind, that introduces laughter and positive sensation back into one's life. We often admire people who seem to have squeezed fun out of their schedules, and then we are shocked if they burn out or succumb to various temptations. We need to make sure that we are not complying with a system that has caused them to never let up and find freedom from all the pressure.

PDI #6: HOLD THINGS LOOSELY

We don't have to study the New Testament characters for very long before we see that they held all things loosely: their material possessions, their jobs, their security and, finally, even their lives. They seem to have seen all things as on loan, ready to be recalled at a moment's notice. There is no protest in them.

This loose holding of all things did not come easily. The struggle was hinted at when Simon Peter said to Jesus, "We have left all we had to follow You!" (Luke 18:28). Several similar comments suggest that the disciples expected at first that they would get a lucrative payback in one form or another for their loyalty to Christ. But the wealth would be computed in forms other than what they expected.

John the Baptizer watched the crowds slip away from him as they followed after Christ. He lost his life to the executioner at the behest of a vengeful woman.

Simon Peter left his business and ended up traveling the world until he was martyred in Rome. St. Paul laid aside his position in the prestigious Sanhedrin when he was converted to Christ and spent his life planting the church in Asia Minor and Europe. He apparently died penniless and might have had reason to wonder if all of his efforts were going to last.

We are very much aware that we follow a Savior who was little more than a pauper during His entire public ministry. He had no home, no wardrobe, no income, no investments. Our faith has little to say about things except to challenge us to hold them loosely and be willing to part with them without warning.

That thought seems to militate against a large part of modern Christianity, and it may be a key reason why men and women end up in broken-world experiences. In fact, it might also be why many churches end up in trouble. When individual Christians and congregations begin to accumulate property, payrolls, and other forms of assets, they increase their vulnerability to conflicts and choices that can lead to broken worlds.

Sin flourishes when people hold on to things tightly enough to compete, to protect, or to covet. And sin flourishes when people become obsessed with the acquisition of things so that their focus moves from the objectives of faith to the goals of things. And in that refocusing, people open themselves for a hundred evils to break forth.

What are the snares that lead toward broken-world choices about material matters? *Debt* and its ability to put us into financial captivity; *pride* and its ability to move us toward measuring ourselves against others; and *greed* and its ability to engender within us a sense of dissatisfaction. We have put a personal defense initiative system into place when we choose to live out of debt, within the confines of our income, and in obedience to the biblical standard of generosity as we give to others in need or in ministry.

PDI #7: BE FILLED WITH THE SPIRIT OF GOD

I left this initiative until last because it is the most important. In the Bible, being filled with the Spirit of God always meant that a person was given extraordinary power to achieve something, or wisdom to discern something, or unusual force of character to be a leader or a prophet.

In the Old Testament, these strange and wonderful experiences occured only for short periods, but the Bible always pointed toward an era when ordinary people would have access to them. And that era began on the day of Pentecost when a group of simple men and women entered the streets of Jerusalem speaking in strange languages and were able to connect with a large crowd of people speaking similar languages who were on pilgrimage from other parts of the world.

From that time forward, the fullness of the Spirit in one's personal world became an issue for Christians. What did it mean to have the life of God within in this special way?

It meant to the New Testament Christians special gifts and capacities, discernment of things not ordinarily understood, and strength to do things that ordinary human beings were not able to accomplish. In other words, people were lifted beyond normal capacity and character.

Jesus spoke of this Spirit who would enter the lives of Christians as One who would guide us into truth, who would bring to mind the teaching of Christ, who would empower us to be spokespersons about faith. At the base of all this was the certitude that when the Spirit of God was at work in believers, He Himself would be the most powerful "weapon" in preventing broken-world choices.

This Spirit could be ignored, squelched, or resisted, St. Paul warned the Thessalonians. And that's what we broken-world people are aware that we did. For a time, we found a way to ignore warnings and rebukes.

The fullness of the Spirit is available to every Christian who simply asks for it on a regular basis. It may ebb and flow in strength and vitality with the follower of the Lord as he or she is conscious of asking and submitting to its direction. And that may be the chief item on the agenda of anyone who pursues spiritual discipline every day.

Among my many friendships is one with an older leader in the Christian church who, when he calls me on the phone, always asks this question: "Gordon, are you filled with the Holy Spirit today?" The first time I heard his question, I recoiled. Was he being nosy? Was the question not a bit trite? But after further thought, I came to realize that it was one of the most important questions anyone might ever ask me. His question was a gesture of Christian affection.

"Are you filled with the Holy Spirit?" is indeed a caring question. And it is a challenging one. I wonder if I should not resolve to ask it of my friends with greater frequency and welcome it when they ask it of me. The question forces an inward look: a quality-control check to see if the life within me is energized by God's purposes or by issues that are less than best.

"Look at the hill from the standpoint of the enemy," Major Bradley told Cadet First Captain Westmoreland. Good advice to a young officer who wants to prevent the enemy from gaining a foothold on the hill he must defend. And it's good advice for believers who wish to prevent the foothold that leads to broken-world choices. Prevent we must, or broken our worlds are likely to be.

And where are the crevices on the hill the enemy is most likely to exploit? The crevice of the *unrepentant heart*. The crevice of the *undisciplined spirit*. The crevice of the *isolated Christian*. The crevice of *undeserved applause*. The crevice of the *tired, overworked mind and body*. The crevice of the *materialistic man or woman*. And the crevice of someone who has never come under the *indwelling power of God*.

How do we prevent worlds from breaking? We seize the Bradley Tutorial: we put ourselves in the position of the enemy. He's likely to attack at one of these points of vulnerability.

PART VI

REBUILDING YOUR BROKEN WORLD

CHAPTER 18

Rebuilt

> BOTTOM LINE #18:
> *The grace that helps to rebuild a broken world is something given: never deserved, never demanded, never self-induced.*

I have imagined the scene on Lake Galilee more times than I could ever estimate. It is early morning, and the sky above the Golan hills to the east hints at a pending sunrise. The lake is dotted here and there with fishing boats, and if you have good eyesight, you can pick out the figures of men working their nets in hopes of a final catch before they have to quit.

One boat holds a group of men who seem tired and depressed. In charge is Simon Peter, and with him are John and several other men who have more recently been known as disciples of Jesus. What could you learn if you could pick their brains? What feelings and what explanations do they toss about in their private worlds as their thoughts keep snapping back to that night not long ago when they utterly failed the Lord? At a moment of supreme test they had simply cut and run when the more valorous thing would have been to take the same bullets the Master was taking. They hadn't, and they were escaping their embarrassment by working hard at something else.

Simon Peter has to be the most thoughtful. In his mind he has to account for absurd promises that never came close to being kept, the drawing of the sword in the garden, and the three-time renunciation of any association with Christ. The cowardice of the others was bad enough, but if there was a prize for the greatest fool, Peter would win it.

Suddenly a voice calls from the shore. "Friends, have you any fish?"

"No," the answer roars back with more than a little irritation. It's been a bad business night.

"Throw your net on the right side of the boat, and you will find some."

They did! And fish fairly leaped into the nets. So many in fact that the net was too heavy to pull over the side of the boat. Some numbers-crunching member of the crew would later determine that they had 153 fish.

John put the sound of the voice and the success of the strategy together and concluded that the Man on the shore was the Lord. "It is the Lord," he said. Was it a triumphant shout or a frightened whisper?

No matter. It was all Simon Peter needed to hear. In seconds he was over the side of the boat swimming with all of his strength toward shore. Again, what went through his mind as he swam? What was he looking for? And what did he anticipate that Jesus might say to him when he arrived?

Did he ponder the possibility that Jesus might say, "I've come to say good-bye"? Did he think that he might hear the Lord say, "Peter, I really tried hard to make you into an effective performer, but I'm afraid you don't have what it takes in you"? Perhaps he might have expected Jesus to say, "We need to sit down and talk about where you went wrong the other night."

But none of those comments were uttered. Instead, when Peter dragged himself on shore, he found the Lord preparing breakfast over a charcoal fire: bread and fish prepared to serve some hungry, cold, and tired men. Think of it: the Son of God cooking breakfast for a group of failures. *That is grace!*

No, Simon Peter heard none of the possible negative comments that any of us might have been prepared to say to him. Rather, he heard a question asked three times: *"Do you love me?"* And three times Peter struggled with the truth that came from insight. No promises this time. Only the truth. "Yes, I love you." *I don't know how that translates into action*, I can sense Peter thinking, *but I will tell you where my heart is.*

Each time Peter responded, he heard words that perhaps he had never thought he would hear again: feed my lambs; take care of my sheep; feed my sheep. *The original call was still in place.* Peter had not been dumped. HE WAS BEING RESTORED. His broken world was being rebuilt.

Every reader of the Bible has a favorite story. This one is mine. It is down to earth; it is emotional; it offers hope. It is a model of what it means to take the gift of restorative grace and press it into the life of a human being who has caused his world to be broken and now needs help in putting things back together again.

I find it insightful that the last chapter of the book of John concludes with the story of the restoration of a close follower of the Lord and that the first chapter of the following book picks up with the story of the evangelization of the world. It all suggests to me that God is in the business of taking broken-world people like Simon Peter and sending them forth to be His agents in kingdom expansion.

Three important things happened that morning on the beach. First, *Jesus came to Peter in his world.* The rebuilder went to the broken-world person knowing, perhaps, that Peter was too wounded to take the initiative himself. Second, *Jesus gave Peter a chance to replace his earlier three denials* with three honest attempts at a reaffirmation of his love for the Lord. And, third, *Jesus reissued His call.* When the beach scene was over, there were no longer any second-class citizens in the community of Jesus.

Among the most precious gifts the church has to offer is restorative grace to the broken-world person. We are talking about a community where one can confess failures, find forgiveness and counsel so that there will not be a repetition of earlier broken-world choices, and then begin to experience usefulness in serving God again. That's what Peter found on the beach, and that's what broken-world people need to find today in the congregation.

In talking about restoration we begin with the assumption that the broken-world person has acknowledged actions and attitudes that have led to consequences and offenses grievous to the Christian community. That is confession and repentance, and no one can do that for the sinner. But conversely, the repentant person cannot restore himself or herself; he or she must be restored by others. Again, I must say that I feel free to write on this subject only because I have received such restoration personally.

Many examples of restoration appear in the Scriptures. The great theme of restoration laces itself throughout Israel's history. Jeremiah could be called the great prophet of restoration; his sermons are saturated with calls for "faithless Israel" to return to the Lord,

> for I am your husband [God says]. I will choose one of you from every town and two from every clan and bring you to Zion. Then I will give you shepherds after my own heart, who will lead you with knowledge and understanding (Jer. 3:14–15).

Again Jeremiah mediated the word of God to adulterous Israel:

> If you repent, I will restore you
> that you may serve me;
> if you utter worthy, not worthless, words,
> you will be my spokesman (Jer. 15:19).

Some of the most wicked kings in Israel's time learned something about God's restorative grace. Manasseh, the king of Judah, probably had more to learn than anyone else.

> Manasseh led Judah and the people of Jerusalem astray, so that they did more evil than the nations the LORD had destroyed before the Israelites. The LORD spoke to Manasseh and his people, but they paid no attention (2 Chron. 33:9–10).

Result? A broken world.

> So the LORD brought against them the army commanders of the king of Assyria, who took Manasseh prisoner, put a hook in his nose, and bound him with bronze shackles and took him to Babylon (2 Chron. 33:11).

But Manesseh repented.

> In his distress he sought the favor of the LORD his God and humbled himself greatly before the God of his fathers. And when he prayed to him, the LORD was moved by his entreaty and listened to his plea; so he brought him back to Jerusalem *and to his kingdom.* Then Manesseh knew that the *Lord* is God (2 Chron. 33:12–14, emphasis mine).

Consequences for Manesseh? Absolutely. But restoration? Absolutely.

St. Paul reflects this theme of a restorative God in several familiar passages as he instructs new Christians on the way of life that is unique to followers of the Lord.

> Brothers, if someone is caught in a sin, you who are spiritual should restore him gently. But watch yourself, or you also may be tempted. Carry each other's burdens, and in this you will fulfill the law of Christ (Gal. 6:1–2).

The key word is *restore*. In other parts of the New Testament the same Greek word speaks to the idea of fixing or repairing or refitting something so that it can become useful again.

Nowhere do we have a better view of what Paul had in mind than when he wrote to the Corinthians about a man in the congregation who had committed a gross immorality. Originally, Paul was greatly upset over the church's failure to surface this sin and discipline the guilty man. But when they acted in discipline, Paul turned to the matter of restoration.

Aware that the man had expressed sorrow and repentance for his act, Paul said,

> The punishment inflicted on him by the majority is sufficient for him. Now instead, you ought to forgive and comfort him, so that he will not be overwhelmed by excessive sorrow. I urge you, therefore, to reaffirm your love for him (2 Cor. 2:6–8).

Forgive and *comfort* appear to be Paul's two-point program for restoration. Forgiveness seems to have been a specific act of declaring that the past would no longer be remembered. Comfort appears to have been an ongoing procedure to provide the man with a defined pathway of reconciliation to those he offended and to help him regain his place of service and fellowship in the congregation.

It looks like *everyone* was called to participate in the restoration process. It was a priority great enough that Paul made it a major issue in his writings. It was important because not to have done it would have permitted the enemy of the church to neutralize the congregation.

> If you forgive anyone, I also forgive him. And what I have forgiven—if there was anything to forgive—I have forgiven in the sight of Christ for your sake, in order that Satan might not outwit us. For we are not unaware of his schemes (2 Cor. 2:10–11).

This would have been a most appropriate time for Paul to say that the man, though forgiven and reconciled, should not be permitted to serve in certain capacities in the church. I find it important that Paul never said anything of the sort. Restoration means full return to congregational life, period.

I am also impressed with the fact that Paul clearly trusted the actions of the Corinthians. I hear him saying, *you have obviously done the right things; I affirm your actions and agree with your conclusions. Count me in as a fellow restorer.*

Stanley Jones writes of a group who understood this process at a crucial moment in his life when he found himself on his way to what could have been a broken-world experience:

For months after [my] conversion, I was running under cloudless skies. And then suddenly I tripped, almost fell, pulled back this side of the sin, but was shaken and humiliated that I could come that close to sin. I thought I was emancipated and found I wasn't. I went to the class meeting—I'm grateful that I didn't stay away— went, but my music had gone. I had hung my harp on a weeping willow tree. As the others spoke of their joys and victories of the week, I sat there with the tears rolling down my cheeks. I was heartbroken. After the others had spoken, John Zink, the class leader, said: "Now, Stanley, tell us what is the matter." I told them I couldn't, but would they please pray for me? Like one man they fell to their knees, and they lifted me back to the bosom of God by faith and love. When we got up from our knees, I was reconciled to my heavenly Father, to the group, and to myself. I was reconciled. The universe opened its arms and took me in again. The estrangement was gone. I took my harp from the willow tree and began to sing again—the Song of Moses and the Lamb, especially the Lamb. The cross was my refuge and my release.

That was a very crucial moment in my Song of Ascents, the moment when I lost my music. *My destiny was in the hands of that group.* I was a very bruised reed; suppose they had broken me? I was a smouldering wick; suppose they had snuffed me out? Just a criticism: "I told you so. Too good to be true. He was riding for a fall." *But they never uttered a criticism, or even thought of one, as far as I could see. The reaction was nothing but redemptive love.* That group became redemptive. I saw and experienced the power of redemptive love incarnate in a group. (*A Song of Ascents*, emphasis mine)

This extraordinary description of a restorative group is beautiful to read. It oozes with grace. It's not a complete story, of course, because there are times when confrontation and critique must take place for the well-being of the broken-world person. But this is a story of the healing dimension that happens when a team of people determine that a broken-world person should be rebuilt. In restoration there are things that only the team or the church can do. The broken-world person's hands are tied.

A number of elements of a full restorative process are helpful to think about. Each fits with the others like pieces in a jigsaw puzzle, and when they are complete, we may see a broken world on its way to rebuilding.

Restoration first requires confession by the broken-world person. The secrets of the heart and of past actions have to be put into the light. That's what David was doing when he finally stopped holding out and admitted to Nathan, "I have sinned." David went further in his confession when he wrote Psalm 51 in which he pours out his heart both to God and to the people about his remorse over what had happened and his desire that his broken world be rebuilt.

This is a confession of guilt and responsibility. It avoids all excuses and rationalizations. It makes no attempt to blame others or to shirk responsibility for what has happened. Until this happens, the healing process has no chance to begin.

A second aspect of the restoration or rebuilding process takes place when the broken-world person and a restoration team take time to go into the history of the events that led to misbehavior. This is an important process, like the drilling of that tooth before the dentist can fill the cavity and rebuild it to former strength. But it isn't a process for a large number of people—perhaps a group of three who are mature enough to sit with someone who has been in trouble and wants to bring the truth to the surface. There is no need for the public to know the details of one person's failures. If there is to be full restoration, however, a few need to come alongside and affirm that the issues have been dealt with.

When I faced a moment like this in my broken-world failure, the three men who formed my original restoration team met with me and engaged in a formal session much like a court. We kept a detailed set of minutes of what we said to one another.

As honestly as I knew how, I opened my life to them. Having heard everything I said, they then knew something of how they could go about helping me find a process of rebuilding. That session ended with a remarkable experience of prayer and forgiveness, the beginning of a healing that goes on until this day.

I must underscore the significance of counseling at this point. Although we may give or receive forgiveness, that is no guarantee that all the roots of misbehavior have been discovered. Counseling from a gifted therapist can go a long way to making sure that the "decay" is treated.

Third, *restoration requires discipline.* The broken-world person cannot take this into his own hands. He needs to trust in a body of mature, godly people whose agenda is rebuilding. Along the way some painful steps must be taken to regain the confidence of others and to experience healing, and the members of the restorative body should determine how much time to allow.

Discipline usually means restrictions: being relieved of certain responsibilities, being asked to account to others on personal spiritual activities, and being required to submit to pastoral oversight or counseling. In some cases, discipline may even require the act of restitution— the formal seeking and granting of forgiveness to offended parties, repayment of monies that have been taken, or agreements that there will no longer be verbal attacks or slanders. As much as possible, discipline will require that damages and offenses are recognized and settled. This is not punishment; but it is a recognition that, for everyone's good, a time of withdrawal is wise so that the rebuilding work of Christ and His church can take place. We do no favors to one another if we rush a wounded soldier back to action.

Then restoration involves comfort. No one but the broken-world person knows how painful can be the humiliation and loss following misbehavior and its consequences. If the Christian community desires to restore an individual, regular attempts have to be made to pour courage and confidence into him.

I have strong memories of the almost daily phone calls that came to our home for Gail and me from the men who set out to help me rebuild my broken world. When they called, they read the Bible to us, having selected passages that they believed would offer hope. They often prayed with one or both of us over the phone, interceding to God in our hearing about our needs. Through the mail came notes, articles, and books for us to read. In every way possible they set out to say, "There is a tomorrow; wait for it."

Samuel Logan Brengle, an evangelist in the Salvation Army, was once called to give such comfort to a colleague serving with him who had hit the bottom in spiritual despair. The man to whom he wrote had been overcome with the conviction that he no longer had any use to Christ. Watch Brengle pour encouragement into him with this letter:

My Dear Troubled Comrade: "Absolutely useless to God and man!" You must please excuse me for breaking in on your rest with this note, but I'm still laughing and rejoicing—laughing at that ridiculous idea born in your tired brain, and rejoicing to think what a black eye the Devil is likely to get.

You say in your note to me: "I was born to the fight"; and now that you are in a real fight you feel that you are absolutely "useless!" No, no, you have often been on dress parade when you thought you were fighting. When you were at the head of a lot of shouting men and women, cheered by thousands, the Devil may have sat down, crossed his legs and watched it all as a pretty performance. But he is on the job now. I imagine that I hear him hiss: "Now I'll crush him! Now I'll smash his helmet of hope! Now I'll rob him of his shield of faith! Now I'll break his sword of the Spirit! Now I'll quench his spirit of prayer;"—and what a Devil he is.

Don't imagine that you are out of the fight. You are in it, and you must fight the good fight of faith now, in loneliness and weakness. But you will triumph.

We Salvationists exalt the active virtues, not too much, but too exclusively. The great battles, the battles that decide our destiny and the destiny of generations yet unborn, are not fought on public platforms, but in lonely hours of the night and in moments of agony.

You were indeed "born to the fight." (*Portrait of a Prophet*)

A fifth aspect of restoration is advocacy. The process of rebuilding always has a stated objective, which is healing and a return to service or usefulness. Those involved in the rebuilding actually take on the responsibility to speak for the broken-world person, to represent the possibilities for his rebuilding to others.

I have heard little in the church about the subject of advocacy. Yet Barnabas, the favorite New Testament character for many of us, was an advocate on at least two occasions we've already looked at. He advocated the interests and growth of Paul before the Jerusalem church when no one wanted to trust the man. And he advocated the interests and possibilities of John Mark before Paul when the old apostle didn't want to trust the younger man.

Who will advocate for the broken-world person? Who will make sure that news about his or her personal world is truthful? Who will stand with the repentant sinner and assure that he or she receives the forgiveness and grace the Scriptures tell us God wishes to give? Having experienced all of this from those who determined to rebuild my personal world and having known its hope-giving value, I wish it for every broken-world person.

Finally, *restoration requires an official declaration when it is accomplished.*

A specific time must come when one is released from discipline. Perhaps this is a public occasion, a time when the advocates of a person's restoration are prepared to say to the world or to those who care: this person is ready once again for responsibility. This can be a small or large service for Christian people. The news of what has happened should be widely circulated since it is usually true that bad news travels far and wide, but good news crawls. It needs to be declared.

I must not dare close these comments on restorative grace in action without saying once more that broken-world people will almost always live with heartbreaks and consequences that inevitably flow from wrong choices. Some, remembering the plight of Jacob who always walked with a limp after he dared to wrestle with God's messenger one night, will suggest that broken-world people will also always walk with a limp of sorts. For the most part the restorative team cannot remove this. But they can ensure that, to the best of their ability, no soldier is ever lost to the fight; no gifts ever wasted; no call, if possible, ever terminated.

There is a sense in which Jesus seems to have done all of these things for Simon Peter when they met on the shoreline of Galilee. What a moment it must have been as Peter stumbled on shore and saw the fire and the food. Was that a hint to him that he was walking not into harshness but into hospitality? Did the three questions—"Peter, do you love me?"—slowly bore into Peter's humiliated private world with the assurance that he was being given a second chance to affirm what he had originally denied? And what must it have meant when he heard the Son of God say, "Feed my lambs"? In a flash he must have known: *the call was still alive;* he still had a chance to go forth and die for this One who had died for him. Grace was real; restoration was an accomplished fact.

> Peter,
> had I
>   followed him as eagerly
>   served him as loyally
>   loved him as utterly
>   agreed to die with him as willingly
> as you,
> and then denied him as dastardly,
>   thrice,
> I would weep when roosters crow.
> But
> because I have done all things
> conservatively
> and have faced death not at all,

I have neither wept
nor been tenderly restored
and called a rock.
(Gerald Oosterveen, *Decision* Magazine)

Epilogue: Finishing the Race

I began this book with the stories of two runners who sustained terrible falls in the middle of races. One got up; the other didn't or couldn't. I might have mentioned a third well-known trackman of recent years who also once took a fall: Jim Ryun.

> BOTTOM LINE:
> *When you have been pushed or have fallen to the ground, there can be only one useful resolve:*
> *GET UP AND FINISH THE RACE!*

Ryun was a favorite in the Olympic 1,500 meters the day he fell. As a massive crowd in the stadium and on television watched, Ryun made his way around the track in a pack of finely conditioned runners. And then, just as it had happened to the others, he crashed to the ground. In a race of that sort, a fall virtually guarantees that it will be impossible to win. And Jim Ryun must have known that as he lay there on the track.

What were the options Ryun sorted through his mind in that moment? Quitting and heading for the locker room and a hot shower? Anger at having trained for so long for this event and now missing the chance for the gold medal? Self-pity over the seeming bad deal he'd gotten by being jostled in the pack?

None of these, apparently. Rather, he seems to have had only one thought that eclipsed all of these possibilities I've mentioned. Getting up and running again; FINISHING, even if he couldn't win. AND THAT IS WHAT JIM RYUN DID. He got up and ran again. Others won medals, but Ryun won a large measure of respect when he determined to finish the race.

Many biblical challenges call us to a performance in the Christian life worthy of a medal. But underlying all of those encouragements is an even more important one: FINISH THE RACE.

This metaphor is also a challenge to the church, to the fellowship of men and women who have found the life of the Cross the only way to live. To them goes my plea: help broken-world people get up and finish the race. Confront them like Nathan confronted David; seek them out like Hosea did his wayward wife, Gomer; forgive them like Paul did the jailer; pray for them like Stephen did for his executioners; rebuild them like Barnabas rebuilt John Mark; and restore them to usefulness whenever possible like Jesus did for Simon Peter.

In recent years we've spent enormous amounts of energy asking how the church in the West might find renewal. We've sought the answers in the pursuit of powerful preaching, evangelistic marketing programs, group dynamics, and upbeat, contemporary public services. Perhaps there is virtue in all of that. But I would like to propose that if we were to rediscover the ministry of restorative grace, we might find an enormous number of people crowding forward to receive what God has offered to give through Jesus Christ. There, in the ministry of restoration, may be a key to renewal.

Both inside and outside the church are broken-world people, and they are there in no small numbers. They yearn for an understanding and wise ear; they dearly wish for an amnesty that would provide the chance to make things right and new. If their spirit is right, they are not asking that their sins be diminished or overlooked; they are not asking that people pretend that nothing has happened. What they seek is what the cross of Christ offered: grace freely given; healing fully applied; usefulness restored.

And to the broken-world people: my brothers and sisters in that worldwide fraternity of those who know what it is like to feel useless and hopeless, there are great things to learn when the heart is sweet and open to the disciplining voice of God. Charles Spurgeon looked back upon dark hours in his own life and said:

> I bear willing witness that I owe more to the fire, and the hammer, and the file, than to anything else in my Lord's workshop. I some times question whether I have ever learned anything except through the rod. When my schoolroom is darkened, I see most.

The objective of rebuilding a broken world is not returning life to business-as-usual as if nothing had ever happened. That could never be.

No, the objective is to come out of a dark time and finish the race with a depth of grace and humility that might not have happened under any other circumstance.

We broken-world people live with a strange irony. Not for one moment would we ever wish to repeat what caused the original collapse. But we cannot ignore the fact that when restoration has had its way, we may be in a better position to offer insight and grace to others than we ever were before. We should never imagine ourselves heroes or worthy of special attention. But we do have a stewardship: a responsibility to testify to the pain, the grace, and the joy of reentering the fellowship of God and His people.

Broken-world people are equipped now to understand other struggling people. We know how to give grace because we have received it. We know how to spot the earliest signs that someone is headed in the wrong direction, and if we are wise and caring, we may be able to help others in ways we wish we'd been able to help ourselves.

All of these things and much more come to individuals who choose, when they have fallen, to get up again and finish the race. Many of the saints in the Scriptures who hit the infield grass can testify to this great grace.

For each broken-world person who has to make the choice to get up and run again, the circumstances of rebuilding will probably be unique to some extent. There will be different kinds of support structures, different kinds of "angels," and different time frames. For me the most important single factor in the rebuilding process was the partnership I share with Gail. We lived through the darkest days *together;* we pursued the Peace Ledge Principles *together;* we walked through the restoration process so graciously overseen by others *together.* Day by day, *together,* we searched the mind of God and we built a refreshed love for one another, stronger than we had ever known before. This partnership we share today is really an uncommon bond: unbreakable and resilient. I would wish for every broken-world person a champion like the one with whom I have shared this dark time.

When I fell to the infield grass and the news later became public, Gail and I were flooded with loving letters from all over the world. Some of them were difficult to open because the envelope was marked with the name of a special person I knew I'd especially let down. But each envelope contained a message of love, and it had to be read.

One such letter came from an old, old friend, a professor from graduate school days of whom I've often spoken because of his modeling of character and godliness. Dr. Raymond Buker had been an Olympic athlete, and strangely enough, he had run in the 1924 Olympic Games where Eric Liddell had made his mark on athletic history.

When Buker wrote to me in some of my darkest hours, it was as if he had been reading my mind because he said:

> Dear Gordon: Back in 1923 I once ran an invitational race (one mile) with Joey Ray and Ray Watson.
>
> We three were members of the relay team that set the world record for the four mile relay held for over twenty years. These two had a better time than I by three or four seconds. They never beat me in a race; I never did well without competition.
>
> Anyhow in this race we three were running along at a mile rate together—the first lap, then the second lap. I suddenly hit a branch of a tree, a solid branch, (with) my left shoulder. It was a terrible blow and stopped me cold. The blow almost knocked me out. For two or three seconds I could not think. I cannot remember whether it knocked me on to the ground, but it knocked me out of my running place, stopped me cold.
>
> I remember trying to figure out what I should do next. How could I ever catch them—should I bother to stay in the race. Everyone would understand that the blow by the tree branch knocked me out.
>
> Somehow I staggered back on the track and stumbled along. I can see them (now) many, many yards ahead of me.
>
> But I remember one clear conclusion. "I must keep going— even if I come in long behind. I must not quit." So I kept going. I won the race.
>
> This then is the lesson I learned: whatever the difficulty—the blow—we must keep on. God will lead to the result that will glorify Him.

It was powerful advice, and I seized it. If you are on the ground today, I hope you will too.

And some who are the most gifted in the things of God will stumble in those days and fall, but this will only refine and cleanse them and make them pure until the final end of all their trials, at God's appointed time (Dan. 11:35 TLB).